Jeannie P. Miller, PhD
Editor

Emerging Issues in the Electronic Environment: Challenges for Librarians and Researchers in the Sciences

Emerging Issues in the Electronic Environment: Challenges for Librarians and Researchers in the Sciences has been co-published simultaneously as *Science & Technology Libraries*, Volume 25, Numbers 1/2 2004.

Pre-publication REVIEWS, COMMENTARIES, EVALUATIONS . . .

"EXTREMELY USEFUL. . . . THOUGHT-PROVOKING AND WELL-WRITTEN. . . . Clearly articulates the issues that librarians and users from many disciplines will be grappling with in the years to come."

Lynne Rudasill, MSLS
*Associate Professor
of Library Administration
University of Illinois
at Urbana-Champaign*

The Haworth Information Press
An Imprint of The Haworth Press, Inc.

Emerging Issues in the Electronic Environment: Challenges for Librarians and Researchers in the Sciences

DATE DUE

Emerging Is...   *enges for*
Librarians a...   published
simultaneous...   lume 25,
Numbers 1/2

Demco, Inc. 38-293

Science & Technology Libraries Monographic "Separates"

Below is a list of "separates," which in serials librarianship means a special issue simultaneously published as a special journal issue or double-issue *and* as a "separate" hardbound monograph. (This is a format which we also call a "DocuSerial.")

"Separates" are published because specialized libraries or professionals may wish to purchase a specific thematic issue by itself in a format which can be separately cataloged and shelved, as opposed to purchasing the journal on an on-going basis. Faculty members may also more easily consider a "separate" for classroom adoption.

"Separates" are carefully classified separately with the major book jobbers so that the journal tie-in can be noted on new book order slips to avoid duplicate purchasing.

You may wish to visit Haworth's website at . . .

http://www.HaworthPress.com

. . . to search our online catalog for complete tables of contents of these separates and related publications.

You may also call 1-800-HAWORTH (outside US/Canada: 607-722-5857), or Fax: 1-800-895-0582 (outside US/Canada: 607-771-0012), or e-mail at:

docdelivery@haworthpress.com

Emerging Issues in the Electronic Environment: Challenges for Librarians and Researchers in the Sciences, edited by Jeannie P. Miller, PhD (Vol. 25, No. 1/2, 2004). *Examines the rapid advances in technology and scientific discovery that have changed the way sci/tech library users seek information and interact with library staff.*

Innovations in Science and Technology Libraries, edited by William Miller, PhD, MLS, and Rita M. Pellen, MLS, BA (Vol. 24, No. 1/2, 2003 and Vol. 24, No. 3/4, 2004). *"An invaluable resource. . . . Tells the stories of innovative libraries and librarians. . . . Strikes a good balance between technical specification and illustration/discussion of strategic issues. . . . Will appeal to a broad range of technologists, reference librarians, and managers." (Michael L. Nelson, PhD, Assistant Professor, Department of Computer Science, Old Dominion University)*

Online Ecological and Environmental Data, edited by Virginia Baldwin, MS, MLS (Vol. 23, No. 4, 2003). *Explores aspects of the online data projects developed in various fields from ecological and environmental research programs.*

Leadership and Management Principles in Libraries in Developing Countries, edited by Wei Wei, MA, MLS, Sue O'Neill Johnson, BA, MLS, MPA, and Sylvia E. A. Piggott, BA, MLS (Vol. 23, No. 2/3, 2002). *Examines case studies of innovative programs from special libraries in developing countries, with a focus on the management and leadersip skills that made these initiatives successful.*

Scholarly Communication in Science and Engineering Research in Higher Education, edited by Wei Wei, MA, MLS (Vol. 22, No. 3/4, 2002). *Examines science and technology libraries' difficulties with maintaining expensive journal subscriptions for both researchers and tenure-ready scholars; offers advice and examples of efficient improvement to make fact-finding and publication easier and more cost-efficient.*

Patents and Trademark Information: Uses and Perspectives, edited by Virginia Baldwin, MS, MLS (Vol. 22, No. 1/2, 2001). *"A lucid and in-depth presentation of key resources and information systems in this area." (Javed Mostafa, PhD, Victor H. Yngve Associate Professor, Indiana University, Bloomington)*

Information and the Professional Scientist and Engineer, edited by Virginia Baldwin, MS, MLS, and Julie Hallmark, PhD (Vol. 21, No. 3/4, 2001). *Covers information needs, information seeking, communication behavior, and information resources.*

Information Practice in Science and Technology: Evolving Challenges and New Directions, edited by Mary C. Schlembach, BS, MLS, CAS (Vol. 21, No. 1/2, 2001). *Shows how libraries are addressing new challenges and changes in today's publishing market, in interdisciplinary research areas, and in online access.*

Electronic Resources and Services in Sci-Tech Libraries, edited by Mary C. Schlembach, BS, MLS, and William H. Mischo, BA, MA (Vol. 20, No. 2/3, 2001). *Examines collection development, reference service, and information service in science and technology libraries.*

Engineering Libraries: Building Collections and Delivering Services, edited by Thomas W. Conkling, BS, MLS, and Linda R. Musser, BS, MS (Vol. 19, No. 3/4, 2001). *"Highly useful. The range of topics is broad, from collections to user services . . . most of the authors provide extra value by focusing on points of special interest. Of value to almost all librarians or information specialists in academic or special libraries, or as a supplementary text for graduate library courses." (Susan Davis Herring, MLS, PhD, Engineering Reference Librarian, M. Louis Salmon Library, University of Alabama, Huntsville)*

Electronic Expectations: Science Journals on the Web, by Tony Stankus, MLS (Vol. 18, No. 2/3, 1999). *Separates the hype about electronic journals from the realities that they will bring. This book provides a complete tutorial review of the literature that relates to the rise of electronic journals in the sciences and explores the many cost factors that may prevent electronic journals from becoming revolutionary in the research industry.*

Digital Libraries: Philosophies, Technical Design Considerations, and Example Scenarios, edited by David Stern (Vol. 17, No. 3/4, 1999). *"Digital Libraries: Philosophies, Technical Design Considerations, and Example Scenarios targets the general librarian population and does a good job of opening eyes to the impact that digital library projects are already having in our automated libraries." (Kimberly J. Parker, MILS, Electronic Publishing & Collections Librarian, Yale University Library)*

Sci/Tech Librarianship: Education and Training, edited by Julie Hallmark, PhD, and Ruth K. Seidman, MSLS (Vol. 17, No. 2, 1998). *"Insightful, informative, and right-on-the-mark. . . . This collection provides a much-needed view of the education of sci/tech librarians." (Michael R. Leach, AB, Director, Physics Research Library, Harvard University)*

Chemical Librarianship: Challenges and Opportunities, edited by Arleen N. Somerville (Vol. 16, No. 3/4, 1997). *"Presents a most satisfying collection of articles that will be of interest, first and foremost, to chemistry librarians, but also to science librarians working in other science disciplines within academic settings." (Barbara List, Director, Science and Engineering Libraries, Columbia University, New York, New York)*

History of Science and Technology: A Sampler of Centers and Collections of Distinction, edited by Cynthia Steinke, MS (Vol. 14, No. 4, 1995). *"A 'grand tour' of history of science and technology collections that is of great interest to scholars, students and librarians." (Jay K. Lucker, AB, MSLS, Director of Libraries, Massachusetts Institute of Technology; Lecturer in Science and Technology, Simmons College, Graduate School of Library and Information Science)*

Instruction for Information Access in Sci-Tech Libraries, edited by Cynthia Steinke, MS (Vol. 14, No. 2, 1994). *"A refreshing mix of user education programs and contain[s] many examples of good practice." (Library Review and Reference Reviews)*

Scientific and Clinical Literature for the Decade of the Brain, edited by Tony Stankus, MLS (Vol. 13, No. 3/4, 1993). *"This format combined with selected book and journal title lists is very convenient for life science, social science, or general reference librarians/bibliographers who wish to review the area or get up to speed quickly." (Ruth Lewis, MLS, Biology Librarian, Washington University, St. Louis, Missouri)*

Sci-Tech Libraries of the Future, edited by Cynthia Steinke, MS (Vol. 12, No. 4 and Vol. 13, No. 1, 1993). *"Very timely. . . . Will be of interest to all libraries confronted with changes in technology, information formats, and user expectations." (LA Record)*

Science Librarianship at America's Liberal Arts Colleges: Working Librarians Tell Their Stories, edited by Tony Stankus, MLS (Vol. 12, No. 3, 1992). *"For those teetering on the tightrope between the needs and desires of science faculty and liberal arts librarianship, this book brings a sense of balance." (Teresa R. Faust, MLS, Science Reference Librarian, Wake Forest University)*

Biographies of Scientists for Sci-Tech Libraries: Adding Faces to the Facts, edited by Tony Stankus, MLS (Vol. 11, No. 4, 1992). *"A guide to biographies of scientists from a wide variety of scientific fields, identifying titles that reveal the personality of the biographee as well as contributions to his/her field." (Sci Tech Book News)*

Information Seeking and Communicating Behavior of Scientists and Engineers, edited by Cynthia Steinke, MS (Vol. 11, No. 3, 1991). *"Unequivocally recommended. . . . The subject is one of importance to most university libraries, which are actively engaged in addressing user needs as a framework for library services." (New Library World)*

Technology Transfer: The Role of the Sci-Tech Librarian, edited by Cynthia Steinke, MS (Vol. 11, No. 2, 1991). *"Educates the reader about the role of information professionals in the multifaceted technology transfer process." (Journal of Chemical Information and Computer Sciences)*

Electronic Information Systems in Sci-Tech Libraries, edited by Cynthia Steinke, MS (Vol. 11, No. 1, 1990). *"Serves to illustrate the possibilities for effective networking from any library/information facility to any other geographical point." (Library Journal)*

The Role of Trade Literature in Sci-Tech Libraries, edited by Ellis Mount, DLS (Vol. 10, No. 4, 1990). *"A highly useful resource to identify and discuss the subject of manufacturers' catalogs and their historical as well as practical value to the profession of librarianship. Dr. Mount has made an outstanding contribution." (Academic Library Book Review)*

Role of Standards in Sci-Tech Libraries, edited by Ellis Mount, DLS (Vol. 10, No. 3, 1990). *Required reading for any librarian who has been asked to identify standards and specifications.*

Relation of Sci-Tech Information to Environmental Studies, edited by Ellis Mount, DLS (Vol. 10, No. 2, 1990). *"A timely and important book that illustrates the nature and use of sci-tech information in relation to the environment." (The Bulletin of Science, Technology & Society)*

End-User Training for Sci-Tech Databases, edited by Ellis Mount, DLS (Vol. 10, No. 1, 1990). *"This is a timely publication for those of us involved in conducting online searches in special libraries where our users have a detailed knowledge of their subject areas." (Australian Library Review)*

Sci-Tech Archives and Manuscript Collections, edited by Ellis Mount, DLS (Vol. 9, No. 4, 1989). *Gain valuable information on the ways in which sci-tech archival material is being handled and preserved in various institutions and organizations.*

Collection Management in Sci-Tech Libraries, edited by Ellis Mount, DLS (Vol. 9, No. 3, 1989). *"An interesting and timely survey of current issues in collection management as they pertain to science and technology libraries." (Barbara A. List, AMLS, Coordinator of Collection Development, Science & Technology Research Center, and Editor, New Technical Books, The Research Libraries, New York Public Library)*

The Role of Conference Literature in Sci-Tech Libraries, edited by Ellis Mount, DLS (Vol. 9, No. 2, 1989). *"The volume constitutes a valuable overview of the issues posed for librarians and users by one of the most frustrating and yet important sources of scientific and technical information." (Australian Library Review)*

Adaptation of Turnkey Computer Systems in Sci-Tech Libraries, edited by Ellis Mount, DLS (Vol. 9, No. 1, 1989). *"Interesting and useful. . . . The book addresses the problems and benefits associated with the installation of a turnkey or ready-made computer system in a scientific or technical library." (Information Retrieval & Library Automation)*

Sci-Tech Libraries Serving Zoological Gardens, edited by Ellis Mount, DLS (Vol. 8, No. 4, 1989). *"Reviews the history and development of six major zoological garden libraries in the U.S." (Australian Library Review)*

Libraries Serving Science-Oriented and Vocational High Schools, edited by Ellis Mount, DLS (Vol. 8, No. 3, 1989). *A wealth of information on the special collections of science-oriented and vocational high schools, with a look at their services, students, activities, and problems.*

Sci-Tech Library Networks Within Organizations, edited by Ellis Mount, DLS (Vol. 8, No. 2, 1988). *Offers thorough descriptions of sci-tech library networks in which their members have a common sponsorship or ownership.*

One Hundred Years of Sci-Tech Libraries: A Brief History, edited by Ellis Mount, DLS (Vol. 8, No. 1, 1988). *"Should be read by all those considering, or who are already involved in, information retrieval, whether in Sci-tech libraries or others." (Library Resources & Technical Services)*

Alternative Careers in Sci-Tech Information Service, edited by Ellis Mount, DLS (Vol. 7, No. 4, 1987). *Here is an eye-opening look at alternative careers for professionals with a sci-tech background, including librarians, scientists, and engineers.*

Preservation and Conservation of Sci-Tech Materials, edited by Ellis Mount, DLS (Vol. 7, No. 3, 1987). *"This cleverly coordinated work is essential reading for library school students and practicing librarians. . . . Recommended reading." (Science Books and Films)*

Sci-Tech Libraries Serving Societies and Institutions, edited by Ellis Mount, DLS (Vol. 7, No. 2, 1987). *"Of most interest to special librarians, providing them with some insight into sci-tech libraries and their activities as well as a means of identifying specialized services and collections which may be of use to them." (Sci-Tech Libraries)*

Innovations in Planning Facilities for Sci-Tech Libraries, edited by Ellis Mount, DLS (Vol. 7, No. 1, 1986). *"Will prove invaluable to any librarian establishing a new library or contemplating expansion." (Australasian College Libraries)*

Role of Computers in Sci-Tech Libraries, edited by Ellis Mount, DLS (Vol. 6, No. 4, 1986). *"A very readable text. . . . I am including a number of the articles in the student reading list." (C. Bull, Kingstec Community College, Kentville, Nova Scotia, Canada)*

Weeding of Collections in Sci-Tech Libraries, edited by Ellis Mount, DLS (Vol. 6, No. 3, 1986). *"A useful publication. . . . Should be in every science and technology library." (Rivernia Library Review)*

Sci-Tech Libraries in Museums and Aquariums, edited by Ellis Mount, DLS (Vol. 6, No. 1/2, 1985). *"Useful to libraries in museums and aquariums for its descriptive and practical information." (The Association for Information Management)*

Data Manipulation in Sci-Tech Libraries, edited by Ellis Mount, DLS (Vol. 5, No. 4, 1985). *"Papers in this volume present evidence of the growing sophistication in the manipulation of data by information personnel." (Sci-Tech Book News)*

Role of Maps in Sci-Tech Libraries, edited by Ellis Mount, DLS (Vol. 5, No. 3, 1985). *Learn all about the acquisition of maps and the special problems of their storage and preservation in this insightful book.*

Fee-Based Services in Sci-Tech Libraries, edited by Ellis Mount, DLS (Vol. 5, No. 2, 1985). *"Highly recommended. Any librarian will find something of interest in this volume." (Australasian College Libraries)*

Serving End-Users in Sci-Tech Libraries, edited by Ellis Mount, DLS (Vol. 5, No. 1, 1984). *"Welcome and indeed interesting reading. . . . a useful acquisition for anyone starting out in one or more of the areas covered." (Australasian College Libraries)*

Management of Sci-Tech Libraries, edited by Ellis Mount, DLS (Vol. 4, No. 3/4, 1984). *Become better equipped to tackle difficult staffing, budgeting, and personnel challenges with this essential volume on managing different types of sci-tech libraries.*

Collection Development in Sci-Tech Libraries, edited by Ellis Mount, DLS (Vol. 4, No. 2, 1984). *"Well-written by authors who work in the field they are discussing. Should be of value to librarians whose collections cover a wide range of scientific and technical fields." (Library Acquisitions: Practice and Theory)*

Role of Serials in Sci-Tech Libraries, edited by Ellis Mount, DLS (Vol. 4, No. 1, 1983). *"Some interesting nuggets to offer dedicated serials librarians and users of scientific journal literature. . . . Outlines the direction of some major changes already occurring in scientific journal publishing and serials management." (Serials Review)*

Planning Facilities for Sci-Tech Libraries, edited by Ellis Mount, DLS (Vol. 3, No. 4, 1983). *"Will be of interest to special librarians who are contemplating the building of new facilities or the renovating and adaptation of existing facilities in the near future. . . . A useful manual based on actual experiences." (Sci-Tech News)*

Monographs in Sci-Tech Libraries, edited by Ellis Mount, DLS (Vol. 3, No. 3, 1983). *This insightful book addresses the present contributions monographs are making in sci-tech libraries as well as their probable role in the future.*

Role of Translations in Sci-Tech Libraries, edited by Ellis Mount, DLS (Vol. 3, No. 2, 1983). *"Good required reading in a course on special libraries in library school. It would also be useful to any librarian who handles the ordering of translations." (Sci-Tech News)*

Online versus Manual Searching in Sci-Tech Libraries, edited by Ellis Mount, DLS (Vol. 3, No. 1, 1982). *An authoritative volume that examines the role that manual searches play in academic, public, corporate, and hospital libraries.*

Document Delivery for Sci-Tech Libraries, edited by Ellis Mount, DLS (Vol. 2, No. 4, 1982). *Touches on important aspects of document delivery and the place each aspect holds in the overall scheme of things.*

Cataloging and Indexing for Sci-Tech Libraries, edited by Ellis Mount, DLS (Vol. 2, No. 3, 1982). *Diverse and authoritative views on the problems of cataloging and indexing in sci-tech libraries.*

Role of Patents in Sci-Tech Libraries, edited by Ellis Mount, DLS (Vol. 2, No. 2, 1982). *A fascinating look at the nature of patents and the complicated, ever-changing set of indexes and computerized databases devoted to facilitating the identification and retrieval of patents.*

Current Awareness Services in Sci-Tech Libraries, edited by Ellis Mount, DLS (Vol. 2, No. 1, 1982). *An interesting and comprehensive look at the many forms of current awareness services that sci-tech libraries offer.*

Role of Technical Reports in Sci-Tech Libraries, edited by Ellis Mount, DLS (Vol. 1, No. 4, 1982). *Recommended reading not only for science and technology librarians, this unique volume is specifically devoted to the analysis of problems, innovative practices, and advances relating to the control and servicing of technical reports.*

Training of Sci-Tech Librarians and Library Users, edited by Ellis Mount, DLS (Vol. 1, No. 3, 1981). *Here is a crucial overview of the current and future issues in the training of science and engineering librarians as well as instruction for users of these libraries.*

Networking in Sci-Tech Libraries and Information Centers, edited by Ellis Mount, DLS (Vol. 1, No. 2, 1981). *Here is an entire volume devoted to the topic of cooperative projects and library networks among sci-tech libraries.*

Planning for Online Search Service in Sci-Tech Libraries, edited by Ellis Mount, DLS (Vol. 1, No. 1, 1981). *Covers the most important issue to consider when planning for online search services.*

Emerging Issues in the Electronic Environment: Challenges for Librarians and Researchers in the Sciences

Jeannie P. Miller
Editor

Emerging Issues in the Electronic Environment: Challenges for Librarians and Researchers in the Sciences has been co-published simultaneously as *Science & Technology Libraries*, Volume 25, Numbers 1/2 2004.

The Haworth Information Press®
An Imprint of The Haworth Press, Inc.

New York • London • Victoria (AU)
www.HaworthPress.com

Published by

The Haworth Information Press®, 10 Alice Street, Binghamton, NY 13904-1580 USA

The Haworth Information Press® is an imprint of The Haworth Press, Inc., 10 Alice Street, Binghamtom, NY 13904-1580 USA.

Emerging Issues in the Electronic Environment: Challenges for Librarians and Researchers in the Sciences has been co-published simultaneously as *Science & Technology Libraries*™, Volume 25, Numbers 1/2 2004.

Library of Congress Cataloging-in-Publication Data

Emerging issues in the electronic environment : challenges for librarians and researchers in the sciences / Jeannie P. Miller, editor.
     p. cm.
     "Co-published simultaneously as Science & technology libraries, Volume 25, Numbers 1/2 2004."
     Includes bibliographical references and index.
     ISBN 0-7890-2577-9 (alk. paper) – ISBN 0-7890-2578-7 (pbk. : alk. paper)
     1. Scientific libraries–Information technology. 2. Technical libraries–Information technology. 3. Science–Electronic information resources. 4. Technology–Electronic information resources. 5. Libraries–Special collections–Electronic journals. 6. Electronic journals. 7. Digital libraries. 8. Communication in the sciences–Technological innovations. I. Miller, Jeannie P. II. Science & technology libraries.
Z675.T3 E48 2004
025'.00285–dc22

2004014895

Indexing, Abstracting & Website/Internet Coverage

This section provides you with a list of major indexing & abstracting services and other tools for bibliographic access. That is to say, each service began covering this periodical during the year noted in the right column. Most Websites which are listed below have indicated that they will either post, disseminate, compile, archive, cite or alert their own Website users with research-based content from this work. (This list is as current as the copyright date of this publication.)

Abstracting, Website/Indexing Coverage . . . . Year When Coverage Began

- *AATA Online: Abstracts of International Conservation Literature (formerly Art & Archeology Technical Abstracts) <http://aata.getty.edu>* **2004**

- *ABC POL SCI: A Bibliography of Contents: Political Science & Government, ABC-CLIO (Now called Worldwide Political Science & Government) <http://www.csa.com>* **2003**

- *AGRICOLA Database (AGRICultural OnLine Access): A bibliographic database of citations to the agricultural literature created by the National Agricultural Library and its cooperators <http://www.natl.usda.gov/ag98>* **1989**

- *AGRIS <http://www.fao.org/agris/>* **1989**

- *Aluminum Industry Abstracts <http://www.csa.com>* **2003**

- *Biosciences Information Service of Biological Abstracts (BIOSIS) a centralized source of life science information <http://www.biosis.org>* **1982**

- *BIOSIS Previews: online version of Biological Abstracts and Biological Abstracts/RRM (Reports, Reviews, Meetings); Covers approximately 6,500 life science journals and 2,000 worldwide meetings* **1982**

- *Cambridge Scientific Abstracts is a leading publisher of scientific information in print journals, online databases, CD-ROM and via the Internet <http://www.csa.com>* **2003**

- *Ceramic Abstracts <http://www.csa.com>* **2003**

(continued)

(continued)

(continued)

Special Bibliographic Notes related to special journal issues
(separates) and indexing/abstracting:

- indexing/abstracting services in this list will also cover material in any "separate" that is co-published simultaneously with Haworth's special thematic journal issue or DocuSerial. Indexing/abstracting usually covers material at the article/chapter level.
- monographic co-editions are intended for either non-subscribers or libraries which intend to purchase a second copy for their circulating collections.
- monographic co-editions are reported to all jobbers/wholesalers/approval plans. The source journal is listed as the "series" to assist the prevention of duplicate purchasing in the same manner utilized for books-in-series.
- to facilitate user/access services all indexing/abstracting services are encouraged to utilize the co-indexing entry note indicated at the bottom of the first page of each article/chapter/contribution.
- this is intended to assist a library user of any reference tool (whether print, electronic, online, or CD-ROM) to locate the monographic version if the library has purchased this version but not a subscription to the source journal.
- individual articles/chapters in any Haworth publication are also available through the Haworth Document Delivery Service (HDDS).

Emerging Issues in the Electronic Environment: Challenges for Librarians and Researchers in the Sciences

CONTENTS

ABOUT THE EDITOR

Jeannie P. Miller, PhD, has been on the faculty of the Texas A&M University Libraries since 1991, when she was hired as Senior Science Reference Librarian. Dr. Miller was tenured in 1997, promoted to Professor in 2003, and is currently Director of Science/Engineering Services in the Sterling C. Evans Library. Her research and publication efforts focus on facilitating access to information sources in the sciences and on promotion and tenure issues for academic librarians. She is active in the American Library Association and the Science and Technology Section of ACRL, and participates on several library and university committees, including the Committee on Appointment, Promotion, and Tenure, and the Faculty Senate. Dr. Miller's previous professional positions include that of Cataloging Librarian at the Memorial Library, University of Wisconsin, Madison, and Reference Librarian at the Michigan State University Library, East Lansing.

Introduction

The objective of this special, thematic volume is to inspire thought and future research on technology-related issues that face both librarians and scientists. Increasingly rapid advances in technology and scientific discovery have dramatically altered the information-seeking behavior of both student and faculty researchers. Concomitant with these changes is a new set of challenges for librarians serving this population of users. Science librarians need not only advanced skills in information technology but also a more in-depth knowledge and understanding of specific subject areas. As the availability of indexes and journals in electronic format increases, so does the ease of conducting a literature review and acquiring journal articles and other pertinent materials. To satisfy the needs of their users, libraries continue to add electronic journals and databases to their collections. At the same time, budgetary constraints have resulted in cancellation of many paper subscriptions in favor of the "more desirable" electronic version. Librarians struggle to locate, purchase, make available, understand, use, and preserve the record of science in both content and format for users they might never see face-to-face. Scientists, too, can easily be overwhelmed when sifting through, organizing, and using the plethora of information published in their fields.

The first paper, "Scientific Communication: New Roles and New Players," by Julie M. Hurd sets the tone of the issue by examining in detail the evolution of information-seeking behavior of scientists from the days of print-based sources to those of electronic media. Elizabeth B.

[Haworth co-indexing entry note]: "Introduction." Miller, Jeannie P. Co-published simultaneously in *Science & Technology Libraries* (The Haworth Information Press, an imprint of The Haworth Press, Inc.) Vol. 25, No. 1/2, 2004, pp. 1-3; and: *Emerging Issues in the Electronic Environment: Challenges for Librarians and Researchers in the Sciences* (ed: Jeannie P. Miller) The Haworth Information Press, an imprint of The Haworth Press, Inc., 2004, pp. 1-3. Single or multiple copies of this article are available for a fee from The Haworth Document Delivery Service [1-800-HAWORTH, 9:00 a.m. - 5:00 p.m. (EST). E-mail address: docdelivery@haworthpress.com].

Digital Object Identifier: 10.1300/J122v25n01_01

Scientific Communication:
New Roles and New Players

Julie M. Hurd

SUMMARY. Communication in science has evolved from a process dependent on print-on-paper to one increasingly reliant on electronic media as databases have replaced indexes and journals have shifted to electronic formats. This migration from print to electronic has transformed the roles of virtually all participants in the system of scientific communication. Scientist-authors, publishers, and librarians have all assumed new duties as the Internet and the World Wide Web have blurred boundaries and realigned responsibilities.

This paper examines some of these changes in detail with reference to a communication model developed during a print-based time by sociologists William Garvey and Belver Griffith. An updated model of the current scientific communication system will be presented that incorporates developments that have changed the very nature of research and publishing and have altered, as well, the ways that libraries and librarians interact with scientists and publishers. The challenges associated with these changes are identified and discussed. *[Article copies available for a fee from The Haworth Document Delivery Service: 1-800-HAWORTH. E-mail address: <docdelivery@haworthpress.com> Website: <http://www.HaworthPress.com> © 2004 by The Haworth Press, Inc. All rights reserved.]*

Julie M. Hurd, PhD (Chemistry), MA (Library Science), is Science Librarian and Coordinator for Digital Library Planning, University of Illinois at Chicago, P.O. Box 8198, M/C 234, Chicago, IL 60680 (E-mail: jhurd@uic.edu).

[Haworth co-indexing entry note]: "Scientific Communication: New Roles and New Players." Hurd, Julie M. Co-published simultaneously in *Science & Technology Libraries* (The Haworth Information Press, an imprint of The Haworth Press, Inc.) Vol. 25, No. 1/2, 2004, pp. 5-22; and: *Emerging Issues in the Electronic Environment: Challenges for Librarians and Researchers in the Sciences* (ed: Jeannie P. Miller) The Haworth Information Press, an imprint of The Haworth Press, Inc., 2004, pp. 5-22. Single or multiple copies of this article are available for a fee from The Haworth Document Delivery Service [1-800-HAWORTH, 9:00 a.m. - 5:00 p.m. (EST). E-mail address: docdelivery@haworthpress.com].

http://www.haworthpress.com/web/STL
© 2004 by The Haworth Press, Inc. All rights reserved.
Digital Object Identifier: 10.1300/J122v25n01_02

KEYWORDS. Communication in science, electronic publishing, scholarly publication

INTRODUCTION

Scientific communication is a complex and interrelated system that has evolved over several centuries. Its origins lie in the first scientific journals that developed in the late seventeenth century from the correspondence of scientific societies comprised of individuals with broad and general interests in scientific discovery. The earliest scientific journals reflected the wide-ranging interests of early society members, but gradually discipline-specific societies were formed, and these associations began to publish their own more specialized journals. As the number of journals increased, indexes and abstracts were created to provide access to the contents of the ever-growing scientific literature; new publishers emerged that specialized in these secondary publications. By the middle of the twentieth century, scientific publishers included both society and for-profit organizations. The latter often produced the most narrowly-specialized titles.

Publishers of scientific journals depend on scientist-authors to provide content for their volumes, and the peer-review process has evolved as a mechanism to validate the quality of the science that is published. The authors of scientific journal articles, in turn, have traditionally relied on the stature of journals in which they publish their research to advance their careers; this is especially the case for those scientists employed in research universities. Initially, scientists were able to purchase all of the publications needed to support their research, but, as the literature grew, they became increasingly dependent on libraries to provide them with needed information, whether primary research journals or secondary service publications. The growth of research libraries during the twentieth century paralleled the growth of both profit-sector and society publishers and resulted in an economic interdependence that continues to the present.

Scientific communication links these very diverse individuals and organizations by the common thread of their shared interests in the outcomes of scientific research. Since the appearance of the first scientific journals in the late seventeenth century, the roles of individuals and organizations within the communication system have been reasonably well understood. This situation shifted dramatically with the emergence of several powerful change agents during the latter part of the twentieth century.

The first catalyst for change was the computer, although its ultimate power to destabilize the communication system wasn't realized initially by most participants. The earliest applications of computers by the publishing industry increased efficiencies in the production process for print materials; for example, computer-driven typesetting reduced the delay in bringing print journals to publication. As secondary publishers adapted computer technology to streamline and speed the publication of print indexes and abstracts, they created bibliographic databases, initially as by-products, that quickly became the preferred mode of searching the scientific literature. Still later, electronic journals would hasten the transformation from a print-based to an electronic system.

The two other major catalysts for change were the Internet and the World Wide Web. The Internet and the Web were both products of scientists seeking to find better ways to facilitate sharing of research results; both developments have had a much broader and disruptive impact on the entire system of scientific communication. This paper focuses on the changing system of scientific communication outlined briefly in the preceding paragraphs and explores how those changes have resulted in new roles for participants and have brought new stake-holders into the system.

COMMUNICATION IN THE PRINT ERA

Sociologists of science William Garvey, Belver Griffith, and co-workers developed a model of a scientific communication system based on their observations of psychologists (Garvey and Griffith 1972; Garvey 1979, and references cited therein). Garvey and Griffith approached the study of scientific communication as a social process, and their investigations produced a model of the communication system in psychology from the initiation of a research project to its ultimate assimilation into the discipline's knowledge base. The Garvey/Griffith model was subsequently demonstrated to be generally applicable across many other disciplines in the physical, life, and social sciences. Figure 1 depicts the Garvey/Griffith model as it was outlined over thirty years ago. The various steps in the creation and dissemination of new knowledge are shown as a timeline. The participants at each stage and their roles in the system are indicated.

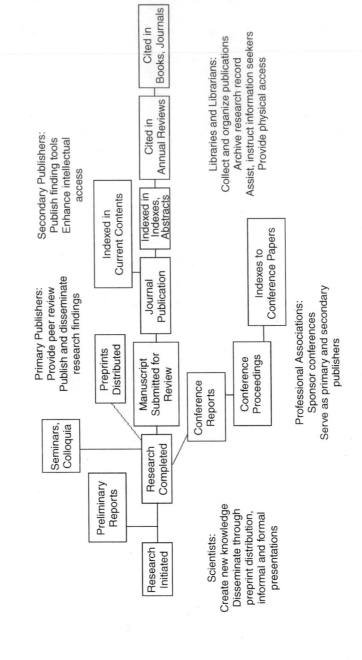

FIGURE 1. Scientific Communication Traditional Garvey/Griffith Model

Participants and Their Roles

The Garvey/Griffith model depicts both formal and informal communication among individuals and groups. It is essentially a sequential process with the central activity publication of research in peer-reviewed scientific journals. After journal publication, other aspects of the model represent the incorporation of the scientist's findings into the discipline's literature through inclusion in indexes, abstracts, annual reviews, and other publications. At each stage, the roles of both individuals and organizations were clearly understood by all system participants; there was little ambiguity in either the sequence or the appropriate actions. For example, a scientist/author knew without question that a manuscript would be submitted to a peer-reviewed scientific journal appropriate for its content. In many scientific specialties, the preferred venue for publication was a journal published by the scientific association in that field: for example, *JAMA* (*The Journal of the American Medical Association*) or the American Chemical Society's *Journal of Organic Chemistry*.

As scientific research became increasingly specialized, for-profit publishers saw opportunities to serve the emerging sub-disciplines and began to publish titles that were intended for a very narrow and focused readership. Both scientific societies and the commercial scientific publishers that emerged mid-twentieth century co-existed and shared the same market for their products, a mix of individual scientists and research libraries. Libraries and librarians occupied a well-established place in the system as well. Libraries acquired and maintained the growing collections of scholarly journals, indexes and abstracts, annual reviews, and textbooks and were committed to archiving knowledge in perpetuity for society. Librarians understood the structure of the literature, built the research collections, and helped scientists locate the materials needed to support their research. Even as Garvey and Griffith were developing their model, however, agents for change were appearing that would eventually prove disruptive to the entire communication system.

TECHNOLOGICAL CHANGE AGENTS

Computers in the Workplace

During the decade following World War II, high-speed computing became generally available to the scientific and business communities. Applications in the research sector were focused on manipulation and

regard for geographic location" (Leiner et al. 2000). They identify four distinct aspects in the origins of the Internet: the technological innovations that permitted open architecture networking, the operations and management contributions to the infrastructure, the social changes that built on e-mail to radically alter communication behavior, and the commercialization that supported the evolution of research results into a broadly used and widely available resource.

The World Wide Web, developed by Tim Berners-Lee and others in the high energy physics community, provided a user-friendly and intuitive interface to link, search, and display Internet-based resources (Internet Pioneers n.d.). Using the Web requires very little understanding of the complexity of the underlying technology; the Web browsers that now exist allow users ranging from children in grade school to research scientists to share information globally on their desktop computers. The ease of use of the Web has encouraged numerous commercial applications including those in electronic publishing, a development that has transformed scientific communication and is the subject of this article.

SCIENTIFIC COMMUNICATION
IN AN ELECTRONIC ENVIRONMENT

Initial predictions of a transformed system of scientific communication were sometimes simplistic and overestimated the rate of change with respect to adoption of innovations. Some visionaries predicted a future that discounted discipline-specific factors that now have been realized as significant. For example, the success of e-print archives in high energy physics suggested a communication model that was based on e-print databases and would eventually replace scientific journals. While a few specializations enthusiastically adopted e-print archives, the vast majority of others did not.

Kling and McKim (2000) provided a thoughtful analysis that takes into account disciplinary differences in communication behavior. Their approach captures the complexities of scholarship and supports a better understanding of what the future might bring. Crawford, Hurd, and Weller (1996) and Hurd (2000) also proposed new models of scientific communication that incorporate discipline-specific attributes.

At this time, electronic journals published on the World Wide Web are the norm in most scientific disciplines. While the demise of the scientific journal was predicted, in fact, that has not yet come to be. Rather, those formerly-print publications are now also published electronically in a format that retains the strengths of print, such as peer-review, but offers new and powerful functionalities such as reference linking. Both scholarly society and for-profit publishers of print journals quickly realized the need to digitize their journals; most of them now offer both print and electronic versions of titles. The business models necessary to support parallel formats have been more difficult to develop, with resulting stresses on both publishers and their library and individual markets.

CHANGING ROLES AND NEW RESPONSIBILITIES

Even as publishers are caught up in the ongoing transformation from print to electronic so are all other participants in the system. What was once a linear process with clearly defined roles has evolved into a more complex and interrelated environment. In this dynamic period, traditional roles have blurred and new roles have emerged, sometimes assumed by familiar players, but other times by new entities. Figure 2 depicts some of this complexity and highlights changes in the process of scientific communication. The rectangular elements in the figure represent enduring activities and functionalities, some of which now incorporate technology. For example, those fields that had a culture of disseminating preprints, have adapted and now utilize e-print archives. Other features of this model, those shown as ovals, were not part of the print-based system and identify new functionalities and new participants.

New collaborations are emerging as a result of changes that potentially involve all participants in the system. Kate Wittenberg, director of an electronic publishing initiative at Columbia University, described some of these from a scholarly publishers' perspective (Wittenberg 2003). She asserted that the changes in scholarly communication were blurring roles and responsibilities for editors and authors, even as technology presented creative opportunities for everyone involved in organizing and presenting new knowledge to readers. She challenged publishers to create an organizational model that fosters collaborations among authors, editors, book designers, technologists, and marketing staff and that builds in formal mechanisms for involvement of scholars, librarians, and educators as well.

The Association of Research Libraries sponsored a forum in October 2001 that examined how "the changes in the environment of scholarly communication were shifting or blurring boundaries of responsibilities within the library, and externally among the many stakeholders in the system" (ARL 2002). The report of papers and discussions from that

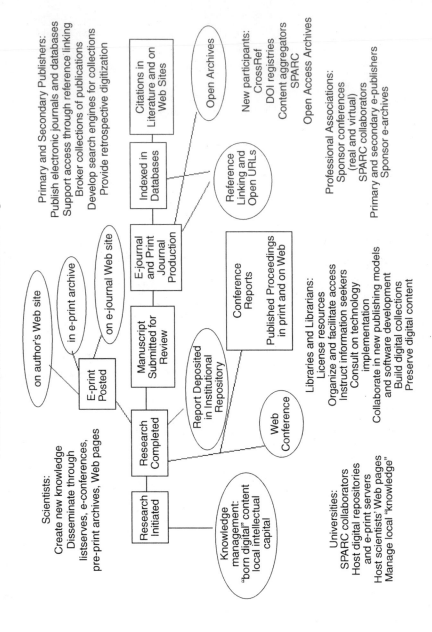

FIGURE 2. Scientific Communication in a Digital World

meeting is a succinct overview of the opportunities and challenges for libraries; the references found in that report link to additional details on many of the issues explored in this paper. Some of the changing roles identified for research libraries include:

- shifting emphasis from building print collections to licensing electronic resources
- participating in initiatives such as SPARC (the Scholarly Publishing and Academic Resources Coalition) that seek to develop affordable publishing alternatives
- digitizing materials and building locally maintained but widely shared digital collections
- collaborating with other units in the organization, or outside, to create virtual collections from dispersed resources
- developing new services, many of them technology-based, to enhance access within the organization and across institutional boundaries.

Brach (2001) and Hurd and Weller (2004) provide analyses of the successes and remaining problems that electronic resources pose for managers of research library collections.

Acquisition of Electronic Resources

The growing emphasis on electronic resources is especially important in science, technology, and medicine (STM). These disciplines were the leaders in electronic publishing, and STM resources are among the most highly developed and costly. Electronic resources require fundamentally different approaches to acquisition than print materials. Library selectors now find themselves going beyond the assessment of content that informed print selection; it is also essential to evaluate the functionality of a user interface and know the hardware and software requirements before deciding to license a resource.

The licenses themselves continue to be one of the more demanding aspects of the evaluation process and frequently require the intervention of the parent organization's legal counsel in order to determine compatibility with the parent organization's policies. It is not unusual to find clauses in a license that are unacceptable and subject to further negotiation and adjustment before signing. Large complex organizations may have facilities in multiple locations; for example, universities with more than one campus or corporations with facilities at multiple sites. In either case, the definition of "site" in a license can be a critical issue. Another area of concern in licenses is restriction on interlibrary lending. Many publishers of e-journals do not permit these items to be used to supply interlibrary loan requests. Other restrictive terms may exist that hinder use in electronic reserve operations or distance education.

Some providers license products for a set number of simultaneous users, for example, *SciFinder Scholar* and the *Web of Knowledge*. This type of resource requires a library to know enough about its user community to make a wise decision about anticipated use. The price of the resource will depend on the maximum number of users supported. If a library makes a "best guess" as to how many "seats" to license, timely use statistics and a flexible agreement with the provider can allow for later adjustment to reflect actual use. At the same time, this type of access may be unfamiliar to users who are turned away and will not necessarily realize the reason. The user interface may not provide a message understandable by users, so this situation represents an area where librarians must educate their constituencies.

As publishers and aggregators increased their e-journal offerings, many began to broker bundled collections that included either their entire product line or discipline-specific groupings. These prepackaged assemblages typically include many titles for which a library lacks a current print equivalent. Kenneth Frazier comments on the disruptive effect of this marketing strategy, which he calls the "big deal," on the library acquisition process (Frazier 2001). He points out that these group licenses typically include constraints on cancellation of the e-journal titles that are included. Bundled titles may dilute a library's collection with titles for which it has no need. The "big deal" favors the larger publishers and may leave a library with insufficient resources to select from the offerings of smaller publishers whose journals may contribute uniquely to a discipline. While patrons may perceive only the short-term gain–the addition of many more e-journals–in the long term, the collection may weaken and lose its special strengths that differentiate it from the collections of other institutions.

The Scholarly Publishing and Academic Resources Coalition (SPARC)

In response to some of these financial pressures, libraries have partnered with small scholarly publishers and presses to develop alternative journals that promise cost savings through SPARC, an initiative of the Association of Research Libraries (http://www.arl.org/sparc/).

SPARC-sponsored STM titles have succeeded in attracting scientists, both as members of their editorial boards and as authors, and include some very remarkable successes such as *Organic Letters*, a collaboration with the American Chemical Society. *Organic Letters*, now in it its fifth year of publication, has the highest impact factor of all journals publishing more than 100 articles per year in organic chemistry for the second year in a row according to the 2002 ISI *Journal Citation Reports* (ACS 2003). Collaborations such as SPARC offer an opportunity for librarians to be active participants in the scholarly publishing process and to shape the future of scientific communication.

Reference Linking

The migration to electronic publishing of journals and databases has made feasible functionalities not possible in a print environment. Reference linking, sometimes known as citation linking, is considered by Priscilla Caplan to be "one of the most important added values to emerge from the rise of electronic scholarly publishing" (Caplan 2001). She defines reference linking "as the ability to go directly from a citation to the work cited, or to additional information about the cited work." Sources of citations include entries in databases, references in a full-text article, or any other clickable link. The targets of these links are generally the articles in libraries' licensed e-journals, but may also include materials on patent office or other government agency Web sites as well as commercial and personal Web pages. In the best of worlds, all this linking would be seamless, activated only by a single mouse click; in the present reality, matters are not yet quite that simple. How reference linking is enabled varies significantly at this time and is not fully realized, but its promise has resulted in new alliances among publishers and other information organizations.

CrossRef, DOIs, SFX, and Open URLs

CrossRef is an initiative directed toward resolving some of the barriers to seamless reference linking. CrossRef (http://www.crossref.org) is a joint effort by major primary and secondary publishers to provide an infrastructure for reference linking through use of the Digital Object Identifier (DOI) (Mader 2001). DOIs are unique identifiers for digital objects such as article text and, possibly, even discrete portions of articles such as figures or tables. DOIs are persistent and are registered by the publisher with the URL where the article resides in a database maintained by the International DOI Foundation. The DOI must be searched in this database to determine the URL, a process referred to as "resolving." CrossRef-participating publishers deposit article bibliographic metadata and DOIs into a database maintained by CrossRef. When a user clicks on a reference that offers a CrossRef-enabled link to full text, the CrossRef switching system "resolves" the DOI by translating it into the correct URL and connects the user to the article on the publisher Web site where the user would be authenticated as a valid subscriber to the journal. The CrossRef database also can be queried by participating publishers to create "actionable" links in lists of references. At this time, CrossRef cannot address the context of the user, i.e., the organizational environment that determines access privileges. CrossRef cannot direct that individual to sources other than the primary publisher. For example, libraries may use aggregators to authenticate users before passing them off to a publisher site, or they may channel users coming from outside the organization's computing network to a proxy server for authentication.

Context-sensitive reference linking tools support the need of many libraries to localize their linking functions by referring their users to the "appropriate copy" of an article, i.e., the copy that has been licensed for that institution's users whether that be from a publisher, an aggregator, or through a consortium. Libraries frequently have more than one choice of provider for a particular resource. The library may also wish to direct users to its print collections for items not available electronically or to document delivery services for items not held locally.

The seamless interconnectivity that is the dream of all users is not necessarily easy for libraries to implement. The first efforts to resolve the "appropriate copy" problem were labor-intensive and often required a library to convey information to a database provider on the source for each and every journal indexed in a database to which the library wished to provide reference linking. Of course, when a library adds or cancels titles or switches providers, holdings information must be updated. For very large libraries, the initial customization can require considerable time up front, with lesser amounts of time required to maintain current holdings information. And this sort of activity would need to be replicated, with variations, in every other database that supports local customization in this fashion. Clearly, this does not scale well in times of tight staffing! The need for scalability has driven the development of products designed to facilitate, at the local library level, the integration of resources acquired from an array of providers.

SFX (for Special Effects) is a proprietary, context-sensitive reference linking product commercially available from Ex Libris, a provider of library integrated systems (http://www.exlibrisgroup.com/sfx.htm). The software makes use of OpenURL, an open source protocol and proposed standard that provides a syntax for the address and other descriptive elements such as the DOI and metadata that identify a specific digital object, e.g., an article in a full-text e-journal. The SFX server, knowing the requester's affiliation, can identify the resources available to that user and determine the location of an appropriate copy/copies. Only the SFX server needs to store the list of preferred providers, and staff do not then need to customize products individually, provided the resources are SFX-aware.

To provide the apparently seamless linking among resources so desired by librarians and users requires the interaction of all the components described above. DOIs must be in place to provide persistent identifiers, and the OpenURL protocol employed to standardize metadata elements essential to locating content. The CrossRef database serves as a reference for DOIs and citation metadata, and SFX (or a similar product) provides resolution and referral at the local library level. Implementing reference linking is a truly collaborative process that involves numerous participants; it has resulted in new responsibilities for primary and secondary publishers and librarians, and generated new organizations to maintain the necessary data.

Building Digital Collections

Linking licensed resources has enhanced access to the published record represented by scientific journals, patents, and government documents. Other initiatives underway are focusing on materials that may be unique to one institution or rare and special in some other way. Many libraries now are pursuing strategies to enhance access to their special collections, whether text, image, or other media. Collaborating with faculty, academic departments, local organizations such as museums, and not-for-profit agencies, librarians are building digital collections that make locally-held or dispersed resources more easily identifiable, searchable, and accessible. The digital repositories that are under development are wide-ranging in content. Some, such as MIT's DSpace, manage local intellectual capital by bringing together university research in digital form, including preprints, technical reports, working papers, conference papers, images, and more (https://dspace.mit.edu/index.jsp).

Other digital repositories are being created from rich and valuable retrospective collections that formerly required scholars to visit the library holding the resources. Many special collections departments have eagerly begun to digitize their holdings thereby making them widely available and supporting their preservation. Librarians participating in digitization projects have acquired new skills related to technology, but have also drawn on their traditional strengths in organizing information and providing instruction to potential users. New infrastructures such as the Open Archives Initiative have emerged to link digital collections by harvesting the metadata that libraries create to describe their digital collections (http://www.openarchives.org/). New standards are being written, and the software is under development to support interoperability and digital rights management. The collaborations that are forming will change how research is done and will make primary sources available to an increasingly diverse audience.

New Services to Users

Technology has made the developments above possible and, in so doing, challenged existing approaches to the provision of library services. As ever more information is available electronically, the concept of place-based services and resources is eroded. If many of a library's users do not need to come into the building to obtain the information they need, then new delivery mechanisms are required. Web-based instruction, possibly integrated with course management software such as BlackBoard, has the potential to reach students who might be in campus residence halls, but could instead be enrolled in distance education programs far from any library. Librarians are partnering with faculty and instructional technology staff to create and develop the tools needed to use digitized resources. Virtual or chat reference represents another approach to reaching off-site users and, in many cases, supports outreach to previously unserved groups. Virtual reference is frequently collaborative, as it may involve referring questions to other libraries to take advantage of special expertise or different time zones to insure around-the-clock services.

FUTURE DIRECTIONS

Scientific communication systems will continue to evolve as the developments outlined above give rise to new approaches to sharing the results of research. We are in the midst of a transformation that has created new roles for authors, publishers, information technologists, and librarians. Technology has been the catalyst and will continue to ensure a fluid environment, with change the only constant. Behavioral determinants will also shape the future as both traditional players and new participants interact to achieve common goals. Organizational cultures are challenged to respond to new participants and increased collaborations. Economic pressures, barely alluded to in this article, will also influence the outcomes. In the words of Jay Jordan, President and Chief Executive Officer of OCLC, "We face some exciting prospects in this new environment of digital collections. . . . Working together, we can help change how people conduct research, scholarship and education, and these changes will have far-reaching benefits for humanity in the years to come" (Jordan 2003).

REFERENCES

American Chemical Society. http://pubs.acs.org/journals/orlef7/ (accessed July 20, 2004).

Association of Research Libraries. 2002. Collections and access for the 21st-century scholar: Changing roles of research libraries. *ARL: A Bimonthly Report on Research Library Issues and Actions from ARL, CNI, and SPARC.* Washington, DC: ARL. no, 225, December 2002.

Brach, Carol. 2001. Electronic collections–Evolution of strategies: Past, present, and future. *Science & Technology Libraries* 21(1/2):17-27.

Caplan, Priscilla. 2001. Reference linking for journal articles: Promise, progress, and perils. *portal: Libraries and the academy* 1(3):351-356.

Crawford, Susan Y., Hurd, Julie M. and Weller, Ann C. 1996. *From print to electronic: The transformation of scientific communication.* ASIS Monograph Series. Medford, NJ: Information Today.

Frazier, Kenneth. 2001. The librarian's dilemma: Contemplating the costs of the "big deal." *D-Lib Magazine,* 7. http://www.dlib.org/dlib/march01/frazier/03frazier.html (accessed July 20, 2004).

Garvey, William D. 1979. *Communication: The essence of science.* Elmsford, NY: Pergamon Press.

Garvey, William D. and Griffith, Belver C. 1972. Communication and information processing within scientific disciplines: Empirical findings for psychology. *Information Storage and Retrieval* 8:123-126.

Hurd, Julie M. 2000. The transformation of scientific communication: A model for 2020, *Journal of the American Society for Information Science* 51(14):1279-1283.

Hurd, Julie M. and Weller, Ann C. 2004. Evolving electronic journals: Accomplishments and challenges. *Journal of Electronic Resources in Medical Libraries* 1(1):31-49.

Internet Pioneers: Tim Berners-Lee. n.d. http://www.ibiblio.org/pioneers/lee.html (accessed July 20, 2004).

Jordan, Jay. 2003. Digital collections, e-learning and libraries. *OCLC Newsletter*, no. 261:2-3.

Kling, R. and McKim, G. W. 2000. Not just a matter of time: Field differences and the shaping of electronic media in supporting scientific communication. *Journal of the American Society for Information Science* 51(14):1306-1320.

Leiner, Barry M., Cerf, Vinton G., Clark, David D., Kahn, Robert E., Kleinrock, Leonard, Lynch, Daniel C., Postel, Jon, Roberts, Larry G., and Wolff, Stephen. 2000. A brief history of the Internet. The Internet Society http://www.isoc.org/internet/history/brief.shtml (accessed July 20, 2004).

Mader, Cynthia. 2001. Current implementation of the DOI in STM publication. *Science & Technology Libraries* 21(1/2): 97-118.

Wittenberg, Kate. 2003. Scholarly editing in the digital age. *The Chronicle of Higher Education* 49(41):B12.

Too Important to Be Left to Chance–
Serendipity and the Digital Library

Elizabeth B. Cooksey

SUMMARY. This article discusses the meaning of "serendipity" in the digital library, with an emphasis on the role of librarians in facilitating conditions of serendipity for a scientific audience. It argues that the digital revolution has created a greater need among scientists for libraries and librarians. Provided a wealth of new resources instantly available online, scientists who miss crucial information by focusing on a small number of resources with which they are familiar need to interact with their librarians on an ever-increasing basis. The importance of providing not only access to digital resources, but also more and more guidance beyond "Google" and its analogs, is required so that scientists can make the connections needed in their information searches. *[Article copies available for a fee from The Haworth Document Delivery Service: 1-800-HAWORTH. E-mail address: <docdelivery@haworthpress.com> Website: <http://www.HaworthPress.com> © 2004 by The Haworth Press, Inc. All rights reserved.]*

KEYWORDS. Library serendipity, information finding practices of scientists

Elizabeth B. Cooksey, MA, MLS, is an Independent Information Professional and Consulting Research Librarian, University of Georgia Marine Education Center and Aquarium, 12708 Sunnybrook Road, Savannah, GA 31419-2420 (E-mail: sciquest@bellsouth.net or askliz@bellsouth.net).

[Haworth co-indexing entry note]: "Too Important to Be Left to Chance–Serendipity and the Digital Library." Cooksey, Elizabeth B. Co-published simultaneously in *Science & Technology Libraries* (The Haworth Information Press, an imprint of The Haworth Press, Inc.) Vol. 25, No. 1/2, 2004, pp. 23-32; and: *Emerging Issues in the Electronic Environment: Challenges for Librarians and Researchers in the Sciences* (ed: Jeannie P. Miller) The Haworth Information Press, an imprint of The Haworth Press, Inc., 2004, pp. 23-32. Single or multiple copies of this article are available for a fee from The Haworth Document Delivery Service [1-800-HAWORTH, 9:00 a.m. - 5:00 p.m. (EST). E-mail address: docdelivery@haworthpress.com].

http://www.haworthpress.com/web/STL
© 2004 by The Haworth Press, Inc. All rights reserved.
Digital Object Identifier: 10.1300/J122v25n01_03

After reading through a score of "library cases," one is tempted to think of library angels in charge of providing cross-references.

–Arthur Koestler (Liestman 1992)

INTRODUCTION

It has been a mantra that the goal of librarianship is to save the patron time–to be the "library angels" who make it easier for information seekers to reach their goals, but some patrons have believed that their success in finding just the right book, article, or bit of information has been due to "serendipity," the happy coincidence of patron and information. Librarians and sophisticated library users, of course, know better. They *expect* serendipity when they browse the shelves, realizing that there is a system and people behind the scenes, preparing the collection for such happy discoveries.

The literature is full of discussions surrounding the definition of "serendipity," and scholars have debated its nature for decades. Consultation of "famous quotations" collections yields "sayings" from the semi-serious to the witty, "Serendipity is too important to be left to chance" (Rhodes 2003); "Serendipity is looking in a haystack for a needle and discovering the farmer's daughter" (Anonymous). The word itself was coined by British wit Horace Walpole, while alluding to a 16th century set of fairy tales, *The Three Princes of Serendip*. As Walpole recalled in a letter to his friend, the diplomat Horace Mann in 1754, "[the heroes] were always making discoveries, by accidents and sagacity, of things they were not in quest of" (Oxford English Dictionary, 2nd ed).

However, the common understanding of a "serendipitous finding" has departed from the sort the princes were stumbling across–the completely unsought for discoveries–and now brings to mind the felicitous finding of something to assist one in reaching an already formulated goal. Some have taken issue with this, offering instead the terms "pseudoserendipity" or "serendipity analog" to represent "accidental discoveries of ways to achieve an end sought for, in contrast to the meanings of (true) serendipity . . . which describes accidental discoveries of things not sought for" (Roberts 1989).

Another way of thinking about serendipity in a way that helps us understand how it works, is to draw an analogy with the metaphor, the rhetorical trope in which one thing is by implication compared with another. Employing metaphor, a poet might write, "My love is a rose."

Here some implicit properties connected with the rose are compared with implicit qualities of the beloved. The metaphor does not tell us how to interpret itself, but it does suggest a range of possibilities. The poet probably does not mean to say that the beloved is covered with rose petals, but rather that the beloved has a quality of delicacy, or softness, or fragrance. On the other hand, a wag might play with the implication of rose thorns, not the poet's original intention, but an interesting new way to look at the situation. The point is that the *linking* of concepts in the metaphor stimulates the reader to make connections. Some of these connections may have been expected, but the real power of a good metaphor is its ability to open the possibility of connections that have not previously been anticipated. That, to use another (tired) metaphor, is what it means to think outside the proverbial box.

This *parallel* with metaphors gives us some sense of the elements of serendipity and how it works. There are not only the circumstances of serendipity, but also the mind that is bringing them together. The librarian, like the poet, helps to set the scene for the metaphor. But it is the reader who makes the connections.

It is assumed that most readers of this journal work with library clientele whose research is in science and technology, so the focus here will be on library serendipity in the lives of such patrons. When asked whether they believe in "serendipity" or "luck," scientists will often respond by recalling important findings such as Alexander Fleming's observation of the antibacterial effects of the mold penicillin, or Wilhelm Roentgen's discovery of X-rays–but in such cases, the discoveries could not have been made without the years of background work leading to the knowledge each discoverer had assimilated before putting it together with the new phenomenon. Those in science have been well schooled in Louis Pasteur's remark that "in the fields of observation, chance favors only the mind that is prepared" (Bartlett 1980). Pasteur's remark underlies two aspects that are of importance here: preparation and minds. It is not the observation or bit of information *per se* that makes knowledge, but the mind that sees the significance and makes the connections. As the old joke goes, Newton's dog also saw the apple fall. But in addition to the mind are the conditions to which the mind responded. What if the apple had not fallen? Serendipity is the happy convergence of the mind with conditions. The scientist provides the mind; the librarian provides the conditions. Whether the scientist proves more like Newton than his dog is contingent on the range and richness of the circumstances that the librarian helps to provide.

How does this carry over into the use of the library by those in science and technology? The question requires a short exploration of the methods by which scientists have traditionally found the information they needed, and how these methods have changed since the advent of digital resources.

Although differences in the ways varieties of scientific specialists have found their information have been examined and expounded, several methods have been shared by scientists in general since the pre-computer age. After their own personal observation of the phenomena studied, they tend to turn to colleagues ("the invisible college") within their fields, sharing information long before it is published. Published studies differ regarding the reliance of biologists, chemists, mathematicians, and engineers on such sharing, but each does turn to colleagues for some knowledge. Personal sharing of this nature occurs both formally, at conferences, and informally, in one-to-one communication. Beyond their personal interactions, scientists move on to the printed word. For instance, according to survey results published in 1999 (Brown 1999), scientists in the disciplines of astronomy, chemistry-biochemistry, mathematics, and physics at the University of Oklahoma all relied heavily on textbooks for support of teaching activities. When asked how they kept current in their fields, these professionals mentioned attendance at conferences, but stressed that surveying the current journals was their method of choice. Those surveyed "overwhelmingly indicated" that they found older information by using the citations at the end of journal articles. The result was that the information they were drawing on followed a long but narrow line that did not go very far from its "box," limiting the potential for serendipitous discoveries. At the time, these faculty members were only vaguely familiar, or not familiar at all, with online databases such as *Carl UnCover* or *Article First*. Some of them had used *Science Citation Index*, and within each field, some had used tools specific to their disciplines (e.g., *Chemical Abstracts* for chemists) but knew little or nothing of tools specific to other disciplines. At the time, nearly all reprints were requested by the scientists themselves directly from their colleagues or through interlibrary loan, and 85% maintained personal collections of such reprints. Three years later, results of a survey of over 3,000 faculty members, graduate and undergraduate students from three types of educational institutions in seven disciplines were asked similar questions. Scientists who taught still reported a preference for printed texts for lecture preparation. The use of electronic materials had soared for other scholarly endeavors, however, with 58.08% of faculty members and graduate students reporting their research needs being met by the Internet. Respondents continued to list interaction with colleagues, professional meetings, and personal subscriptions as ways they kept current, but by this time had added the "open" Internet, department and library Web pages, and on-line alerting services (Friedlander 2002).

Precipitating this and further reports of adoption of e-resources (see below) was the sudden escalation of availability and acceptance of electronic versions of peer-reviewed journals. Between 1998 and 2002 the percentage of journals in science, mathematics, and medicine in the *Science Citation Index* available online jumped from 30% to 75% (Van Orsdel and Born 2002).

By 2003, Tenopir et al. reported a gigantic leap in use of electronic journals among scientists in the previous two years. In a study conducted in three phases beginning in 1990-1993 (with 862 respondents) and ending in 2001-2002 (with 508 respondents), scientists surveyed reported an increase from 0.3% to 79.5% in the number of articles they obtained electronically. In the same study, scientists reported a decrease of more than 50% in personal subscriptions since 1977, and their browsing for appropriate reading was evolving into searching for particular articles, although they preferred browsing current issues in print (Tenopir et al. 2003). Tenopir and her colleagues concluded that this change in citation discovery methods has been accompanied by more reliance on libraries. Access to the articles discovered is actually moving more and more into the library's hands, as scientists identify articles in journals they or their colleagues no longer, or never subscribed to. So, while e-journals have enabled faster and often cheaper article access to the patron, access is more than ever through library collections, which are able to provide much more comprehensive digital e-journal collections than any individual could subscribe to.

TRUE SERENDIPITY

But what of true serendipity? Does the digital library fall into Karen Lawrence's lyrical definition: "For a good library invites students to browse among books not assigned, to discover writers out of fashion, writers who may be valued by future generations, as well as writers valued in the past. It is precisely this kind of potential that a major research library must nurture, and far from a luxury, this is the lifeblood of intellectual activity" (Lawrence 2002).

In the infancy of computerized library databases, Russell Doll (1980) worried that "reliance upon data bases [sic] for research may, in a subtle fashion, narrow the possibility of research questions by eliminating the important albeit overlooked aspect of serendipity in research . . . the computer is dumb. It does not provide the interplay of search and serendipity. Browsing in the indexes and doing a manual search has, on a number of occasions, led to a complete change in question, an opening of new possibilities, and opened up related but previously overlooked variables."

While at first glance it may seem that Doll's fears were not unfounded, recent users of many online OPACs and a good number of online databases have been provided with cross-links to promote his "interplay of search and serendipity." OPAC searchers, while looking at the record for one work, find links to take them to other works on the same subject, the same author(s), within the same series, if applicable, or even to those works sitting on the shelf on either side of the work at hand. Users of *WorldCat*, for instance, can link not only to other books on a subject, but also to screens that will guide them in the ways the old "see also" and "see" catalog cards did. More recently, they can even link to *WorldCat*'s "Hot Topics" links–following the trend displayed by commercial search engines such as Yahoo and Google. Many databases provide thesauri to help the searcher settle on the most successful term for a search–"oncology" instead of "cancer," for example. And more and more commonly, citation indices lead not only to other pertinent citations, but also to digital full text of the articles themselves.

Altruistic serendipity–the sharing of information one comes across with another person whom the information-finder thinks it might interest–has been enhanced by the built-in "send e-mail" choices in many library databases. Twidale et al. (1995) call this a mode of collaborative browsing, the extension of the old-style browsing and discovery to include others, pointing out that the digital search strategies themselves, as well as their results, can often be forwarded by e-mail.

If true serendipity is one's discovery of something new, combined with the realization of a connection between it and something one already knew, perhaps the library user's discovery of the existence of entire databases is a form of serendipity. A scientist who for years relied chiefly on the handful of key journals in one specialty will, by using an online journal citation index, discover the existence of pertinent and worthwhile journals hitherto unknown to him/her. Scholars who were heretofore dependent on the print indices which only deigned to cover the "prestigious" journals can now find a world of small, specialized, but quite useful publications, some of which might contain articles key to their interests. Librarians in major libraries have used print analogues to some of these indices (e.g., *The Access Index to Little Magazines*), but in general the habits of the library user would not have made the use of these commonly known at the user level.

ROLE OF LIBRARIANS

And so, digital browsing, then, not only provides serendipity, but enhances it. "Library angels" have not retired with the onset of the digital revolution! But their work would seem to have become more and more centralized, sent from afar through the ethernet. With computers helping users help themselves, and other users helping users help themselves, what is the place of the on-site librarian in the current picture? By their very efforts to streamline the finding and delivery of information for patrons, do on-site librarians thus work themselves into obsolescence?

While some anticipated that the digital library might signal the end of the print collection, it is in many places supplementing it. In the many libraries whose resources have expanded several hundredfold by the addition of e-journals and the indices to search them online, librarians find that they are needed more, not less. As practitioners, they develop the skills needed to be successful with the variety of approaches required as one moves from database to database. Infrequent use of more than two or three of these databases by patrons often results in frustration if they attempt to move out of their comfortable "ruts," and so the explosion of information needed by many, especially competitive research scientists, requires the librarian's guidance more than ever.

What is our future as librarians for scientists? Put another way, what is the function of a librarian in a research institute where the patrons are already (supposedly) trained in the art of research? Scientists tend to work in teams, with each member of a laboratory responsible for distinct tasks to achieve the overall result. It is impossible for any scholar to keep up with all the literature in his field these days, let alone all the new library resources. As one scholar recently remarked, "Having a billion new library resources that I don't know how to use, is no better than having just three that I do!" (Cooksey 2003). So if the apple falls, but Newton is distracted by his picnic basket, serendipity cannot occur. The librarian can join a scientist's team by doing whatever is possible to eliminate the distractions from the source of new connections.

Librarians have seen all too frequently the library users who miss valuable resources in the mistaken belief that what has always worked for them surely cannot be improved upon. When they are content with their two or three comfortable databases, and believe they are too busy to meet with their librarians for advice, too often they are limiting their possibilities for serendipity.

Librarians must find those individuals who have settled for less and teach them more. The "path of least resistance" is alive and well among our library users, from the freshest of freshmen to the directors of our institutions. In any institution where a new user arrives, there will of course be the need to teach the use of the resources. The challenge in these days of "instant Google satisfaction" is several-fold: students who turn first to the "open" Internet may be joined by many professionals (including librarians), but the similarity stops there. Librarians know to go beyond Google and its analogs to the "deep Web," well-screened online resources often purchased by libraries for reliability and solid scholarship. It is essential that the existence, value, and use of these databases be advertised to library users, and that users find librarians ready to teach them how to maneuver around successfully. Long more than storehouse keepers and organizers for print material, librarians have been expert advisors, interpreters, and evaluators of information for centuries. Time possibly snatched from the decrease in physical processing required in the new library is now required to interpret vendor contracts and solve computer network issues, among other duties.

CONCLUSION

In the best of worlds, digital communication has not replaced face-to-face interaction, but enhanced it. Many libraries have adopted e-reference services, allowing many more of their users to reach them more easily from off campus. For campuses with large distance learning components, this willingness and availability of the librarians to continue their traditional roles as expert advisors prevents the off-site students and faculty from settling for the often less reliable answers they might get on their own, or (possibly worse), from unknown paid-by-the-answer search engine hirees. In the study by Tenopir and others cited above, faculty and graduate students did not "perceive a competition between library-based information and information they find on the Internet through search engines, the library's Web site, and other tools." These subjects reported a healthy skepticism as to the credibility of

Internet-based information, with 98.2% of all surveyed agreeing with the statement "My institution's library contains information from credible and known sources" (Tenopir et al. 2003). The availability of digital communication, well used by librarians, assists with these laudable opinions.

The role of the librarian is not to discover scientific knowledge, but to facilitate the discovery, by providing the conditions for knowledge to happen. The librarian provides sources and materials as well as an intuition of what's "out there," based on experience. It is the scientist who makes the connections and sees the implications that mark scientific discovery. It is the librarian who expands the conditions that facilitate serendipity. Just as the poet sets up a metaphor in juxtaposing items, so it is the reader (the scientist) who discovers possibilities and meanings beyond the original intention.

REFERENCES

Bartlett, John. 1980. *Familiar Quotations*, 15th ed., edited by Emily Morison Beck. Boston: Little Brown, p. 591 (Louis Pasteur).

Brown, C.M. 1999. Information seeking behavior of scientists in the electronic information age: Astronomers, chemists, mathematicians, and physicists. *Journal of the American Society for Information Technology* 50(10): 929-943.

Cooksey, T. L. Personal interview with author, 16 July 2003.

Doll, Russell. 1980. Speculations on unanticipated outcomes of data base research. *Journal of Library Automation* 13(1): 49-55.

Rhodes, Bradley. 2003. "Opportunity." E-knowledge, http://www.e-knowledge.ca/wisdom/opportunity.html (accessed August 2003).

Friedlander, A. 2002. Dimensions and use of the scholarly information environment: introduction to a data set assembled by the Digital Library Federation and Outsell, Inc. http://www.clir.org/pubs/reports/pub110/introduction.html#observations.

Lawrence, K. 2002. *Reinvention of the Library: Looking Forward While Looking Back.* Excerpts of keynote speech given at the dedication of the Marriott Library addition, University of Utah http://www.alumni.utah.edu/continuum/winter96/library.html (accessed August 2003).

Liestman, D. 1992. Chance in the midst of design. *Reference Quarterly* 31: 524-532.

Oxford English Dictionary, 2nd ed. Online (accessed via password to the GALILEO Consortium): http://www.galileo.usg.edu/.

Roberts, R. 1989. *Serendipity: Accidental Discoveries in Science.* New York: John Wiley and sons. Quoted in http://www.chemalliance.org/Columns/Networking/Tips_and_techniques.asp (accessed August 2003).

Sandstrom, P.E. 1994. An optimal foraging approach to information seeking and use. *Library Quarterly* 64(4): 414-449.

Tenopir, C., King. D., Boyce, P. and Grayson, M. 2003. Patterns of journal use by scientists through three evolutionary phases. *D-Lib Magazine* 9: 5. http://www.dlib.org/dlib/may03/king/05king.html.

Twidale, M.B, Nichols, D.M., Mariani, J.A., Rodden, T. and Sawyer, P. 1995. Supporting the active learning of collaborative database browsing techniques. *Association for Learning Technology Journal* 3(1): 75-79.

Van Orsdel, L. and K. Born. 2002. Doing the digital flip. *Library Journal* 7: 51-56.

For Better or for Worse:
The Joys and Woes of E-Journals

Linda L. Eells

SUMMARY. As electronic journals, or e-journals, have become more prevalent, publishers, libraries, and users have all had to adapt to a new paradigm, to new methods for publishing, acquiring, providing access to, preserving, and searching for research articles. Publishers offer new and constantly changing subscription and pricing models, and the prices of many commercial journals have been increasing at rates far exceeding the rate of inflation. The resulting budget crunch has driven significant changes in the way libraries develop their collections as they strive to reformulate their traditional role as provider and preserver of information. Some libraries are working more in consortium with other libraries to purchase large bundled journal packages now offered as one of the new subscription models developed by publishers. While this appears to be a win-win situation for libraries and users in the consortium, potential drawbacks to e-journals and the big bundled packages may impact libraries and researchers alike. This study investigates some of the potential effects of a move toward e-journal only collections, large bundled journal packages, and consortial purchasing including archival, economic, content, and research impact issues. Fu-

Linda L. Eells, MLIS, MS (Conservation Biology), is Social Sciences/Science Librarian, Magrath Library, University of Minnesota, St. Paul, MN 55108 (E-mail: lle@umn.edu).

[Haworth co-indexing entry note]: "For Better or for Worse: The Joys and Woes of E-Journals." Eells, Linda L. Co-published simultaneously in *Science & Technology Libraries* (The Haworth Information Press, an imprint of The Haworth Press, Inc.) Vol. 25, No. 1/2, 2004, pp. 33-53; and: *Emerging Issues in the Electronic Environment: Challenges for Librarians and Researchers in the Sciences* (ed: Jeannie P. Miller) The Haworth Information Press, an imprint of The Haworth Press, Inc., 2004, pp. 33-53. Single or multiple copies of this article are available for a fee from The Haworth Document Delivery Service [1-800-HAWORTH, 9:00 a.m. - 5:00 p.m. (EST). E-mail address: docdelivery@haworthpress.com].

http://www.haworthpress.com/web/STL
Digital Object Identifier: 10.1300/J122v25n01_04

33

ture predictions are difficult in the current, rapidly changing scholarly publishing environment, but a number of initiatives provide hope for the future of academic libraries and their users. *[Article copies available for a fee from The Haworth Document Delivery Service: 1-800-HAWORTH. E-mail address: <docdelivery@haworthpress.com> Website: <http://www.HaworthPress.com> © 2004 by The Haworth Press, Inc. All rights reserved.]*

KEYWORDS. Electronic journal, Big Deal, e-journal, consortia, collection development, scholarly communication

INTRODUCTION

Commercial and society publishers have been quick to capitalize on the Internet and the possibilities inherent in linking technology by publishing increasing numbers of journal titles electronically. Researchers have come to expect desktop access to electronic scholarly articles from wherever they may be, at home or in the office. Libraries increasingly are responding to this market shift by "acquiring" access to ever greater numbers of these electronic journals, or e-journals. This trend is of great benefit to users, but it has become a major challenge for libraries trying to absorb annual journal price increases that have, over the past 15 years, consistently exceeded the rate of inflation, in many cases by four or five times. Library budgets have not, of course, grown to accommodate such huge increases, and the resulting budget crunch is driving many libraries to develop new journal collection policies. Many large academic libraries are choosing to purchase electronic access to large, bundled journal packages, while concurrently canceling the print subscriptions to most of the bundled titles. These bundled packages consume large proportions of library collection budgets, and, as one cost saving measure, libraries cancel "marginal" journal titles that are not considered "core" resources for their faculty members. We are now effectively moving from a collection model centered around each institution's unique research population and information needs to a model driven primarily by economic considerations. Often this leads libraries to increase their participation in consortial purchasing agreements. What are the current and long-term economic and sociological effects of this model? The benefits to users seem clear, but at what cost to collective and individual identities? Librarians should be aware of the pinnacles and pitfalls that lie ahead if all collect the same bits and bytes at the expense of less transient media. As we dive headlong into an electronic future, a review of some potential effects of the movement to all-electronic journal collections should help to illuminate the present situation and inform future collection development decisions.

The costs and benefits of electronic journal collections are dependent on the form of the e-journal and on the manner in which a title is "acquired." As online publishing has come of age, the e-journal has morphed several times and is now available for purchase in several different formats, all with different associated pricing and access terms. E-journals have developed very quickly along an evolutionary pathway that is still changing rapidly, with new publishing models constantly being tested and proposed. A brief discussion of the different e-journal forms and pricing models, and specification of the form of e-journal under scrutiny in this article, will place the rest of the discussion in the proper context.

ELECTRONIC JOURNALS:
THREE PERMUTATIONS

Journals are currently published following three primary models. The first e-journals were traditional print publications that were simply scanned and converted into electronic format, with no variation or enhancement, and published online either in PDF or HTML format. This initial transformation was quite similar to the major media change that transpired when microfilm and microfiche were invented, and newspapers and other documents were reproduced in micro format. This first type of e-journal is still published in print format, but can also be purchased in an electronic format if desired. Most electronic versions are now produced in html, SGML, or XML format and thus typically include a number of enhancements not available in PDF, such as links between the references and the text or links to other documents or articles. Other enhanced features e-journals offer to users include the ability to mark, save, and e-mail articles, export the bibliographic data to citation software, etc. Traditional print journals that have migrated to electronic format typically retain the familiar ISSN, volume, issue, and page numbers as reference points and citation parameters for researchers, thus maintaining the identity of the journal with its readers. This is currently the predominant publishing model, not only for commercial publishers but also for academic publishers like Stanford University's *Highwire Press* that are actively promoting the online publication of print journals deemed most important to the scholarly community.

A second permutation or publication model is the e-journal that is published only online, i.e., this title has never existed in print but rather was "born digital." This type of journal sometimes may not possess familiar identifiers from the print-publishing tradition, such as volume, issue, and page numbers. Instead, online publication dates and unique URLs serve as the primary access points and identity markers. One example is *Psycoloquy*, "a refereed international, interdisciplinary electronic journal" (http://psycprints.ecs.soton.ac.uk/) sponsored by the American Psychological Association (APA). This journal does not exist in print format, yet it does have an ISSN (1055-0143), is peer-reviewed, and is indexed in both the APA's *PsycINFO* database and the Institute for Scientific Information (ISI) citation indexes. Another scholarly society moving in this direction is the American Institute of Physics (AIP), which is offering a number of new titles that will be published *only* online.

Most recently, a third category of e-journal has emerged, one that began life and is intended to exist primarily as an e-journal, but which is produced rather tangentially, and one suspects only for the short term, in print format (e.g., *PloS Biology*). The Public Library of Science (PLoS; http://www.plos.org) initiative has the potential to fundamentally and drastically alter publishing models and scholarly publishing traditions, as the scholarly community reacts to shifts in the publishing industry that have been inspired by the evolution of the e-journal.

SUBSCRIPTION AND PRICING MODELS

As the different publishing models have evolved, so have subscription models changed over time. Publishers now offer scholarly articles in a number of new access models that do not necessarily contain familiar references to a print document or even lead directly to a specific journal title. Montgomery and King (2002) list four different electronic journal subscription types: individual subscriptions, publishers' packages (e.g., *ScienceDirect*), aggregator journals (e.g., *JSTOR*) and full-text database journals (e.g., *Lexis/Nexis*). Individual subscriptions may be available from one scholarly association that produces one journal for its members, or they may be offered by a publisher who produces many journal titles for a number of smaller associations. An example of the latter is the AIP, which offers subscriptions to a large suite of journal titles that can be purchased in print, online, CD, and microfiche formats, with optional backfile access available for an additional fee. The purchase of [access to] e-journals follows a variety of different models as well. The journal title may be subscribed to on an individual basis directly from the commercial or scholarly publisher; it may be part of a package of various titles from different publishers handled by an intermediate subscription agent (e.g., Harrassowitz); or it may be a part of a very large bundled package of many titles offered by a specific publisher, as with *ScienceDirect* from Elsevier.

Publication modes have changed, subscription models have evolved to accommodate those changes, and new pricing models for those subscriptions have evolved as well. Electronic journal pricing has changed significantly over the years, with a complex variety of pricing models being offered by different publishers. A common misconception that seems to be held by many virtual library users is that, regardless of who supplies a journal title for purchase, the subscription cost is simple: one base price for print, with the electronic version thrown in for free. This pricing model is becoming more rare every year, with publishers revising the model in response to steeply increasing user preference for electronic content. Typically, subscribers now pay one price for access to current (usually the current calendar year) journal content in electronic-only format, a slightly higher price for print-only, and the highest price for both print and electronic current versions. In addition, as libraries today know too well, the association between purchase and ownership has been replaced by an assumption that purchase may be related only to current access–or access to "current" volumes, as the case may be. Libraries often have to pay extra for access to "archival" content, or content published in previous years. Again, libraries may subscribe to a print version, an electronic version, or both print and electronic. If a library has gone "all-electronic," it may need to purchase not only the current year's content, but also access to previous years, since it has at some point cancelled the print but still wishes to have archival access to content published in the intervening years. That is, access to full electronic backfiles of issues published prior to the libraries' current e-access will cost extra, unless the library held a subscription to the print version for the previous years of interest.

The latest pricing model is a new open-access author-fee publishing model undergoing a trial run by the Public Library of Science, with their journal *PloS Biology*. This journal offers "a new model for scientific publishing in which peer-reviewed research articles are freely available to read and use through the Internet. The costs of publication are recovered not from subscription . . . but from publication fees paid by authors out of their grant funds and from other revenue sources."

Clearly, different cost/benefit issues will arise depending on a variety of factors specific to various publication and subscription types. This article focuses primarily on the costs and effects of libraries moving to purchase large bundled e-journal packages, while canceling "duplicate" or marginal print titles. While this is a fairly narrow and specific example of the possible collection choices a library might make in the current complex and increasingly dynamic academic publishing climate, it is a choice that is becoming increasingly popular and thus bears closer scrutiny.

PUBLISHING ECONOMICS

Many researchers have written about the escalating costs of journals in the electronic environment, with some attempting to relate the price increases to production cost increases. However, this is a difficult, if not impossible, task given the complex variables at work in the scholarly publishing industry. As with most commercial vendors and their products, publishers are much more willing to discuss costs than revenue, leaving subscribers to analyze the publishing puzzle with many of the pieces missing. Some commercial publishers attempt to justify wildly escalating subscription prices by asserting that their pricing reflects cost increases incurred in adding electronic production to their publishing profile. Karen Hunter (at the time a Vice President at Elsevier) represented a common publisher's lament in stating that "the simplistic view that electronic journals are paper journals without the paper and postage is naive because it overlooks all of the new, additional costs that go into creating innovative electronic projects [and] maintaining two product lines simultaneously" (Hunter 1999). Publishing cost assessment is also complicated by the fact that publishers prefer to maintain confidentiality about their revenue and circulation/subscription data. However, it is quite clear that the price increases imposed on libraries by commercial (and in some cases scholarly) publishers over the past two decades have far exceeded the increases seen in earlier decades, especially in comparison to the rate of inflation. An example of the disparity between inflation and journal prices is vividly illustrated by the difference between the Consumer Price Index and serial increases in ARL libraries between 1986 and 2002. During that period, the CPI increased by 64%, an average annual increase of 3.2%, while serial expenditures increased an astonishing 227%, or an average annual increase of 7.7% (Kyrillidou and Young 2003).

Although publishers and libraries frequently disagree on the rationale and justification for the current pricing of e-journals, research data indicates that the increased costs do not in many cases reflect increased costs of production. Halliday and Oppenheim (2001) explored journal pricing and found "no relationship between production costs and subscription prices of scholarly journals." As these researchers noted, the move from print to digital publishing has provided little change in the discrepancy between production costs and pricing. At first glance this is not surprising, since the primary cost savings between digital and print publishing of scientific and technical journals resides primarily with content distribution, not with the format of the publication. Early in the e-publishing timeline, Lorrin Garson of the American Chemical Society noted that "Eighty percent of our production cost is for the first copy. Twenty percent . . . is whether the information is delivered by petrochemicals on crushed trees or sent electronically" (Garson 1995). Noll (1995) agreed, stating that "for the vast majority of scientific and technical journals, the first copy costs account for on the order of 80 to 85 percent or more of the total cost of production and dissemination." Publishers have used these figures to support the assertion that their costs are not significantly reduced as a result of the move toward electronic distribution of journals. However, assuming that costs have remained steady, or even increased by having to produce duplicate versions of each publication, the huge profits being reaped by some of the academic publishing giants appear symptomatic of an industry with a captive audience and little competition. Elsevier, for example, recorded "significant growth, with revenues up 24.9% and operating profits up 26%" in 2002. Crispin Davis, CEO of Reed Elsevier, acknowledged that even though this growth occurred during "extraordinarily difficult years economically and politically, I don't think it's unreasonable that we should be able to maintain that level of growth" (Reed Elsevier finishes 2002 on a strong note, sets sights on 2003). Odlyzko (1999) points out great disparities in costs among journals and argues that this is a "sign of an industry that has not had to worry about efficiency." He also states that the existence of large profits, both in the commercial sector and in professional societies, is evidence of "an industry with little effective competition." One researcher has even produced evidence of actual price discrimination by publishers against libraries, and has developed a "robust selection tool to compare actual prices to model-predicted prices among the subscriptions . . . and to predict those that, statistically, are significantly overpriced" (Meyer 2001).

ECONOMICS IN LIBRARIES

Regardless of the justification for the price increases, there is no question that the rising costs of serials over the past two decades have had an unprecedented impact on library budgets. Increasingly, large research libraries in particular are being pressured by publishers and vendors to accept exceedingly large, expensive bundled electronic journal packages, while fighting to retain "privileges" such as access to archival copies and the ability to cancel individual titles. Some libraries have tried to balance the costs more widely by entering into consortial agreements with other institutions. This provides a wider range of institutions with access to titles they never had before, while distributing the cost among several institutions. The problem is that the prohibitive cost of these large bundled packages, sometimes referred to as the "Big Deal" (Frazier 2001), still forces libraries to cancel access to print titles in order to afford the bundled packages. Libraries are reacting differently to the Big Deal-type licenses depending on specific licensing terms, local library administrative philosophies, and the ability or willingness to accept the astronomical costs of these packages. A recent Academic and Research Libraries (ARL) survey of its members reflects the difficulty libraries are experiencing with this decision (Case 2003). At one extreme are the 39% of responding libraries that plan to cancel or consider canceling a bundled package this year, with 72% of that group (16 of 22 libraries) indicating that they could no longer afford the package. At the other extreme are the 44% (25 of 57 total respondents) who are subscribing only to electronic versions when both print and electronic exist.

The variety of different pricing models currently available to libraries results in a very unclear picture of the long-term economic costs of choosing a "Big Deal" package over the maintenance of individual subscriptions to journals. Measuring the economic impacts is difficult in the current, changing environment. Costs will vary depending on such factors as: how a library purchases its electronic journals, i.e., whether or not it is a member of a consortium; how it measures use, i.e., whether it evaluates the cost per use of each title in a package individually or averages usage statistics over all titles or some combination, including electronic use measures; whether the "cost" of missing (e.g., deleted) content is considered; and whether a library values and purchases archival access for their users.

Drexel University Case Study

At this point it may be instructive to briefly examine the experience of one library that has chosen to move to an all-electronic journal collection, and to think about how their experience can be translated in the context of other libraries. Drexel University is among a number of research institutions that have taken a concrete leap into an all-electronic future, committing to the collection of electronic journals while canceling subscriptions to the print versions of those titles. The U.S. Institute for Museum and Library Services (MLS) funded a study at Drexel's W. W. Hagerty Library to study the impact of this shift on staff and associated costs. The conclusion of this case study was that, for this particular institution, the decision to migrate to an all-electronic collection was more cost effective both for the library and for the users, especially in terms of space and cost per use (Montgomery and King 2002).

However, Montgomery and King acknowledge that their data may not translate directly to other institutions due to some of the specific conditions of the situation at Drexel. For instance, Drexel does not factor in any archival costs (e.g., storing, serving, and migrating content) because their stated philosophy is that this issue should be addressed by other organizations, including "publishers, large vendors and professional organizations, foundations, and major research libraries." Relying on publishers, large vendors, or professional organizations to protect archival content and provide reasonably-priced access into perpetuity seems at best naïve. Also, if large academic research libraries are to be held responsible for handling archival issues, then those libraries do need to consider this rather significant cost factor when evaluating the impact of a massive migration to an all-electronic journal collection. Drexel was also able to considerably reduce costs by reducing the amount of staffing time needed for serials processing. This was made possible by their decision not to catalog electronic journals, using instead a Web-based system to provide access to these resources. Again, this decision resulted in significantly lower cost calculations than would likely be incurred by a library choosing to catalog their electronic journals.

Finally, even though the authors of the Drexel study acknowledged some of the serious contextual drawbacks to large e-journal databases, such as the volatility of content, missing visuals, and lack of access to back issues, they did not place any monetary value on these drawbacks. Some of these negative drawbacks involving contextual issues may be considered a more serious deterrent by other libraries. Thus, while

Drexel may have made a good decision relative to their situation and their users, many universities that are larger or that must make different choices about cataloging and archival issues will not experience the same perceived or actual cost savings.

ARCHIVAL CONCERNS

Archival access to journal content remains a huge concern for academic librarians faced with the decision to go all-electronic. The archival situation is a very complex, evolving issue deserving of its own separate discussion, but it is an issue of great concern and import as libraries move to electronic-only journal collections. This concern is also increasingly noted by users as they become more experienced with, and savvy about, differences between electronic and print versions of the same titles. For example, respondents to Schottlaender's University of California/CMI e-journal use study cited some of the same concerns about content as were mentioned by Drexel's users. While nearly half of the UC users preferred to access journals electronically, they also cited content coverage and short back files as a major barrier to electronic journal use (Schottlaender 2003).

What if large numbers of research institutions follow Drexel's lead in eliminating archival access to journal content, under the assumption that someone else will step forward and secure and ensure that access for the future? Libraries concerned about this issue are pushing publishers to provide future archival access to current volumes as part of their electronic license agreements, but this does not guarantee that access to the information will be preserved in perpetuity. If libraries purchase access to "current" (i.e., this calendar year) content, will they still have access to that content five years from now? Where will archival issues be stored and "served up"? If this is handled locally, libraries must assume the costs of long-term storage and systematic migration of the archival content to new formats, in order to ensure continued access in response to inevitable changes in technology. This access simply cannot be guaranteed by commercial interests, in spite of licensing agreements that appear to provide that assurance. If the publishers are responsible for maintaining the archives, how stable is that content and how accessible will that content remain? Commercial publishers have not, to date, shown a great deal of interest in spending money to maintain archives, simply for the sake of preservation. They may, however, see fit to preserve that access if they can at some point make a profit in doing so. Libraries and consortia have begun to formulate their own solutions, with initiatives like *JSTOR* and *Project MUSE* providing encouraging examples of what libraries can do if they make an effort to address and resolve archival issues on a concerted, organized, national or international scale (Friedlander and Bessette 2003). Although these initiatives have relieved the concerns of many, serious concerns still remain regarding archival access to e-journal content.

CONTENT STABILITY

While the archival issue is perhaps the most significant concern for many libraries teetering on the brink of an all-electronic future, a closely related concern of note regarding electronic-only access to material is the instability of content in today's volatile publishing environment. What happens when a library purchases a subscription for access to a journal, and the publisher changes ownership or the society publishing a journal decides to move their contract to a different publisher? This situation was difficult enough in a print environment, but it becomes more problematic when a library is dealing with a packaged bundle containing up to 1,500 individual titles, with a license specifying (for instance) that no refunds will be provided for any specific titles that are cancelled. There is no guarantee that the access you purchase today will be the access that you maintain over the course of that license or contract. In recent years, for example, many libraries who had signed license agreements with Academic Press for current and archival access to their rather sizeable journal bundle rather suddenly found that all bets were off, their license was negated, and access terms were no longer valid. The entire license had to be renegotiated because that publisher was acquired by another company.

Another form of content instability made possible by electronic-only content delivery was demonstrated by Elsevier during the period 2000-2003 when they quietly withdrew dozens of journal articles from *ScienceDirect* for no apparent stated reason. Elsevier claimed that the articles involved copyright problems or scientific misconduct and were removed for legal reasons. They noted that the excised material amounted to a very small percentage of the database, about 30 articles out of the millions contained therein. Elsevier was not alone in removing previously published material, as apparently LexisNexis and Westlaw removed an article from their databases for an even more questionable reason.[1] There was no proof of plagiarism or other scholarly misconduct or misinformation. The article was, to all outward appearances, removed because powerful entities were unhappy with the opinions expressed by the author. This form of "editing" is simply not possible in a print journal, and librarians, science historians, and many other publishers agree that expunging published articles without providing any reason or reference to the removed material is very dangerous, regardless of the reason for the removal. "As more and more scientific literature is moved from print to a digital environment, they fear, holes in databases could leave researchers ignorant of why certain articles were considered questionable. . . . And, scholars ask, shouldn't researchers be warned about authors who plagiarize, or commit scientific fraud or misconduct?" (Foster 2003b).

Librarians were reassured by Elsevier's response to negative feedback from the scholarly community, when in February 2003 the publishing giant released to librarians a new plan for handling problematic articles in its database (Foster 2003a). It is distressing, however, that Elsevier did not from the beginning simply follow the "gold standard" of guidelines for content removal that had already been established by *Medline*.

USERS NEEDS

While archival and content issues are of concern to users and libraries alike, other issues important to libraries were brought to light in the recent ARL survey, as noted by Mary Case in an e-mail message to ARL Directors (Case 2003). This survey included a list of "bottom-line positions that will make or break a deal" for the purchase of a huge bundled package of journals (e.g., *ScienceDirect*), including governing law and venue, remote access, indemnifications, and price. While these concerns are certainly important, notably absent from the list is any mention of use issues or user community considerations. Of course, collection decisions have always been bounded to some degree by economic constraints. But when the needs of our local user community do not appear at all on the list of factors affecting a collection decision that will consume such a huge chunk of our budget, one could ask what that means for the future of our individual collections. Librarians also may want to consider what this dynamic implies about future relationships between academic libraries and the academic community they are intended to serve.

HOMOGENEITY OF COLLECTIONS

Focusing only on the bottom line and reacting by purchasing packages in cooperation with local consortia may result in decisions that are beneficial to the consortial partners as a whole but are in fact detrimental to primary users. There is danger in smaller universities like Drexel relying on larger universities for breadth and depth, while also implicitly relying on them as the only institutions who can afford the "Big Deal." These may not appear to be mutually incompatible dependencies, but large libraries cannot do it all with the budgetary pressures inherent in the current economic environment. Breadth and depth are demonstrated by comprehensive collections that contain many "low-use," esoteric, or "marginal" titles not included in these expensive bundled packages. Committing an ever-increasing percentage of our collection budget to the purchase of that large, bundled package ensures that subscriptions to those marginal titles will have to be cancelled–hence the dichotomy.

As these bundles devour acquisition budgets, less and less funding is available for the purchase of other materials, whether produced in print or electronic format. Libraries are increasingly responding to this budget crunch by participating in large consortia, often anchored by one large research institution, that are all purchasing these same large bundled packages with a relatively limited degree of variation within the packaged bundle. Perhaps one of the greatest dangers of a wholesale move toward the "Big Deal," and an associated increase in consortial collection development, may be the loss of individual, institutional identities. Research collections have long been developed in response to and in support of "local" departmental and institutional programmatic priorities and strengths. Publishers can argue that they are providing increased access to marginal materials by making huge journal packages including both core titles and lesser-used titles available to large consortia. But is the large research institution purchasing access to titles that users at their institution do not want or need, at the expense of non-packaged titles that those users consider critical to their research? The result could be that smaller or more marginal journals that are not a part of the big bundles may be cancelled by subscribers who can no longer afford both the big bundles and the title-by-title subscriptions to journals with more limited or local appeal. The problem is that these journals may be highly important to one field of research, albeit to a relatively small number of researchers in one single library in a consortia. The potential problem of local identity loss was explicitly identified by Elsevier's Karen Hunter when she asked some of the publishers' electronic-only library customers what concerns they had in making the decision to stop receiving paper. Some institutions that had elected to purchase the electronic-only option cited the "risk with large consortium agreements that take large parts of library budgets is that there will be fewer resources available to build local collections. Non-core material disappears and the collections become more and more similar" (Hunter 2001). We could ask, to what degree does consortial purchasing contribute to any one member of the consortium, and to what degree does this type of purchasing result in a watered-down, homogenized collection of titles, with everyone having access to the same titles as everyone else?

Clearly, librarians can no longer all afford to own every title available, and they cannot continue to function in a development culture in which duplicates abound even as library funding grows increasingly tight. "Lots of Copies Keep Stuff Safe (LOCKSS)," a well-known e-journal archive initiative (Reich and Rosenthal 2000), is a catchy moniker that articulates a traditional and appealing philosophy. Librarians are aware, however, that in the current fiscal environment they will have to work more cooperatively with regional partners and be happy with a philosophy that fewer copies, if held relatively locally, are better than none. The caveat to this awareness is that cooperative collection development should not lead to each member of the cooperative developing the same collection as every other member. In the rush to work together and thus save money, each institution should beware of developing a smaller collection of titles that is, ironically, the same collection that exists in every other institution of the same type and size. "If libraries continue down the path of least resistance and fold into larger and larger consortia to help negotiate mega-databases and electronic journal packages, will we all become the same library?" (McGinnis 2000). The end result could indeed be a homogenized collection and a concurrent loss of identity for the individual members of the consortium.

As decisions are made on how to configure collections, and on how to distribute limited library funding, librarians must maintain a strong connection to their users and an awareness of their preferences and needs. Barton et al. (2002) found that users at the University of Iowa, while enamoured of electronic resources, "would [still] like the Libraries to invest more in the acquisition of print books and journals, in addition to electronic journals and expanded remote access." In a survey at the University of Maryland, researchers found that faculty members' preferences with regard to format were dependent on the importance of a title to their area of research (Dillon and Hahn 2002). Faculty preferred to maintain access to titles in print as well as electronic if those titles were critically core to their research and teaching, with a preference towards electronic-only access for lesser-used titles.

TECHNICAL AND COGNITIVE IMPACTS

While "journal literature is essential and transcends the medium that delivers it to users" (Tenopir 2000), choices users make between the print and electronic format do differ in different situations. A conflicting dichotomy currently exists between what format users want when they do their research, and what they want as authors. As researchers, they prefer "free and fast access to the publications of others, but as authors they . . . above all want to get published in high prestige journals, even at the expense of rapid publication and easy access for others" (Bjork 2001). Many articles and studies have investigated the use of e-journals compared to print journals, with most coming to the definite conclusion that users increasingly prefer to access the research literature online. In a survey of the faculty at the University of Tennessee, Tenopir (2000) found that over 50% prefer e-journals over the print format. Johns (2003) provides compelling data indicating that electronic journals are the format of choice across disciplines at the California Digital Library, UC Santa Barbara, albeit with some remaining drawbacks and problems. The University of California Collections Management Initiative (UC/CMI), funded by the Mellon Foundation, confirmed other studies with data showing that "digital use of journals was considerably higher than print use" (Schottlaender 2003). The latter finding is very significant due to the design and the size of the study, with 300 journal titles and over 3,000 respondents (30% response rate) across four general subject areas including arts and humanities, life and health sciences, physical sciences and engineering, and social sciences. Additionally, UC was able to maintain a control campus with copies of print and electronic versions of titles, and an experimental campus that migrated the print versions of their journals to storage. This enabled the researchers to measure use as affected by the proximity of print journals rather than just their availability in the system.

Impact–Research

However, a disturbing result of the UC/CMI study that has implications for future research is that researchers elected to consult print articles *only* when access to that content was nearby, relying almost totally on electronic articles if the print was located offsite. This result contradicts the assertion that collaborative collecting and interlibrary loan are the answer to our budgetary woes, i.e., that libraries can cancel lesser-used titles with little impact on researchers, because the few faculty who need those will get them from other institutions. In fact, the faculty at UC did not choose to follow this model, i.e., they *did not* pursue the interlibrary loan option for the print. The underlying implication is that the unavailability of (or reduced access to) back issues could potentially have an impact on the quality and nature of the research process as e-journals become more prevalent. That is, if researchers find it too troublesome to obtain print articles, they may fail to seek out and incorporate into their work the historical content that has traditionally provided the ongoing basis and context for future research. Concerned academics have begun to assess the impact of the paradigm shift from print to electronic on how research is performed and evaluated (Thorin 2003). Tenopir (2000) also speculated that faculty may not search for older issues of journals, even though research indicates that older articles are more important than recent articles in certain kinds of research. The "slippery slope" implication is that the choices libraries make today between different publishing and subscription options could indirectly, yet fundamentally, alter the nature of scientific research in the future.

Impact–Reward and Tenure

A related question paramount in universities today is, how will the movement to e-journals impact the academic recognition, reward, and tenure system? E-journals are very slowly gaining acceptance and credibility in the academic community, with that acceptance being enhanced by the support of large scholarly associations that are widely respected and continue to maintain the same standards for their online publications as they would for a print publication (e.g., the American Chemical Society or IEEE). However, the primary limiting factor in the wide acceptance of these models is the reluctance of faculty members to fully support publications and peer-review models that operate in electronic-only format due to the status and importance of certain journal titles in the academic review and tenure process. The Andrew W. Mellon

Foundation recently awarded the Committee on Institutional Cooperation (CIC) a grant to study the role of scholarly publishing in the tenure
process of selected disciplines at the CIC's twelve research institutions.
While this effort is focused on analyzing the tenure process for humanities and social sciences disciplines, Dr. Lou Anna Kimsey Simon, CIC
Chair, notes that this partnership "provides an extraordinary opportunity to . . . create a new paradigm for scholarly communication and its
assessment" (Allen 2003).

NEW DIRECTIONS?

The academic community is reacting to an increased awareness of
the serials crisis by moving to examine traditional methods for evaluating scholarly potential and progress in academia. Review and tenure
procedures grounded in the publication of journal articles in core
peer-reviewed journals are being re-evaluated in light of the astronomical price increases some scholarly publishing firms have imposed on institutions over the past few decades. The potential for self-publishing,
whether by an institution or by an individual, has resulted in the proliferation of a number of relatively new and different publishing models.
Institutional pre-print repositories are becoming increasingly popular,
for example. Commercial publishers, scholarly associations, academic
and scholarly consortia, university presses, and individuals are all potential publishers of electronic journals. Open access publishing initiatives (e.g., the Public Library of Science) are gaining momentum and
credibility, with backing from the Scholarly Publishing and Academic
Resources Coalition (SPARC), and support from highly credible institutions such as the Wellcome Foundation, and the Howard Hughes
Medical Foundation. SPARC is also supporting scholarly societies in
the production of new online journals that are successfully competing
with commercial journals in impact factor rankings. One of the most
successful of these initiatives is the journal *Organic Letters*, published
by the American Chemical Society beginning in 1999, which was initiated with a specific goal of competing with *Tetrahedron Letters*, a
high-impact Elsevier title in the field. As noted by ACS (#84) in 2003,
"In only its second year with a fully calculated impact factor, *Organic
Letters* (3.670 impact factor) increased in impact factor by 9% over the
previous year. Conversely, *Tetrahedron Letters* (2.280 impact factor)
decreased in impact factor by 9% over the same period."

These new directions in scholarly publication could conceivably result in a concerted move by academia away from the dissemination of research via expensive commercial journals and toward the online dissemination of free (or at least reasonably priced) articles produced by associations, universities, or scholarly consortia. An alternative new direction in publishing could be driven not by the academic or commercial community, but by formal governmental legislation. The scholarly publishing community was recently shaken and awakened by a new measure, the Public Access to Science Act, that was introduced in Congress by Representative Martin O. Sabo (DFL, Minnesota). The intent of this legislation is to place the results of all federally funded research in the public domain, where it will be freely available to the public (Leary 2003). This initiative "reflects the spreading frustration that papers based on some of the $50 billion in scientific and medical research funded by U.S. taxpayers every year aren't freely available to the people who paid for them" (Begley 2003). Initiatives like this have also been inspired in part by the frustration of researchers who freely sign away their copyright for the publication of results of their federally funded research, only to be forced to purchase access to that research back again from private publishers reaping huge profits.

CONCLUSION

The future of scholarly publishing is impossible to predict, with innovative new scholarly publishing models emerging that demonstrate a publishing industry clearly at a crossroads. We did not see these "e-journals" coming, and we are not sure where they are going, but the electronic article is surely here to stay for the foreseeable future. Indeed, as the possibilities for online publishing continue to be explored and exploited, thus changing the nature of scholarly publication, e-journals that are published following the traditional print format could in the future be rendered obsolete. One shift that seems inevitable, for example, is for the journal *article* rather than the journal as a *collection of articles*, to become the primary unit of publication and value. Karen Hunter of Elsevier Science commented on this, noting that "while the brand name of the journal remains important for authors and readers, *the article becomes more and more the unit of interaction*" (italics added by this author) (Hunter 2001).

Library collections will probably someday appear to the universe of users as one homogenized mass of information, with tools in place that will allow those users to create unique subject collections that meet their individual needs. The location of the resources that comprise any given subject collection will be irrelevant to the user, and irrelevant with respect to the strength of the collection. However, the uniqueness and depth of resource collections in specific subject areas will, ironically, be diluted if individual libraries do not continue to identify their priorities and strengths, and focus their funding on collections of resources that provide depth and diversity to their unique corner of the universe of information. Librarians should remain true to their mission which includes collecting, providing access to, and preserving as much of the knowledge of our civilization as is technologically possible, including the corners and the fringes. To choose to limit the vast scope of the knowledge produced today in our quest to preserve only the core, would be choosing to deny future generations full access to their history.

NOTE

1. The expunged article was critical of multinational corporations, particularly Boise Cascade, which reacted harshly and whose response led the publisher, the University of Denver, to successfully pressure LexisNexis and WestLaw to remove the article.

REFERENCES

Allen, Barbara. 2003. *Mellon Foundation awards CIC funds in support of scholarly summit*, Committee on Institutional Cooperation. Available from http://www.cic.uiuc.edu/groups/CICMembers/archive/PressRelease/MellonFoundationScholarlySummit15Jul03.pdf (accessed October 3, 2003).

Barton, H., J. Cheng, L. Clougherty, J. Forys, E. Hammond, D. Persson, C. Walters, and C. Washington-Hoagland. 2002. Faculty and staff use of academic library resources and services: A University of Iowa libraries' perspective. *portal: Libraries and the Academy* 2, no. 4: 627-46.

Begley, Sharon. 2003. Scientists challenge costly medical journals. *Wall Street Journal*, June 26. D.3.

Bjork, B. C. 2001. Internet and the economics of the scientific publication process. *Ekonomiska Samfundets Tidskrift* 54, no. 1: 5-.

Case, Mary M. E-mail message to ARL Directors Discussion List, July 14, 2003.

Dillon, I. F., and K. L. Hahn. 2002. Are researchers ready for the electronic-only journal collection? Results of a survey at the University of Maryland. *portal: Libraries and the Academy* 2, no. 3: 375-90.

Foster, Andrea L. 2003a. Elsevier announces new procedures for retracting online articles. *The Chronicle of Higher Education*: 35.

Foster, Andrea L. 2003b. Elsevier's vanishing act: To the dismay of scholars, the publishing giant quietly purges articles from its database. *The Chronicle of Higher Education*: 27.

Frazier, Kenneth. 2001. The librarians' dilemma: Contemplating the costs of the "Big Deal." *D-Lib Magazine* 7, no. 3. http://www.dlib.org/dlib/march01/frazier/03frazier.html.

Friedlander, Amy, and Randi S. Bessette. 2003. The implications of information technology for scientific journal publishing: A literature review. Available from http://www.nsf.gov/sbe/srs/nsf03323/start.htm.

Garson, Lorrin R. 1995. Can e-journals save us? A publisher's view. Paper presented at the Challenging Marketplace Solutions to Problems in the Economics of Information Conference, Washington, D.C., Sept. 18-19.

Halliday, L., and C. Oppenheim. 2001. Developments in digital journals. *Journal of Documentation* 57, no. 2: 260-83.

Hunter, Karen. 1999. The effect of price: Early observations. In *Technology and Scholarly Communication*, edited by Richard Ekman and Richard E. Quandt, 145-57. Berkeley: University of California Press.

Hunter, Karen. 2001. Going "electronic only": Early experiences and issues. *Journal of Library Administration* 35, no. 3: 51-65.

Johns, Cecily. 2003. Collection management strategies in a digital environment. *The Serials Librarian* 43, no. 3: 83-87.

Kyrillidou, Martha, and Mark Young. 2003. *ARL Statistics 2001-2002: Research Library Trends* [html]. Association of Research Libraries. Available from http://www.arl.org/stats/arlstat/02pub/intro02.html (accessed July 6, 2003).

Leary, Warren E. June 26, 2003. Measure calls for wider access to federally financed research. *The New York Times* 22.

McGinnis, Suzan D. 2000. Selling our collecting souls: How license agreements are controlling collection management. *Journal of Library Administration* 3, no. 2: 63-76.

Meyer, R. W. 2001. A tool to assess journal price discrimination. *College & Research Libraries* 62, no. 3: 269-88.

Montgomery, Carol Hansen, and Donald W. King. 2002. Comparing library and user related costs of print and electronic journal collections: A first step towards a comprehensive analysis. *D-Lib Magazine* 8, no. 10. http://www.dlib.org/dlib/october02/montgomery/10montgomery.html.

Noll, Roger. 1995. The economics of information. Paper presented at the Challenging Marketplace Solutions to Problems in the Economics of Information Conference, Washington, D.C., September 18-19.

Odlyzko, Andrew. 1999. The economics of electronic journals. In *Technology and scholarly communication*, edited by Richard Ekman and Richard E. Quandt, 380-93. Berkeley: University of California Press.

Organic Letters publishes its 100th issue, leads all Letters journals in impact, American Chemical Society. Available from http://pubs.acs.org/orgfam/ol_lead.html (accessed October 29, 2003).

Reed Elsevier finishes 2002 on a strong note, sets sights on 2003. *Electronic Information Report* 24, no. 9: 7-8. *Business Source Premier* Accession #9216460 (accessed November 11, 2003).

Reich, Vicky, and David S.H. Rosenthal. 2000. LOCKSS (Lots Of Copies Keep Stuff Safe). Paper presented at the Preservation 2000: An International Conference on the Preservation and Long Term Accessibility of Digital Materials, York, England.

Schottlaender, Brian E.C. 2003. University of California Collections Management Initiative (UC/CMI). Paper presented at the Association of Research Libraries Annual Meeting, Lexington, KY, May 13-16.

Tenopir, Carol. 2000. Moving toward electronic journals. *Library Journal* 125, no. 12: 36-.

Thorin, Suzanne E. 2003. Global changes in scholarly communication. Paper presented at the Workshops on Scholarly Communication in the Digital Era, Feng Chia University, Taichung, Taiwan, August 11-24.

Scan It and They Will Come . . .
But Will They Cite It?

Michael Fosmire

SUMMARY. As the number of retrospective digitization projects of journal content increases, there is a need to assess the impact of these projects on the productivity of researchers. Librarians making collection development decisions about acquiring these back files need to know how useful they are to researchers. This study provides data on usage of a range of years of the *Physical Review*, and citation information from *Physical Review Letters* to other *Physical Review* articles. The usage of the online archive of *Physical Review* articles indicates that articles are accessed all the way back to the first issue, with an average number of downloads on the order of ten per article per year. Both usage and citation rates show exponential decay rates, however, with different intrinsic time scales. The citation half-life is consistent with previous studies of the physics literature, while the usage half-life computed here is in conflict with older analyses of print usage of the physics literature, although in line with some recent online usage studies in medicine. An analysis of the citation data indicates a potential order of 10% enhancement in citations to articles available in the online archive, but the sta-

Michael Fosmire, MS (Physics), MLIS, is Assistant Professor and Science Librarian, Purdue University, West Lafayette, IN (E-mail: fosmire@purdue.edu).

The author is indebted to Martin Blume, Mark Doyle, Claire O'Neill, and Gerald Young for providing generous amounts of usage and citation data for the APS journals.

[Haworth co-indexing entry note]: "Scan It and They Will Come . . . But Will They Cite It?" Fosmire, Michael. Co-published simultaneously in *Science & Technology Libraries* (The Haworth Information Press, an imprint of The Haworth Press, Inc.) Vol. 25, No. 1/2, 2004, pp. 55-72; and: *Emerging Issues in the Electronic Environment: Challenges for Librarians and Researchers in the Sciences* (ed: Jeannie P. Miller) The Haworth Information Press, an imprint of The Haworth Press, Inc., 2004, pp. 55-72. Single or multiple copies of this article are available for a fee from The Haworth Document Delivery Service [1-800-HAWORTH, 9:00 a.m. - 5:00 p.m. (EST). E-mail address: docdelivery@haworthpress.com].

Digital Object Identifier: 10.1300/J122v25n01_05

tistical error is of the same magnitude, so no firm conclusions can be drawn from that data. A few more years of citation data may be able to resolve the question of impact of the online archive on citation rates. *[Article copies available for a fee from The Haworth Document Delivery Service: 1-800-HAWORTH. E-mail address: <docdelivery@haworthpress.com> Website: <http://www.HaworthPress.com> © 2004 by The Haworth Press, Inc. All rights reserved.]*

KEYWORDS. Scientific journals, citation analysis, online usage

INTRODUCTION

It is hard to believe that only five years or so ago electronic journals were still a novelty and not a way of life for researchers. Now that almost all STM publishers publish online versions of their journals, the next decision that the industry is facing is what to do about material that predates their online publishing initiatives, i.e., whether they should digitize their back files. And, for librarians, the relevant question is, should librarians purchase this retrospective content, and what would be a fair price? What added value does the online content for older material provide, in terms of additional productivity for researchers? Despite initial skepticism on the part of many publishers, who didn't believe anyone would use the old stuff, the results of the American Physical Society's conversion of its entire journal run show that, if you scan it, they will come (see Figure 1).

However, the downloading of articles is only one measure of the usefulness of a journal back file. Another is the rate at which scientists integrate older materials into their research, compared to the rate they did when the articles were only available in print. If a goal of digitization is to increase productivity by allowing the older material to more easily be integrated into current research, one way that may show up is by an increased level of citations to the older literature.

A quick look at Thomson ISI's *Journal Citation Reports* shows that the *Physical Review*'s article half-life (an indication of how long an article is relevant to research) has increased, fairly monotonically, from 1998 to 2002. *Physical Review D* hasn't seen a change in the article half-life, but the other sections have seen a 5% to 40% increase in their half-lives. This may indicate that the older material is being used increasingly over time, coincident with the arrival of the online back files. However, data prior to 1998 was not available to the author, so it is un-

FIGURE 1. Downloads from *Physical Review* journals per article published that year, per year, averaged over 2001 and 2002. Guidelines are provided for the two characteristic half-lives.

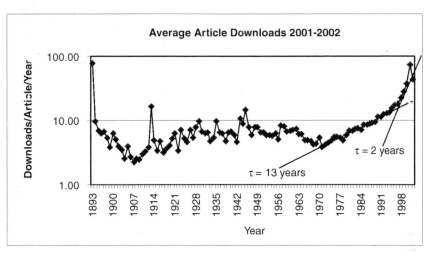

(Raw data courtesy of the American Physical Society)

clear whether this increase was already taking place prior to the existence of the online back file.

Several studies have looked at the obsolescence of the physics literature. Gupta's (1990) citation study found an exponential decrease over time in the density of citations to the *Physical Review* from 15 major journals in physics, and found a half-life in the citation density (Gupta's density corrects for the effect of growth in the literature over time) of about five years. Chen's (1972) shelving study found an obsolescence rate of about 14.5 years, and Sandison (1974) reinterpreted the results to show that there was no obsolescence rate at all, that is, the physics literature remains relevant and its utility doesn't decay over time. However, the Chen and Sandison studies were limited by low statistics and, potentially, systematic sources of error, and did not rigorously correct for changes in the gross research output published in physics at that time.

Brown (2001a) has investigated a situation (e-prints from arXiv.org) where convenient online access to physics research is available, albeit unrefereed. She sees large citation rates for these preprints, where, for example, about two-thirds of all articles submitted to the high-energy theory preprint server were ultimately cited somewhere in the time interval investigated. Electronic preprints may be cited at a high rate because they are the newest research available, or they may be cited preferentially because they are easily and freely available. This study may help to disentangle those two drivers of research citation patterns. If the former is a main driver of citing behavior, there should be little effect on the overall citation rate from access to the *Physical Review* back file. If the latter is more valid, there should be some noticeable result.

Also, if the information system of physics has been efficient in communicating relevant results through time (through complete and accurate referencing, for example), then perhaps having an easily searchable and accessible back file is less important, since relevant research has already been identified. However, if transmission of the relevant results is imperfect, or if research in new fields, or new discoveries, require use of previously unused data, then an increase in citation levels might appear.

METHODS

The American Physical Society's (APS) journals were chosen as subjects to look for potential citation behavior changes as a function of access to the online version of the journal. Since the APS was the first major physics publisher to provide online access, and the first to make their entire back file available online, the statistics on their journals are the most complete. As premier journals in physics, the *Physical Review* sections also provide a good cross-section of high-quality research in all areas of physics. The APS, unlike some of the latecomers to the archival market, has also made their back file available at a reasonable rate to the library and research community, so access to the back files of their articles is as widespread as for any publisher.

However, compiling the citing data manually appeared to be a daunting task. In 2002 alone, over 17,000 articles were published in the *Physical Review*. As tracking a statistically significant subset of these articles, over several years, did not appear feasible, the publishers at the APS were asked whether they already had some of that data and if they were willing to share it. Editor-in-Chief, Martin Blume, and Manager of Product Development, Mark Doyle, explained that, since they had created Digital Object Identifiers (DOIs) for all of their articles, and linked all of their references to other articles in the APS online journal platform, they had all citation information in their publication database and could run a query to extract the information needed for this study.

The ability to automatically process the over three million such links made the execution of this project a reality, and certainly of a much higher quality than could have been achieved manually.

To get the largest possible statistics of citations to the *Physical Review* database, one logical place to go would be the *Web of Science*, since it is the largest citation database. The *Web of Science* indexes several thousand journals, while this paper only analyzes the citations of one journal. However, that would have required manually tracking citations for tens of thousands of articles, which was a prohibitive endeavor. Furthermore, since the annual output of scientific papers is constantly increasing, an extra variable is introduced if only bulk citation counts are tabulated. One would not be able to disentangle the possibility that citation numbers had increased due to the fact that more papers were being published, or if they were just being cited more often than previously. Since APS had all the data in-house, both citations and total publishing output, and it was manipulable in an automated fashion, analyzing citations from the APS journal articles to APS journal articles constituted a much more controlled environment. This decreased the overall statistics in the sample, but it did reduce the number of uncontrolled variables in the analysis. The next question then became, which APS articles to use in this analysis.

SELECTION OF JOURNALS FOR STUDY

The APS publications contain three general types of journal articles. Lengthy review articles are published in *Reviews of Modern Physics*, full-length research articles are published in *Physical Review* sections *A-E*, and shorter communications are published in *Physical Review Letters* (and some short communications are published in the other *Physical Review* sections as well).

In analyzing citation patterns, attempts were made to limit potential systematic sources of error. Admittedly, that is a difficult task, and can be only imperfectly done. For example, hot topics change from year to year, and, consequently, the citation pattern may change due to the different research histories in those areas. Also, the relative number of long or short articles would likely have different average numbers of citations, and would change the rate of citations per article from year to year.

Reviews of Modern Physics (*RMP*) was eliminated from the analysis, since only a few articles, relatively speaking, are published in that journal. With only on the order of 50 or 60 articles published per year, an analysis of the citation patterns would likely be dominated by the differences in subject matter published from year to year. Additionally, with the number of citations per paper significantly greater than in the rest of the APS publications, differences in the relative number of papers published in *RMP* versus the *Physical Review* sections, for example, would skew the citation rates of articles if they were lumped in with the rest of the *Physical Review* sections, so *RMP* was taken out of the mix entirely.

The *Physical Review A-E* sections have short communications and longer, full, research articles, so if the relative concentration of the two changes over time, that also would yield different results in the citation rates by year. Also, in 2002, coincidentally, the APS synchronized its online and print publishing cycle, so that an article's publication date corresponded to its online publication, rather than its publication in a print issue (which is typically on the order of a month or so later). The result is that the print version now comes out later than it did (and, for example, articles that might have appeared in the January 2003 print issue were placed in the December 2002 issue). This led to a 13% increase in articles published in 2002 over 2001, compared to a 3% increase in articles published in the previous year. Since the citation rate decays rapidly with time, the effect of the publication date shifting alone would lead to lower citation rates in 2002 relative to previous years.

However, the *Physical Review Letters* (*PRL*) did not see the same increase, and in fact had 3% fewer articles published in 2002 than in 2001. Since the *PRL* did not seem to be as affected by the change in publication cycle (and in general *PRL* has a shorter time from acceptance to publication than the other sections of the *Physical Review*, so it shouldn't have been as affected), the citation behavior of just *PRL* was analyzed. Also, the research in *PRL* is generally composed of exciting new findings, while the other sections of the *Physical Review* are more exhaustive treatments of an experiment or theory. Thus, the gestation period of the experiment is likely shorter for *PRL* than for other articles, and one would be able to see the effect of online access sooner in *PRL* than in the other sections of the *Physical Review*. In general, the curves of citation data were fairly similar between *PRL* and the other sections of *Physical Review*, so the qualitative conclusions would probably not have changed if the entire *Physical Review* had been analyzed. The *PRL* also has a tightly constrained article length of four pages, so the articles are very similar in size, and the variation due to article types mentioned above should be minimized by just analyzing those articles. The total number of *PRL* articles published per year is around 3,000, which contain about 20,000 citations to APS articles (see Table 1).

TABLE 1. Citation rates for *Physical Review Letters* to other articles in the *Physical Review*, by year.

Year	Articles	Citations	Citations per Article	Citations/Article/ Article
1995	2,574	12,707	4.9	2.2E-5
1996	2,636	12,957	4.9	2.1E-5
1997	2,632	14,519	5.5	2.2E-5
1998	3,045	18,422	6.0	2.3E-5
1999	2,822	18,263	6.5	2.0E-5
2000	3,001	19,426	6.5	2.2E-5
2001	3,055	20,378	6.7	2.2E-5
2002	2,986	20,136	6.7	2.1E-5

PROCESSING THE DATA

The APS, from its publication database, provided the total number of articles published in each year from 1893-2002, which established a normalization baseline for this study. Also provided was a report of the number of citations from *Physical Review Letters* articles published in 1995-2002 to *Physical Review* articles in previous years (a composite of all sections), and, for comparison, the total number of citations from both *Physical Review A-E* and *Letters* to all articles in previous years.

In order to increase the statistics for relevant time periods, the data were combined from different years into three time periods, corresponding to the availability of portions of the back files. The chronology of events in the digitization process for APS is as follows. In 1998, the APS announced it had digitized and made available its back file to 1985. At the end of 2000, they had digitized materials back to 1975, and in May of 2001, had completed the digitization back to Volume 1 in 1893. Data were combined from 1995-1997 to use as the control group, corresponding to no access to the electronic backfile. Data from 1999-2000 constituted a second portion, where access back to 1985 was available. Finally, 2001-2002 provided a sample of data with access back to 1975, and, for 2002, back to 1893. Since the statistics before 1975 were rather small and didn't warrant a separate analysis, the 2001 and 2002 data were combined. The 1998 data were not analyzed, since that was a transition year, with online access being made available in the middle of the year.

In order to compare apples to apples over time, two normalization procedures for the raw citation information were carried out. First, since different numbers of articles were published each year, the raw citation information was divided by the number of articles published in the year being analyzed. This quantity was then divided by the number of articles published in the year of the cited article. This provides a double-normalized citation rate, c_{dn}, as follows, for example, for citations from 2002 articles to those in 1977:

$$c_{dn\,2002} = \frac{c_{raw\,2002}}{N_{2002} \cdot N_{1977}},$$ where N_X = number of articles published in year

X, and c_{raw} is the gross number of citations from 2002 articles to those published in 1977. In the graphs of citation data that follow, all data are doubly normalized in this way.

Also, since citation rates decay (rather steeply) with time (see Figure 2, with a factor of three decrease in citation rates after seven years), the appropriate comparison of data between years was to graph the rates as a function of Years Since Publication.

For regimes of the usage and citation data where exponential behavior was observed, a least-squares fit was done to compute a half-life τ, where the half-life is the time it takes for a citation rate to become half of what it was originally. Using a functional form of

$$c_{dn}(t) = c_{dn}(0)e^{-ln(2)t/\tau},$$

a least-squares fit of the natural logarithm of the doubly normalized citation rate c_{dn} to the year (t), yields a slope of $ln(2)/\tau$.

Before discussing the results, a few caveats and details about the data are given. The APS data treats any object with a DOI as an article. Thus, in the early years of the *Physical Review*, for example, the book review section was counted as an article in the statistics, and some 'Minor Contributions' were indexed as one article, even though several small articles were lumped under that heading. Also, until 1897, the *Physical Review* had an 'academic' publishing year. So, 1893, for example, runs from July of 1893 to June of 1984. The year 1897 contains only a half-year's worth of articles, as the APS synchronized their volumes to the calendar year. All of these discrepancies are fairly minor, in the gross analysis, but they do lead to small changes in the 'actual' citation rates of the data.

RESULTS

The usage statistics, provided by Claire O'Neill, Data Analyst at APS, and detailed in Figure 1, show that users download articles from

FIGURE 2. Citations from *Physical Review Letters* articles in 2002 to all sections of the *Physical Review*. Data is doubly normalized by dividing by the number of articles published in 2002 and the number of articles published in the year plotted. Guidelines are provided for the two characteristic half-lives.

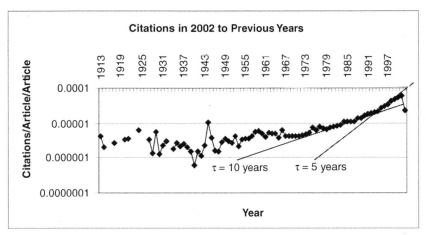

(Raw data courtesy of the American Physical Society)

every year, with even the early years showing about three downloads per article per year. The first few volumes of the *Physical Review* show much larger download rates.

When looking at the download data, there appear to be two exponential trend lines. In the first four or five years, the exponential has a large decay rate, which is overtaken by a slower decay process that extends to the end of the statistically significant portion of the data. The half-lives computed for these two processes are two years and 13 years, respectively.

The associated citation information, as visualized in Figure 2, of 2002 citation data, shows similar trends to the downloads, although, notably, no citations to articles before 1913. The citation curves for all years (1995-2002) look qualitatively the same, as can be seen in Figure 3. The peaks and valleys of the download and citation data in the area prior to approximately 1950 are fairly randomly distributed relative to one another, and are likely just random fluctuations. Indeed, plotting an average of all years of this study smoothes out the peaks in the citation data. The citation data also show two exponential dependencies, with a knee in the exponential curves around seven years from the publication

FIGURE 3. Doubly normalized citation rates from *Physical Review Letters* articles to all sections of the *Physical Review*, for three time intervals. The years 1995-1997 correspond to no access to an online back file, 1999-2000 correspond to access to an online back file to 1985, and 2001-2002 correspond to access to a back file at least back to 1975.

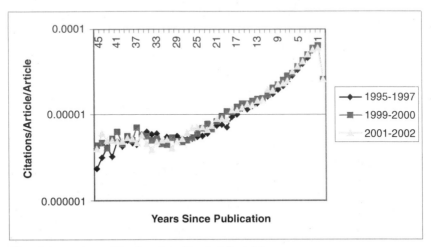

(Raw data courtesy of the American Physical Society)

date. The half-lives of these processes are 5 years and 10 years, respectively. Before 1960, the total number of citations is at most of order 30, so random fluctuations wash out any signal in that time interval.

In addition to year-by-year results of citation rates, the total number of citations were computed for each year from 1995-2002. The third column of Table 1 shows an apparent dramatic increase in citations per article published between the pre-electronic access regime, and the era since the complete back file was made available, with a sharp transition during the years when the back file was implemented. However, when one factors in that, each year, several thousand more articles have been published and thus are available to be cited (see the last column of Table 2), the citation rate per article published that year per article in the *Physical Review* from 1893 to that year is very consistent. Thus, one needs to continuously cite more and more articles in the reference section of a paper in order to maintain the same overall citation rate over time.

Finally, the original purpose of this paper was to analyze what difference in citation behavior online access to the journal may provide. Figure 3 shows data plotted for the time intervals when no online access

TABLE 2. Increased citation rates for years with online access available, compared to the 1995-1997 'Background' with no online access. The 15-year window corresponds to data since 1985 for 1999 data, and the 25-year window to 1975 data. These correspond to the two years for which back files were posted, in 1998 and 2000, respectively.

Year	Mean Enhancement (less than 15 years from publication)	St Dev (σ) (less than 15 years from publication)	Mean enhancement (15-25 years)	St Dev (σ) (15-25 years)
1999-2000	2.7E-6	1.4E-6	1.6E-6	.99E-6
2001-2002	1.9E-6	1.3E-6	1.2E-6	.45E-6
Combined	2.3E-6	1.1E-6		

was available to the back file (1995-1997), access was available back to 1985 (1999-2000), and access was available at least back to 1975 (2001-2002). Although the data look almost the same, there is a small enhancement of citation rate in the more recent data, as Figure 4 shows, when the 'background' citation rate from 1995-1997 is subtracted from the other years' data. The average of the enhancement shown in Figure 4 is computed and tabulated in Table 2.

DISCUSSION

It is very interesting that both the download rates and the citation rates show two exponential trends. It is certainly reasonable to assume that there are many different ways the literature is consulted and cited, and that each one may have its own decay curve. Burton and Kebler (1960) created a robust analogy between radioactive half-life and the half-life of literature. Fitting citation patterns for several disciplines, Burton and Kebler actually determined that their data did not fit one exponential curve, and hypothesized a citation format with two exponentials, one with twice the decay rate of the other. Although there was no intrinsic motivation given for using that particular functional form to fit the data, the concept that literature is made up of many kinds of articles, each with its own half-life, is compelling.

Burton and Kebler posit that 'classic' literature has a long half-life, while 'ephemeral' literature has a much shorter half-life. Thus, with enough statistics, one could easily expect different half-lives for citation and usage data. Potentially, there are many ephemeral papers with short

FIGURE 4. Differential doubly normalized citation rates from *Physical Review Letters* articles to all sections of the *Physical Review*, for the intervals 1999-2000 and 2001-2002 (i.e., subtracting the rate for 1995-1997).

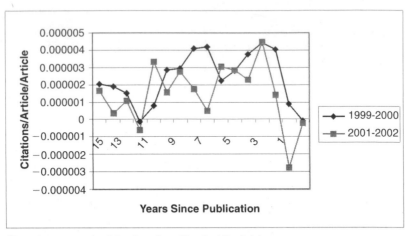

(Raw data courtesy of the American Physical Society)

half-lives that dominate the statistics for short time periods, but after several years, their usage disappears, and the usage of the 'classic' papers with long half-lives becomes the dominant process. Just as Gupta's (1990) paper proclaims the first conclusive evidence of an exponential decay rate in the citation of the physics literature, the present study is the first one the author is aware of that shows evidence of two distinct exponential decay rates, as first predicted by Burton and Kebler, and these decay rates show up in both usage and citation data.

To provide motivation for the existence of multiple usage rates, one may consider the following. In the first year or so of an article's life, it may be browsed in a current awareness capacity. One would expect a very short half-life for this activity, maybe as short as a few months (and, indeed, the download rate for the first year after publication is much higher than that of the preceding years, even steeper than a two-year half-life would indicate. Monthly, or even weekly, data would need to be analyzed to determine this very brief usage process). This current awareness browsing behavior would not be restricted to a scientist's specific research area, so one would expect a lot of amplitude in this channel.

Another use of the literature is as background for a specific research project, perhaps the result of a literature search. This would have less total amplitude than the current awareness use, so it would not be visible in the data from the early years. But, over time, classic results stay relevant, so the half-life of usefulness would be much longer, perhaps the ten years computed here. There are also probably classes of articles, ranging from the seminal article which can be cited for hundreds of years, to the more incremental and applied, Burton and Kebler's ephemeral article, which has a short shelf life until a seminal article comes along and makes that article irrelevant for future research. Perhaps the five-year window of the two-year half-life reflects the usage of the ephemeral articles, while the ten-year half-life refers to use of the seminal articles, whose usage will dominate the statistics when the ephemeral articles have ceased to be useful. Or, perhaps the five-year window still reflects a general browsing behavior of users, and the second decay rate reflects usage related to actual research purposes. More detailed study of specific articles and correlation with citations would shed more light on the actual processes yielding these characteristic lifetimes.

Other usage studies of the physics literature, notably Chen (1972) and Sandison (1974), show usage obsolescence rates of 14.3 years and infinity (and even negative half-lives), respectively. Thus, this study's initial download half-life of two years is much different than those results, and is more in line with other reports of online usage (for example, Anderson et al. 2001, for the journal *Pediatrics*). However, the longer half life shown in Figure 1 compares with Chen's findings for obsolescence.

Print-based usage surveys have significant systematic sources of error, however. For example, the most highly used issues are only shelved a finite number of times per day, and several people may have consulted the issue between reshelvings. Also, a browser would perhaps consult many articles within a recent issue, but only one use is credited in the study. However, for earlier years, a reader is likely to only consult one article per use of a volume, in answer to a specific information need. Finally, researchers with personal subscriptions will show no usage in the library. Researchers are less likely to have older issues of journals in their possession than newer ones, so, again, the bias points to more library usage of older journals, increasing the apparent usage half-life. Thus, it is conceivable that Chen's study is not sensitive to current awareness browsing, but is sensitive to slower processes. However, for example, Chen's data does not take into account the increase in the total volume of literature published, which is corrected for in this study, and when Sandison takes that into account, in a very crude fashion, Chen's half-lives become infinite, or, indeed, the usage density (per article) in fact becomes larger with time. The findings here definitely do not support Sandison's conclusion.

The online usage data from this paper eliminate many of the systematic problems of earlier usage studies. First, it measured all online usage of the *Physical Review*. This eliminates the variation in local journal usage studies caused by an institution having strength in one particular field and not another. It also compiles usage for everyone, everywhere in the world, and thus gives a good description of the behavior of all users of the physics literature. It is irrelevant whether a researcher has a personal subscription or an institutional subscription, since all uses are counted. The only data neglected are for people who browse the print collection. This is a non-trivial loss of data, but, as has been reported elsewhere (for example, Morse and Clintworth 2000), online usage swamps whatever numbers are gained in a journal sweep.

At Purdue University, I have noticed that *Physical Review* is not being reshelved nearly as often as in previous years, as users have switched to reading it online. Indeed, since the library ran out of space to house the entire print run locally, pre-1990 issues were moved into local storage without a peep from users. This is from a library in which, in the early 1990s, a considerable uproar was made when the subscription went from two print copies of the *Physical Review* (in one physical location) to one. An especially robust usage study of the medical literature by Tsay (1999, 1998) also shows an exponential usage rate for print materials, with a mean use half-life of 3.43 years, much closer to the findings of this paper than those of Chen or Sandison.

The citation rates contain similar exponential decay rates, again with two characteristic half-lives. The initial decay rate of this study, at five years, is fairly consistent with the results of Gupta's (1990) 4.9 years, and Burton and Kebler's (1960) 4.6 years for the physics literature. That these half-lives are so consistent is, in some ways, amazing, since they sample citation patterns of authors from the 1950s, the 1980s, and, here, the 21st century. Over 50 years, the half-life of the literature has remained constant, despite the many changes in the way physics is done and the kinds of problems that are being tackled.

Gupta points out that, comparing results to the work of Chen (1972) and Sandison (1974), perhaps the citation and usage data are not measuring the same thing. Tsay (1998) qualitatively supports this supposition of a difference, for the field of medicine, albeit with much different qualitative results than Chen or Sandison, and the current study confirms a difference in the data for physics. With such different characteristic time scales, the activities have some fundamental differences. For example, current awareness searching has no direct effect on citation habits–one reads many papers that don't end up being cited. And subtracting out the body of articles with half-life zero (i.e., are never cited) would tend to increase the effective half-life of citation data over direct usage data.

However, the fairly close correspondence between the longer half-lives for usage and citations (13 years and 10 years, respectively) is interesting. Perhaps this does show that usage and citation rates are measuring the same fundamental process for use of seminal articles of the literature. More investigation of that connection is necessary to draw any firm conclusions, however.

The tails of the distributions in Figures 1 and 2, the peaks and valleys from 1893-1950, are relatively randomly distributed. Indeed, when 1995-2002 citation data are averaged, the peaks and valleys pretty much disappear entirely. Also, the high download rates (up to 100 downloads per article per year) for early issues of the *Physical Review* are likely due to curiosity and/or historical research, rather than to any relevant results for current research, as evidenced by a lack of citations in *PRL* in that time interval to any articles before 1911.

Another difference between the Gupta results and those from this study is that the peak citation rate here comes at one year after publication. Gupta sees the second year having more citations than the first after publication. This is a reasonable difference, because *PRL*, as a Letters journal, has a quick turnaround, and is meant for rapid communication of new developments, while the physics literature as a whole (which was sampled by Gupta) contains predominantly articles that are exhaustive examinations of a topic, and thus take longer to carry out, analyze, review, and get published. Thus, the second year enhancement in the Gupta data is likely due to this gestation period of carrying out research and getting it published. Indeed, when I looked at citations from all sections of the *Physical Review* to the *Physical Review*, the citation rates were about equal in year one and year two after publication, generally consistent with the Gupta results, and different from Tsay (1999) who found a maximum citation rate in the third year after publication in medicine.

The next step is to see whether detailed analysis of the citation levels in recent years shows any enhancement over the control years. The relative citation rates between the pre-electronic access period, the initial back file, and the complete back file look very similar (see Figure 3). In order to identify potentially small differences in the citation patterns, the 'background' of the average data from 1995-1997 was subtracted, and the difference was plotted for the two sets of data corresponding to the availability of the online backfile (see Figure 4). This shows that there is a net positive effect in both the 1999-2000 and 2001-2002 time intervals for citing materials that were available online. The mean values of this enhancement are given in Table 2. This is about a 10% effect on the total citation rate (the subtracted background). As can be seen, there is a weak positive correlation between online access and increased citation level, significant to two standard deviations for the combined data.

Checking before 1985 (the last two columns of Table 2), as a control to see if there is any systematic increase in citation rates irrespective of online access between those years, one finds that there is still a positive enhancement. For the 1999-2000 data, which is the control, it is a slightly lower level of significance than for the 1985-present data, while the 2001-2002 data, which should provide whatever signal is available, have a lower absolute enhancement, but the error is much smaller, yielding results of three standard deviations significance. The results from 1975-1985 show that there could likely be another factor at work in the enhancement of citation rate, since there should be no enhancement for the 1999-2000 data, and yet one shows up. The 2001-2002 data for this time interval have an anomalously low error level compared to the error levels of the other data, so it is perhaps just the result of a fluke correspondence in the data and is without real statistical significance.

Before 1975, the potential enhancement computed is a factor of ten smaller than the error, so no signal is apparent. As mentioned before, the total number of citations in a year up through 1960 is, at most, of order 30, so attempting to find a signal is extremely difficult.

One thing that should be noted is that the 2002 data (like the 1996 data) have a lower absolute citation rate than the other years (see Table 1). I believe this leads to some of the reduced enhancement in citation rates for the 2001-2002 data compared to the 1999-2000 data. Whether this is a fluke for 2002, or a real trend, it will take more years of data to determine (and again, the effect of the changed publishing cycle for 2002 is unknown). Perhaps a study with a few more years of data would produce enough statistics to provide more solid answers, and it should be easier to determine whether the decrease in the citation/article/article rate is real or not. The fact that each four-page *Physical Review Letter* article averages over six references to *Physical Review* articles, leads one to wonder whether the increase can continue indefinitely, or whether, as some pundits have noted, papers will eventually just become a collection of references to other work.

One unresolved question is the effect of e-print citing on the overall citation rate for *Physical Review* articles. The APS suggests that authors submit their papers to arXiv.org before submitting them to the *Physical Review*. This allows for an informal period of peer review before proceeding through the official certification process, and major errors can be corrected outside of the formal process of peer review. It leads to faster editorial reviews for the *Physical Review*, but it also means papers might be citing the e-print version of an article that ends up in the *Physical Review*, rather than the final, published version, and this might erode the overall citation rate for APS articles. As Brown (2001b) has discovered, the citation rate for arXiv papers is substantial and still increasing with time (Brown 2001a). The effect of e-print citing habits is another topic worthy of investigation.

CONCLUSION

The usage data in Figure 1 do show that, 'if you scan it, they will come.' The APS back files are being used frequently, and, if nothing else, at least make it convenient for authors to actually consult the older articles they cite. The citation data further show that articles are still cited in *Physical Review Letters* back to the early 1910s. Double exponential behavior was seen in both download and citation data, which give a flavor of how long articles are useful for reading and citing, and show that there are likely multiple processes involved in the usage of the journal information. For example, with the download data, the large exponential decay rate is likely due to general browsing, while the smaller rate process is more likely related to focused research activities. The overall half-life for citation rates is consistent with previous studies (Gupta 1990; Burton and Kebler 1960), while the usage half-life is similar to recent online usage studies (Anderson et al. 2001; Tsay 1998), and markedly different from previous print usage studies in physics (Chen 1972; Sandison 1974).

The citation data are tantalizing but are not conclusive in determining whether online access to an electronic back file has affected citation rates. One would not expect a huge effect on citation rate, since scientists have always been citing prior research, and, one assumes, already know most of the relevant results, from their own prior research and papers where they've cited past work. So, the 10% enhancement that is observed is perhaps of the right order of magnitude, or even higher than might be expected. However, as seen by the enhancement of the data in pre-1985 years for the 1999-2000 citation data, there might be some other systematic enhancement going on that this research was unable to discriminate. Perhaps future study of this type of data will be able to determine more definitively the nature of the observed enhancement.

REFERENCES

Anderson, Kent, John Sack, Lisa Krauss, and Lori O'Keefe. 2001. Publishing On-line-Only Peer-Reviewed Biomedical Literature: Three Years of Citation, Author Perception, and Usage Experience, *Journal of Electronic Publishing* 6(3). http://www.press.umich.edu/jep/06-03/anderson.html.

Brown, Cecelia. 2001a. The E-volution of Preprints in the Scholarly Communication of Physicists and Astronomers, *Journal of the American Society for Information Science and Technology* 52(3):187-200.

Brown, Cecelia. 2001b. The Coming of Age of E-Prints in the Literature of Physics, *Issues in Science and Technology Librarianship* 31. http://www.istl.org/01-summer/refereed.html.

Burton, R.E. and R.W. Kebler.1960. The 'Half-life' of Some Scientific and Technical Literatures, *American Documentation* 11: 18-22.

Chen, C.C. 1972. The Use Patterns of Physics Journals in a Large Academic Research Library, *Journal of the American Society for Information Science* 23:254-265.

Gupta, Usha. 1990. Obsolescence of Physics Literature: Exponential Decrease of the Density of Citations to Physical Review Articles with Age, *Journal of the American Society for Information Science* 41(4): 282-287.

Morse, David H. and David A. Clintworth. 2000. Comparing Patterns of Electronic and Print Journal Use in an Academic Health Science Library, *Issues in Science and Technology Librarianship* 28. http://www.istl.org/00-fall/refereed.html.

Sandison, A. 1974. Densities of Use, and Absence of Obsolescence, in Physics Journals at MIT, *Journal of the American Society for Information Science* 25:172-182.

Tsay, Ming-Yueh. 1998. Library Journal Use and Citation Half-life in Medical Science, *Journal of the American Society for Information Science* 49(14):1283-1292.

Tsay, Ming-Yueh. 1999. Library Journal Use and Citation Age in Medical Science, *Journal of Documentation* 55(5): 543-555.

The Use of Online Supplementary Material in High-Impact Scientific Journals

Thomas Schaffer
Kathy M. Jackson

SUMMARY. An increasing number of journals are allowing scientists to submit supplementary material with their articles. The presentation of supplementary information is characterized by a variety of technologies and formats. This study examines the use of supplementary material in a selective sample of high-impact journals from the pure and applied sciences. The authors review publishers' policies concerning the submission of supplementary material and discuss the formats permitted. Recommendations for enhancing access to supplementary material and insuring its effective use by scholars are provided. *[Article copies available for a fee from The Haworth Document Delivery Service: 1-800-HAWORTH. E-mail address: <docdelivery@haworthpress.com> Website: <http://www.HaworthPress.com> © 2004 by The Haworth Press, Inc. All rights reserved.]*

Thomas Schaffer, MLS, is Assistant Professor and Social Sciences Reference Librarian (E-mail: tschaffer@tamu.edu), and Kathy M. Jackson, PhD, is Associate Professor and Chemistry Librarian (E-mail: kathy-jackson@tamu.edu), both at Sterling C. Evans Library, Texas A&M University, College Station, TX 77843-5000.

The authors wish to thank Lisa Craig-Young for her assistance with the tables for this article.

[Haworth co-indexing entry note]: "The Use of Online Supplementary Material in High-Impact Scientific Journals." Schaffer, Thomas, and Kathy M. Jackson. Co-published simultaneously in *Science & Technology Libraries* (The Haworth Information Press, an imprint of The Haworth Press, Inc.) Vol. 25, No. 1/2, 2004, pp. 73-85; and: *Emerging Issues in the Electronic Environment: Challenges for Librarians and Researchers in the Sciences* (ed: Jeannie P. Miller) The Haworth Information Press, an imprint of The Haworth Press, Inc., 2004, pp. 73-85. Single or multiple copies of this article are available for a fee from The Haworth Document Delivery Service [1-800-HAWORTH, 9:00 a.m. - 5:00 p.m. (EST). E-mail address: docdelivery@haworthpress.com].

Digital Object Identifier: 10.1300/J122v25n01_06

KEYWORDS. Scientific journal publishing, electronic journals, online supplementary material

INTRODUCTION

Most reference librarians probably have helped users find elusive supplementary material located on an author's Web page. Frequently, the page is no longer available at the URL given in the article's list of references. Now, journal publishers are allowing authors to post supplementary material on the publisher's Web site. A large variety of materials are being posted, and the treatment of supplementary material varies widely by publisher. Long tables and data sets, microarrays, color photographs, and other graphical material that would be expensive to publish in print are appearing as supplementary material on publishers' Web sites. Authors may now submit video and audio supplementary materials to some journals. Such data can greatly enhance articles in ways not previously possible. In this article, the authors look at the use of supplementary material by high-impact journals in astronomy, biochemistry, chemistry, chemical engineering, mathematics, mechanical engineering, physics, and statistics.

RELATED RESEARCH

Few articles provide an extensive discussion of supplementary material. Most library and information science articles that mention supplementary material rarely devote more than a few paragraphs to the subject. For researchers interested in the topic of supplementary material in science journals, Web sites that address the electronic publication of scientific information, articles that provide insight into the evaluation of electronic information, or articles that examine the formats and technologies that characterize supplementary material offer the most pertinent information.

Two Web sites created by McKiernan (2001a; 2001b) offer considerable information concerning the use of supplementary data in scientific publications. "EJI (sm): A Registry of Innovative e-Journals Features, Functionality, and Content" includes 20 pages filled with examples of electronic publishing in science. The site provides links to instructions for the submission of supplementary data from titles like *Science Magazine* and the Institute of Physics' electronic journals. "M-Bed(sm): A

Registry of Embedded Multimedia Electronic Journals" lists 62 science journals that make use of imbedded multimedia files. The site includes hyperlinks to the Web site of each title and an extensive bibliography of articles related to embedded multimedia.

Hurd et al. (2001) advocated a user-center methodology for evaluating electronic journals. Based on the Kano model of customer expectations, the methodology adopts Kano's three-level approach to user satisfaction. In a paradigm that includes basic (expected) needs, performance (normal) quality, and exciting quality, the authors identified links to data repositories or other supplementary data as exciting quality. The authors offered *Science Magazine Online* as an example of a journal that includes innovative features that increase reader satisfaction. The methodology postulates that, over time, exciting features migrate to become normal expectations.

Research articles that focus on Web-based content in electronic journals often address issues encountered in examinations of supplementary material. Three of the most important issues characterizing discussions of Web-based content include the use of links to navigate between sets of data, the use of multimedia, and the need to archive these materials. Stankus (1999) considered multimedia presentations atypical of most Internet publications. He felt that, at present, the willingness of editors to use HTML to create interlinked data provides the most important benefit to scientists. Boyce (1999) noted that the readers of *The Astrophysical Journal* chose HTML versions of articles over PDF files more than 80% of the time. He also considered interlinked data a crucial benefit to scientists. He noted, however, that in the future, multimedia formats like video clips and three-dimensional representations would "profoundly increase the ability to transfer concepts from the author to the reader." Resh (1998) stated that the editors of the *Annual Review of Entomology* encouraged authors to submit multimedia content for posting on the publication's Web site, noting that ". . . if an electronic version was available, sounds of crickets chirping, endless photographs, even a video of a crucial experiment would be possible." McKiernan (2002) considered computer code or programs valuable types of supplementary data, and noted that some e-journals included output files, data sets, and text appendices as supplementary material.

Bachrach and Heller (2000) described the creation of a completely Web-based chemistry journal. They noted that from the journal's inception, the editors of the *Internet Journal of Chemistry* encouraged authors to submit supplementary material with their articles. Editors welcomed the inclusion of large data sets, and encouraged the use of multimedia and interactive tools. Bachrach and Heller also regarded enhancements to tabular data as one of the journal's most important features, since Web-based tables could be imported easily into readers' own spreadsheets.

Boudoin (2003) noted that the inclusion of supplementary material gave some journals an enhanced Internet presence. Yet these same journals invariably relied on print versions as archival copies. She identified three different technological approaches to archiving Web-based data, and hoped that solutions could be devised to preserve the most dynamic scholarly information. Brown and Duda (1996) noted that OCLC's Electronic Collections Online creates archives of electronic journals at no cost to publishers, offering a potential source of archival subscriptions for libraries. Quoting Ken Metzner (1966), the authors noted that adding multimedia features could double the size of research articles. Keller (2000) related the findings of an expert panel of 45 scientists, librarians, consultants, and representatives of journal publishers. The panel submitted several scenarios for the future evolution of electronic journals, but also focused on two models that addressed the problem of archiving non-textual material. Both models rejected commercial publishers as "suitable archiving partners," preferring to rely on national depositories or international cooperatives. The panel expressed confidence that, within fifteen years, the average journal article would contain so much interactive and multimedia content that printed journals could no longer adequately serve as archival copies.

METHODOLOGY

A major goal of the present study was to determine how prevalent the use of supplementary material is in key journals in disciplines for which one of the authors has collection development and reference responsibilities. Those journals with the highest ten impact factors in 2001 and 2002 were selected for the study from the *ISI Journal Citation Reports Science Edition* lists for the following subject categories: (1) Astronomy & Astrophysics; (2) Biochemical Research Methods; Biochemistry & Molecular Biology; (3) Analytical, Applied, Inorganic & Nuclear, Medicinal, Multidisciplinary, Organic, and Physical Chemistry; (4) Chemical Engineering; (5) Mechanical Engineering; (6) Mathematics; Applied Mathematics; Interdisciplinary Applications; (7) Applied, Mathematical, Nuclear & Multidisciplinary Physics; Atomic, Molecular & Chemical Physics; Condensed Matter Physics; Fluids & Plasmas; Particles &

Fields; (8) Statistics & Probability; and (9) ISI's "All" category, not broken down by subject. Some journals appeared on more than one list, and for the purpose of this study, such journals were assigned to the subject category in which the journal had the highest ranking. ISI's "All" listing provides the impact factors for all science and engineering titles in the ISI database. The authors wanted to be sure to include those journals with the highest impact factors, regardless of discipline.

The resulting sample included 105 titles from 41 publishers. Of these, 11 were excluded because the authors did not have access to the electronic versions, or the authors did not have access to the titles that only existed in print. The remaining 94 titles from 34 publishers were included in the study.

The study included the following steps: (1) the instructions for authors for each journal were reviewed for information about supplementary material; (2) recent online issues were checked for supplementary material; (3) for those journals for which the author instructions made no mention of supplementary material and examination of the recent online issues revealed none, an inquiry was made via e-mail or phone as to whether the publisher permitted the use of supplemental material.

RESULTS

As shown in Table 1, 65 (69%) of the 94 journals allowed supplementary material to be posted on the journal or publisher's Web site. When actual issues were examined, less than half of the journal titles actually showed evidence of supplementary material being used in recent issues.

From the communications the authors received from some publishers, it was clear that authors are being encouraged to submit supplementary material to enhance their articles and to help restrict the size of print issues of journals. Reed Elsevier, for example, is in the process of revising the instructions for authors for the recent additions to the Reed Elsevier journal family to include information on supplementary material (Laura Hassink, e-mail message to author, August 16, 2003). In those instances in which the publisher stresses that certain types of material should (or must) be treated as supplementary material, authors take note, and the volume of supplementary material associated with articles increases. *Science Magazine*, for example, now requests that "authors place the bulk of their description of materials and methods online as supporting material, providing only as much methods description in

TABLE 1. Study Results by Subject

Titles	ISI Subject Categories				
	All	Astronomy	Biochemistry	Chemistry	Chemical Eng.
Total number of titles in sample	11	13	12	12	10
Excluded	0	2	0	1	2
Titles included in study	11	11	12	11	8
Titles allowing supplementary material	9	9	12	6	6

Titles	ISI Subject Categories				
	Math	Mechanical Eng.	Physics	Statistics	Total
Total number of titles in sample	13	12	12	10	105
Excluded	3	2	1	0	11
Titles included in study	10	10	11	10	94
Titles allowing supplementary material	5	6	10	2	65

the print manuscript as is necessary to follow the logic of the text" (*Science Magazine*).

The 65 journals permitting supplementary material are listed in Table 2. Also provided are the publisher and the ISI subject category for each title. Twenty-four publishers are represented. Among the publishers with more than one title on the list are the American Chemical Society, the American Physical Society, Blackwell, Cell Press, Reed Elsevier, Kluwer, Nature, and the University of Chicago Press.

Many of the instructions to authors studied by the investigators went into considerable detail about the types of supplementary material that could be accepted. Very specific instructions were provided for each type and format of material. It is illuminating to look at the various types and formats and how they are used. The most frequent category of supplementary material encountered was textual material. Its treatment and use is discussed first.

TABLE 2. Titles Whose Publishers Allow Use of Supplementary Material (65 Titles)

Title	Publisher	ISI Subject
Accounts Chem Res	Amer Chemical Soc	Chemistry
Acta Astronom	Reed Elsevier	Astronomy
Adv Nucl Phys	Kluwer	Physics
Adv Phys	Taylor & Francis	Physics
Angewandte Chemie	Wiley	Chemistry
Ann Math	Ann Mathematics	Mathematics
Annu Rev Cell Dev Biol	Annual Reviews	Biochemistry
Annu Rev Astron Astr	Annual Reviews	Astronomy
Annu Rev Biochem	Annual Reviews	Biochemistry
Annu Rev Bioph Biom	Annual Reviews	Biochemistry
Annu Rev Earth Pl Sc	Annual Reviews	Astronomy
Annu Rev Immunol	Annual Reviews	All
Annu Rev Neurosci	Annual Reviews	All
Annu Rev Nucl Part S	Annual Reviews	Physics
Annu Rev Phys Chem	Annual Reviews	Chemistry
Annu Rev Plant Phys	Annual Reviews	Biochemistry
App Compu Harmon A	Reed Elsevier	Mathematics
Astron Astrophys	EDP Sciences	Astronomy
Astropart Phys	Reed Elsevier	Astromony
Astrophys J	Univ Chicago Press	Astronomy
Astrophys J Suppl S	Univ Chicago Press	Astronomy
BBA-Rev Biomembranes	Reed Elsevier	Biochemistry
Catal Today	Reed Elsevier	Chemical Engineering
Cell	Cell Press	All
Chaos	Amer Inst Physics	Mathematics
Chem Rev	Amer Chemical Soc	Chemistry
Chem Soc Rev	Royal Soc Chemistry	Chemistry
Combust Flame	Reed Elsevier	Chemical Engineering
Embo J	Oxford Univ Press	Biochemistry
Int J Heat Fluid F	Reed Elsevier	Mechanical Engineering
Int J Plasticity	Reed Elsevier	Mechanical Engineering
Intl J Heat Mass Tran	Reed Elsevier	Mechanical Engineering
J Aerosol Sci	Reed Elsevier	Mechanical Engineering
J Am Math Soc	Amer Math Soc	Mathematics
J Catal	Reed Elsevier	Chemical Engineering
J High Energy Phys	Int Sch Advanced Stud/IOP	Physics
J Membrane Sci	Reed Elsevier	Chemical Engineering
J Roy Stat Soc A Sta	Blackwell	Statistics
J Roy Stat Soc B	Blackwell	Statistics

TABLE 2 (continued)

Title	Publisher	ISI Subject
J Supercrit Fluid	Reed Elsevier	Chemical Engineering
J Thermophys Heat Tr	AIAA	Mechanical Engineering
Mat Sci Eng R	Reed Elsevier	Physics
Moll Cell	Cell Press	Biochemistry
Mon Not R Astron Soc	Blackwell	Astronomy
Nat Cell Biol	Nature	Biochemistry
Nat Genet	Nature	All
Nat Immunol	Nature	All
Nat Med	Nature	All
Nat Rev Mol Cell Bio	Nature	Biochemistry
Nat Struct Biol	Nature	Biochemistry
New Astron	Reed Elsevier	Astronomy
New England J Med	Mass Med Soc	All
Phy Rep	Reed Elsevier	Physics
Phys Rev Lett	Amer Physical Soc	Physics
Physica D	Reed Elsevier	Mathematics
Physiol Rev	Amer Physiological Soc/Highw.	All
Plant Cell	Amer Soc Plant Biol/Highwire	Biochemistry
Plasma Chem Plasma P	Kluwer	Chemical Engineering
Prog Energ Combust	Reed Elsevier	Mechanical Engineering
Prog Nucl Mag Res Sp	Reed Elsevier	Physics
Prog Surf Sci	Reed Elsevier	Physics
Rev Mod Phys	Amer Physical Soc	Physics
Science	Amer Assn Advance Science	All
Surf Sci Rep	Reed Elsevier	Chemistry
Trends Biochem Sci	Reed Elsevier	Biochemistry

Tables, Lists, and Textual Documents as Supplementary Material

Much of the supplementary material examined by the authors was a textual extension of the article itself. A recent three-page *Angewandte Chemie International Edition* article serves as a typical example. The article's 23 pages of supplementary material included seven pages of experimental procedures, six pages of chemical data on peptides, two pages of biological data on peptides, and three pages of NMR spectra (Fujii et al. 2003).

Publishers' practices vary regarding limits of file sizes for supplementary material and on the number of items an author may submit. We found some publishers that limited the number of items to eight or less. One publisher allowed 18 items. *Science Magazine* editors urge authors to "make every effort to keep file sizes reasonable and carefully consider whether the material is genuinely essential to the paper in question" (*Science Magazine*). Later in the instructions for preparing supporting online material for *Science Magazine*, file size limits of 6 MB for a single item and a total of 50 MB for all supplementary material are given (*Science Magazine*). *Annual Reviews* states that "supplemental material must not exceed a total of 7 MB or 30 files (including graphic files)" (*Annual Reviews*).

In "ApJ: Supplementary electronic materials philosophy," authors are cautioned about the "potentially sticky issue of how much material can be included before the boundary between a journal and data repository is crossed" (*Astrophysical Journal*).

Machine readable files and computer source codes are also included as supplementary material in some journals. Generally, executable files or copyrighted material may not be included.

Multimedia as Supplementary Material

The use of multimedia to supplement print and online journal articles enhances an author's ability to convey information to readers. Those publishers that allow multimedia objects as supplementary material have even more specific instructions for it than for print supplementary material. Types of multimedia supplementary material encountered by the authors included sound, video, animations, and 3D objects. The supplementary material for an article on transient laser frequency modulation spectroscopy (Hall and North 2000) is representative of material found in this category. This 31-page article in the *Annual Review of Physical Chemistry* is linked to a visual tutorial that uses animation to show waveforms and to explain the particular spectroscopy technique discussed in the paper. Also included is a diagram of the apparatus used for the measurements.

The instructions for authors for *The Plant Cell* state that "One traditional still image of the author's choosing for each video must be included as a figure in the article. The figure should include three frames of the video, indicating the beginning, middle, and end. This image will be published to act as a link from the text to the full video file. It will also appear in the text of the printed journal in place of the video" (*The Plant Cell*). The inclusion in the print journal of stills from the video is useful to those users of the print journal who do not have immediate access to the online supplementary material. It is also useful for archival purposes.

Most videos are short, 30 to 60 seconds long with no sound. The most common video formats used for supplementary material are MPEG and QuickTime. The Author Gateway for Elsevier journals indicates that two other formats, Microsoft Audio/Video Interlaced format and CompuServe GIF, are acceptable for video (Reed Elsevier 2003). Authors submitting videos to the *Physiological Reviews* are asked to keep video files below 10 MB in size and to include a written caption with each video file, explaining what is happening in the video (*Physiological Reviews*).

Photographs as Supplementary Material

Color photographs are expensive to print in journals, and scholarly scientific journals often require authors to cover the cost of including color photographs. The substitution of black-and-white photographs means that a great deal of useful information may be lost to the reader. Posting color photographs online as supplementary material provides authors the opportunity to share photographs without loss of data and without incurring a large cost.

An Electronic Journal with No Print Equivalent

One physics journal in our sample, the *Journal of High Energy Physics* (*JHEP*), has no print equivalent. Its impact factor placed it fifth among physics journals in 2001 and ninth in 2002. *Journal of High Energy Physics* is owned by the International School for Advanced Studies and published by Institute of Physics (IOP) Publishing. According to the editorial information on the journal's home page, "The objective in running the journal is to capitalize on the innovative advantages of the new media: rapidity of communication, broad diffusion and the ability to run and distribute a journal solely by electronic means" (*Journal of High Energy Physics*). When the user views an abstract in *JHEP*, one of the buttons displayed at the bottom of the screen is the Multimedia button. Like other IOP titles, articles are available free for the first 30 days after they are published. It is a good example for study if someone wants to see an advanced electronic journal without a print counterpart.

RECOMMENDATIONS

Some journals make supplementary material easier to locate and to navigate than others. Below are recommendations for improving the accessibility of supplementary material:

- List all supplementary material that has appeared in the journal on the journal home page, with, at minimum, the author's name, the location of the article in the journal, and links to the article summary, to the article, and to the supplementary material. Allow free access to supplementary material to enable subscribers and readers of the print edition to gain access to this data. The Institute of Physics and the American Chemical Society are two examples of publishers that allow free access to supplementary material and provide an up-front list of all supplementary material available for each journal.
- The fact that an article has supplementary material available should be indicated in the table of contents of the issue.
- There should be links from the article to the supplementary material and from the supplementary material to the article.
- A statement indicating where the supplementary material may be found needs to appear in the appropriate place in the text, along with the URL.
- Supplementary material requiring special applications for use or viewing should clearly specify what is needed.
- In online journals, supplementary material should be as fully searchable as the rest of the article that it accompanies.
- The instructions to authors and the editorial policy should clearly state whether supplementary material is peer reviewed or whether it receives editorial review.
- The archiving of supplementary material needs to be clearly addressed by each publisher, and the publisher's policy needs to be stated in the journal for the benefit of both authors and subscribers.

CONCLUSION

This study identifies several trends that will continue to influence scientists' reliance on supplementary material. Instructions for the submission of supplementary material are being encountered with greater frequency on publishers' Web sites. As authors respond to these instructions, the number of articles that include supplementary data will increase. Electronic journals will continue to evolve to make maximum use of the advantages offered by Web-based publishing. The use of existing technologies like computer code, audio files, and three-dimensional imaging will become more commonplace and authors will adapt new technologies to facilitate scientific communication. The authors believe that researchers' interests will expand as electronic journals have an increased impact on their lives and work. We would like to suggest the following topics relating to supplementary material for further study: (1) publishers' archiving practices for supplementary material; (2) editorial review policies for supplementary material; (3) accessibility issues for subscribers to print versions; and (4) the indexing of supplementary material.

REFERENCES

Annual Reviews. Supplemental material policy. Annual Reviews, http://www.annualreviews.org/authors/supp.asp (accessed September 2, 2003).

Astrosphysical Journal. Supplementary electronic materials. University of Chicago Press, http://www.journals.uchicago.edu/ApJ/ematerials.philosophy.html (accessed September 2, 2003).

Bachrach, Steven M. and Stephen R. Heller. 2000. The Internet Journal of Chemistry: A case study of an electronic chemistry journal. *Serials Review* 26(2): 3-14.

Boudoin, Patsy. 2003. Uppity bits: Coming to terms with archiving dynamic electronic journals. *The Serials Librarian* 43 (4): 63-72.

Brown, Elizabeth W. and Andrea L. Duda. 1996. Electronic publishing programs: Issues to consider. *Issues in Science and Technology Librarianship* (Fall 1996). Available http://www.istl.org/96-fall/brown-duda2.html (accessed November 14, 2003).

Boyce, Peter. 1999. Scholarly journals in the electronic world. *The Serials Librarian* 36(1-2): 187-198.

Fujii, Nobutaka, Shinya Oishi, Kenichi Hiramatsu, Takanobu Araki, Satoshi Ueda, Hirokazu Tamamura, Akira Otaka, Shuichi Kusano, Shigemi Terakubo, Hideki Nakashima, James A. Broach, John O. Trent, Zi-xuan Wang, and Stephen C. Peiper. 2003. Molecular-size reduction of a potent CXCR4-Chemokine antagonist using orthogonal combination of conformation- and sequence-based libraries. *Angewandte Chemie International Edition* 42 (28): 3251-3253. Supplementary information available at http://www.wiley-vch.de/contents/jc_2002/2003/z51024_s.pdf (accessed September 2, 2003).

Hall, Gregory E. and Simon W. North. 2000. Transient laser frequency modulation spectroscopy. *Annual Review of Physical Chemistry* 51: 243-274, http://80-arjournals.annualreviews.orgezprox.tamu.edu:2048/doi/full/10.1146/annurev.pphychem.51.1243 (accessed September 2, 2003).

Hurd, Julie M., Deborah D. Blecic, and Ann E. Robinson. 2001. Performance measures of electronic journals: A user centered approach. *Science & Technology Libraries* 20(2/3): 57-71.

Journal of High Energy Physics. International School for Advanced Studies, http://www.iop.org/EJ/journal/JHEP (accessed July 20, 2004).

Keller, Alice. 2000. Future development of electronic journals: A Delphi survey. *International Journal of Specialized Libraries* 34(3-4): 197-193.

McKiernan, Gerry. 2002. E is for everything: The extraordinary, evolutionary e-journal. *The Serials Librarian*, 43(3-4): 293-321.

_____. 2001a. *EJI (sm): A Registry of Innovative E-Journals Features, Functionality, and Content*, Iowa State University Library, 10 August 2001, http://www.public. iastate.edu/~CYBERSTACKS/EJI.htm (accessed August 30, 2003).

_____. 2001b. M-*Bed(sm): A Registry of Embedded Multimedia Electronic Journals*, Iowa State University Library, 6 July 2001, http://www.public.iastate.edu/ ~CYBERSTACKS/M-Bed.htm (accessed August 30, 2003).

Metzner, Ken. 1996. Re[2]: Kick off discussion: Archiving. ARL_EJOURNAL. [arl-ejournal@cni.org]. November 20, 1996. Quoted in Elizabeth W. Brown and Adrea L. Duda. 1996. Electronic publishing programs: Issues to consider. *Issues in Science and Technology Librarianship* (Fall 1966): 2-3. Available http://www.istl. org/96-fall/brown-duda2.html (accessed November 14, 2003).

Physiological Reviews. Instructions for preparing your manuscript. Data supplements. The American Physiological Society, http://www.the-aps.org/publications/i4a/prep_ manuscript.htm#data_supplements (accessed September 2, 2003).

The Plant Cell. Instructions for authors. American Society of Plant Biologists, http:// www.plantcell.org/misc/ifora.shtml (accessed September 2, 2003).

Reed Elsevier. 2003. Author artwork instructions. Multimedia files. Author Gateway. http://authors.elsevier.com (accessed November 14, 2003).

Resh, Vincent H. 1998. Science and communication: An author/editor/user's perspective on the transition from paper to electronic publishing. *Issues in Science and Technology Librarianship* 19 (Summer 1998). http://www.istl.org/98-summer/article3. html (accessed September 2, 2003).

Science Magazine. Preparing your supporting online material. American Association for the Advancement of Science, http://www.sciencemag.org/feature/contribinfo/ prep/prep_online.shtml (accessed September 2, 2003).

Stankus, Tony. 1999. *Electronic Expectations: Science Journals on the Web*. New York: The Haworth Information Press.

Challenges and Opportunities for Bibliometrics in the Electronic Environment: The Case of the *Proceedings of the Oklahoma Academy of Science*

Tony L. Bremholm

SUMMARY. The digitization of back issues of print journals creates opportunities for bibliometric analysis using the electronic text files. Using readily available software, simple methods, and a little creativity, librarians can extract and manipulate information from database search results and from digitized journals for analysis of publication and citation behavior. The current study describes methods and results from a bibliometric and citation analysis of the electronic version of the *Proceedings of the Oklahoma Academy of Science*. This study illustrates the opportunities as well as the challenges for bibliometrics and citation analysis in the electronic environment. As more journals migrate to the digital environment, issues of access, copyright and fair use, on-

Tony L. Bremholm, MLIS, MA (History of Technology and Science), MS (Botany, Major in Water Resources), BS (Biology), is Assistant Professor and Life Sciences Librarian, Science/Engineering Services, Texas A&M University Libraries, 5000 TAMU, College Station, TX 77843-5000 (E-mail: bremholm@tamu.edu).

[Haworth co-indexing entry note]: "Challenges and Opportunities for Bibliometrics in the Electronic Environment: The Case of the *Proceedings of the Oklahoma Academy of Science*." Bremholm, Tony L. Co-published simultaneously in *Science & Technology Libraries* (The Haworth Information Press, an imprint of The Haworth Press, Inc.) Vol. 25, No. 1/2, 2004, pp. 87-107; and: *Emerging Issues in the Electronic Environment: Challenges for Librarians and Researchers in the Sciences* (ed: Jeannie P. Miller) The Haworth Information Press, an imprint of The Haworth Press, Inc., 2004, pp. 87-107. Single or multiple copies of this article are available for a fee from The Haworth Document Delivery Service [1-800-HAWORTH, 9:00 a.m. - 5:00 p.m. (EST). E-mail address: docdelivery@haworthpress.com].

line file formats, and idiosyncrasies in the digital files may limit the opportunities for bibliometric analysis. *[Article copies available for a fee from
The Haworth Document Delivery Service: 1-800-HAWORTH. E-mail address:
<docdelivery@haworthpress.com> Website: <http://www.HaworthPress.com>
© 2004 by The Haworth Press, Inc. All rights reserved.]*

KEYWORDS. Bibliometrics, citation analysis, scientific communication, electronic publishing

INTRODUCTION

The delivery of print journal content via the World Wide Web is becoming the norm in academic libraries. As patrons increasingly demand the electronic format and shun print journals, the digitization of
long runs of print journals could be a boon for bibliometric research.
Bibliometrics is defined as the mathematical and statistical analysis of
patterns in the publication and use of documents. Citation analysis is a
subset of bibliometrics that examines patterns in the citation of documents (Diodato 1994). Librarians use such studies for collection development, while other disciplines use them for evaluating the quality of
journals, researchers, and institutions. Using readily available software
and relatively simple techniques, extracting information directly from
the digital files can automate many of the data collection tasks that made
bibliometrics a daunting and tedious process in the age of print journals
and print indexes. These techniques are particularly useful for journals
not fully covered by abstracting or citation indexing services. Such
journals may also have a small circulation but regional or local importance.

This paper describes the methods and selected results from a bibliometric study of such a small-circulation journal, the *Proceedings of the
Oklahoma Academy of Science* (*Proceedings*) (ISSN: 0078-4303). The
method illustrates the opportunities for bibliometric analysis created by
the recent digitization of several years of back files of the *Proceedings*,
which is not indexed in the *Science Citation Index* and is indexed only
in part by several bibliographic databases. The research also raises several issues for the future of bibliometrics in an increasingly digital publishing environment. Paradoxically, while the digitization of journal
back files creates new opportunities, human factors related to copyright,
access, file formats, and the imperfect digitization process raise ques-

tions about the long-term outlook for implementing the technical solutions described here. First, a brief discussion of the scope of electronic journal delivery and recent applications of bibliometrics in library practice provides the context for the present study.

EVOLUTION IN SCIENTIFIC COMMUNICATION: THE MIGRATION FROM PRINT TO ELECTRONIC

The World Wide Web is becoming the favored delivery mechanism for academic library users seeking scholarly research literature. Faculty members rarely visit the library now that they have access to hundreds of journals from their home or office. Students have come to expect full text online, and increasingly decline to use print sources in their research assignments. Those expectations have added to the complexity of serials management in libraries and are reshaping business models in the publishing industry.

Librarians overwhelmed with the daily demands for electronic access, and users who enjoy nearly seamless access to electronic journals tend to forget that scholarly journals in electronic format have developed over a relatively short period of time. The number of peer-reviewed journals available electronically is difficult to know precisely, at least in part because of definitions. While the distinctions between journals that existed solely in print or electronic format were clearer in the past, the shift to electronic delivery of print journals has quickly given way to journals existing simultaneously in both the print and electronic formats. Even for those, however, the electronic versions are generally not the same as the print. Recognizing the differences between print and electronic formats, the latest edition of the *Chicago Manual of Style*, 15th ed., recommends including the URL when citing articles from print journals that are delivered via the Web as HTML or PDF files.

The first peer-reviewed electronic journals appeared in the 1990s. The number of such journals grew from 7 in 1991 to 29 in 1993. During that time, the journals were ASCII text or *LaTeX* files delivered by e-mail, electronic bulletin board systems (BBS), FTP, Gopher, or diskette (Strangelove and Kovacs 1992, 1993; Tenopir and King 2000). With the introduction of the World Wide Web as a delivery mechanism and HTML, PostScript, and PDF file formats, the number of peer-reviewed electronic journals grew rapidly from 73 in 1994 to 100 in 1995, 1,049 in 1997, and 3,915 in 2000 (King and Kovacs 1994, 1995; Tenopir and

King 2000; Woodward and McKnight 1995; ARL 2000). Some 8,000 journals were available electronically by 1999, although not all were academic or peer-reviewed (Tenopir and King 2000; Stankus 1999).

Current estimates of the number of journals available electronically, including online versions of print journals and those available only in electronic format, vary widely. A National Science Foundation report estimated 3,200 to 4,000 electronic journals in the first half of 2003 (National Science Foundation 2003). The July 2003 edition of *Fulltext Sources Online* (v. 15 no. 2) lists 12,783 titles with ISSNs, which include electronic magazines, journals, newspapers, newswires, newsletters, and transcripts, but again, peer-reviewed scholarly journals are just a fraction of those. In October 2003, Bowker's *UlrichsWeb.com* online database listed 10,915 active, academic or scholarly, peer-reviewed journals with online full text or online full content. While the exact number of journals available electronically varies with the definition, method of counting, and with the source of data, it is clearly growing rapidly.

BIBLIOMETRICS AND CITATION ANALYSIS: METHODS AND APPLICATIONS

Bibliometrics and particularly citation analysis have found applications in the study of scholarly communication, in evaluating journal quality and the research output of individuals, institutions, and nations. As the systematic study of patterns in publication and documents, bibliometrics has much to offer librarians. Examples of bibliometric studies from the library literature emphasize its value for collections management, and particularly serials management. Traditional bibliometric methods have required collecting data from print sources and keying it by hand. Those tedious methods have required relatively small sample sizes. The advent of citation indexes, and particularly electronic databases, has harnessed the data manipulation capabilities of computers. Recent studies also exemplify the use of a variety of methods and software to collect and process bibliometric data.

Citation analysis is the subset of bibliometrics that has found the most applications in library collection management. Serials managers often look at citation counts as a sign of the use or relative importance of a journal. Such information can help librarians decide whether to acquire a particular journal, maintain a subscription, or weed journal back files. Many librarians look to the Institute for Scientific Information

(ISI) *Journal Citation Reports* (*JCR*) and citation indexing databases such as *Science Citation Index* (*SCI*) and *Social Sciences Citation Index* (*SSCI*) for data. Those citation databases also allow searching for papers published by local researchers. Applications in this area include comparisons of print and electronic journal usage on campus (Parker, Bauer, and Sullenger 2003). For publications not indexed by ISI, librarians use citation data gleaned from theses and dissertations completed at the home institution (Edwards 1999), extract references from large numbers of journal issues (Black 2001), or develop other creative methods of journal ranking (Dilevko and Atkinson 2002).

A second major application of bibliometric analysis in collection management is identifying the components of a core collection. Core collections vary by institutions, change over time, and obviously vary by discipline. In times of limited resources for journal collections, only those journals that provide the greatest use at the least cost can be retained. In addition, the use of journals typically follows Bradford's Law of journal scatter, also known as the 80/20 rule, in which about 20% of the journals in a collection account for about 80% of total journal usage (Diodato 1994). Determining important journals for a local community of researchers and faculty can benefit from the quantitative methods offered by bibliometrics. One approach to measure campus relevance is to identify those journals where faculty and researchers are publishing the majority of their research (Davis 2002).

Librarians have used a range of methods to collect and manipulate bibliometric data, but the development and widespread availability of computers and software applications have increased the feasibility of such studies for many collection managers. Studies of print resources still require sifting through pages of references and hand keying data (Edwards 1999), but database, spreadsheet, and even word processing applications can automate many tasks. Those using the citation indexes from ISI have imported the results using a citation management application such as EndNote®, then converted the data into a Microsoft Access® database (Parker, Bauer, and Sullenger 2003; Davis 2002). Researchers studying electronic journals have been among the early adopters of software to automate some of the bibliometric tasks, including using Web search engines to identify electronic journals, batch downloading of the HTML files comprising the journals, using Perl scripting techniques to extract URLs and other data from the raw HTML files, or using UNIX and Microsoft Excel® to remove duplicates and count occurrences of titles (Harter and Ford 2000; Davis 2002).

The weaknesses of bibliometrics, which may discourage more librarians from undertaking such studies, are in collecting and processing data and interpreting the results. Researchers must select a sample size that is statistically valid but that is also manageable for data collection and analysis. Acquiring the sample population, hand keying data, and making sense of idiosyncratic and erroneous citations can consume time, resources, and patience. Other librarians may balk at the quantitative and statistical analysis required for interpretation. There are also questions as to the reliability of citations, including the various reasons authors have for citing the work of other researchers and the too common practice on the part of some researchers of citing sources that they may never have read. The existence of journals or dissertations in electronic format offers a solution to the tedious processes of data collection and processing. As the study described below suggests, however, the migration to electronic journals presents its own set of problems that may overshadow the technological promise.

PROCEEDINGS
OF THE OKLAHOMA ACADEMY OF SCIENCE:
A SMALL CIRCULATION JOURNAL
MEETS THE WORLD WIDE WEB

The *Proceedings* is the official publication of the Oklahoma Academy of Science (OAS). The OAS was founded in 1909 to publicize and advocate for science in the state, to educate the public on the value of science for studying the state's natural resources, and to advise leaders on scientific matters. The *Proceedings* was first published in 1921, 12 years after the founding of the Oklahoma Academy of Science, and has been published annually since then, except for small gaps. Bowker's *UlrichsWeb.com* lists the *Proceedings'* circulation as 800 unspecified in October 2003, and OCLC's *WorldCat* lists holdings in 196 libraries during that same period.

The first volume included papers presented at OAS meetings between 1910 and 1921. The *Proceedings* includes peer-reviewed research and descriptive papers, although it has not always been peer-reviewed, and the date of initiation of peer review is not clearly stated in histories of the OAS. Papers cover a wide range of research and descriptive studies in biology, geology, social science, and science education. Some issues also include lists of titles or abstracts of papers presented at the annual meeting, although those papers are not published. The *Proceedings* also includes information on OAS activities and business, including lists of officers, awards, and memorials. The OAS also publishes the *Transactions of the Oklahoma Junior Academy of Science,* the *Annals of the Oklahoma Academy of Science,* and the *Newsletter of the Oklahoma Academy of Science* (Oklahoma Academy of Science n.d.; Shannon 1921).

The Oklahoma State University Library Electronic Publishing Center has undertaken the digitization of a number of publications significant to Oklahomans, including the *Proceedings.* Posting those sources on the Web has made them available to a wider audience than the original print sources. The OSU Library Electronic Publishing Center has taken an incremental approach to the *Proceedings* digitization project. To date, the tables of contents of all volumes are posted online, with full text available for the issues published since 1976. *WorldCat* did not have a record for the electronic version of the *Proceedings* as of October 2003, but Google has indexed a substantial portion of it, thereby providing article-level access. The *Proceedings* is not indexed in the ISI *Science Citation Index* or the *Social Science Citation Index,* and is only partially indexed in a number of topical bibliographic databases discussed below.

The study presented herein represents a portion of the research done by the author for the MLIS degree and subsequent studies of the scholarly communication between the OAS and the larger scientific community. The present study generally asks whether the research published in the *Proceedings* is of interest to scholars outside of Oklahoma and how they learn about it. The emphasis here is on the relationship between indexing and citations received and the relationship between geographic focus of the research and citations received.

Specifically, the current study asks the following four questions:

- Which journals are cited in the *Proceedings*?
- Which journals cite the *Proceedings*?
- Does indexing have any relationship to citations received by the *Proceedings*?
- Are articles published in the *Proceedings* that are about Oklahoma cited more or less often than those with a broader subject focus?

METHODS

Which Journals Are Cited in the Proceedings?

Because the *Proceedings* are not indexed by the ISI citation indexes, references were extracted from the individual articles in the online full-text version, volumes 56 (1976) through 82 (2002). Data extraction began by downloading copies of the HTML files for the *Proceedings* tables of contents, volumes 1 through 80 (1921-2000). The freeware program URL2File® allows batch downloads by reading from a list of URLs (Chami.com 1998). The URLs for the *Proceedings* table of contents follow a sequential pattern beginning with http://digital.library. okstate.edu/oas/oas_htm_files/v1/index.html. The general method uses Perl scripting to extract information based on the patterns in the HTML tagging and the output of citation indexes. Perl's strengths for these applications are in its capabilities for matching text strings and for extracting the text between two other text strings. Perl scripts were used to extract the URLs for individual articles from the tables of contents of those volumes with full text. The full text of all of the articles in volumes 56 through 82 were downloaded as HTML files (ActiveState Tool Corp. 1996-2001).

Perl scripts were then used to extract all references from the articles based on the HTML tagging convention used to indicate references. File names were output along with the references in order to keep track of which volume the references came from. The results were stripped of the HTML tags using the Find and Replace functions in Microsoft Word®. Those results were exported into Excel® where the individual elements of the references were parsed into separate fields, then the COUNTIF function was used to count the number of occurrences of each cited journal title.

Which Journals Cite the Proceedings?

As already noted, the *Proceedings* are not indexed by the ISI citation databases, but a search of the Cited Works field returns articles published in other journals that have cited the *Proceedings*. Citation counts were extracted from *SciSearch®*, the Institute for Scientific Information's citation database, accessed through Dialog® files 34 and 434. At the time of access, in March 2002, *SciSearch* included articles published since 1974. The search was limited to articles published between 1974 and 2000. The journal name of the *Proceedings* was abbreviated 17 different ways in *SciSearch*, requiring multiple Boolean queries and checking the results for duplicates (Bremholm 2003). Subsequent searches of the Web version of ISI *Science Citation Index* (*SCI*) and *Social Science Citation Index* (*SSCI*) were done to get citations for 2001 and 2002 and to get all available citations from the *SSCI* that were excluded from the

Dialog searches. Again, the results were examined to remove duplicates. Because not all of the records retrieved through the Dialog searches included references and the author no longer had access to Dialog, in the end, 485 records had adequate information to complete this phase of the study.

Perl scripts were used to extract the bibliographic information for the articles citing the *Proceedings* and the citations themselves. Those results were pasted into Excel spreadsheets for parsing into author, title, source, volume, page, etc., fields and then exported to an Access Database. Queries of the database produced lists of journals citing the *Proceedings*. The summary functions in Access counted the number of occurrences of each title.

Does Indexing Have Any Relationship to Citations Received by the Proceedings?

Six bibliographic databases–BIOSIS Previews, CAB Abstracts, GeoRef, PsycINFO, Wildlife & Ecology Studies Worldwide, and Zoological Record–were selected based on their inclusion of 50 or more articles from the *Proceedings*. Searches by journal title or ISSN returned lists of all indexed *Proceedings* articles, and the results were imported into text files. The results were entered into an Access database that already contained bibliographic information for articles published in the *Proceedings* and the number of times those articles had been cited in the *SCI* or *SSCI*. Queries of the database then identified which articles were indexed and which were cited.

Are Articles Published in the Proceedings That Are About Oklahoma Cited More or Less Often Than Those with a Broader Subject Focus?

This study used the same database that was created for the previous studies. The criterion used for determining whether articles were about Oklahoma was whether they had the word Oklahoma in the title. The methodology consisted of querying the article titles field for the word Oklahoma and combining that with queries of the citation field.

RESULTS AND DISCUSSION

Which Journals Are Cited in the Proceedings?

Extracting the references from all articles in the online full text of the *Proceedings* volumes 56 (1976) through 82 (2002) found 499 articles out of 637 that had references. Those 499 articles included 6,841 references. Twenty-eight journals were cited five or more times. Together, those 28 journals accounted for 1,411 references, or about 21% of all of the references. The *Proceedings* was the journal cited the most often, with an average of 0.9 references to the *Proceedings* per article (Table 1).

The list of frequently cited journals reflects the regional and topical focus of the *Proceedings*. Five of the journals (*Proceedings of the Oklahoma Academy of Science, Southwestern Naturalist, Texas Journal of Science, Great Basin Naturalist, Oklahoma Ornithological Society Bulletin*) have a distinct state or regional emphasis. Another two have an implied geographical emphasis based on the topic (*Journal of Range Management, Prairie Naturalist*). *American Midland Naturalist* began as a regional journal, but no longer has that geographical emphasis.

The topical emphasis on natural history, ecology, and wildlife is indicated by the *American Midland Naturalist, Prairie Naturalist, Great Basin Naturalist, Southwestern Naturalist, Ecology, Ecological Monographs, Journal of Ecology, Journal of Wildlife Management, Journal of Mammalogy, Canadian Journal of Zoology, Copeia* (fish), and *Hydrobiologia*. Four journals (*Wilson Bulletin, Condor, Auk, Oklahoma Ornithological Society Bulletin*) deal with ornithology. Another major emphasis in the plant sciences is evident in *Phytopathology, Oikos, Annual Review of Plant Physiology, Journal of Vegetation Science, Canadian Journal of Botany*, and *Phytochemistry*.

The remaining journals, *Poultry Science, Journal of Immunology*, and *Journal of Nutrition*, may represent specific research areas of prolific authors. For example, as the author discovered in earlier research, one of the more prolific authors publishing in the *Proceedings* worked in chicken immunology as part of federally funded research into human immunization (Bremholm 2003). One puzzling gap in the list requires explanation. Geology is a major topic in the *Proceedings*, and the lack of any geology journals in the list of highly cited journals suggests that those studies either cite other *Proceedings* articles or are descriptive in nature without many references to the journal literature.

Which Journals Cite the Proceedings?

There were 733 articles published between 1974 and 2000 in journals indexed by *SciSearch* that cited the *Proceedings*. Those articles cited the *Proceedings* 879 times, which included citations to 467 unique *Proceedings* articles or abstracts (14% of the total articles and abstracts

TABLE 1. Journals Cited Five Times or More by Articles Published in the *Proceedings of the Oklahoma Academy of Science*, Volume 56 (1976) Through Volume 82 (2002)

Journal Cited	Times Cited	Percent of All 6,841 References
Proc. Oklahoma Academy of Science	457	6.68
Southwestern Naturalist	146	2.13
American Midland Naturalist	104	1.52
Ecology	103	1.51
Phytopathology	73	1.07
Journal of Mammalogy	67	0.98
Journal of Wildlife Management	61	0.89
Copeia	47	0.69
Hydrobiologia	44	0.64
Phytochemistry	38	0.56
Wilson Bulletin	29	0.42
Auk	28	0.41
Journal of Range Management	24	0.35
Texas Journal of Science	22	0.32
Ecological Monographs	21	0.31
Journal of Ecology	19	0.28
Journal of Immunology	18	0.26
Oklahoma Ornithological Society Bulletin	15	0.22
Condor	15	0.22
Canadian Journal of Botany	13	0.19
Great Basin Naturalist	12	0.18
Journal of Nutrition	10	0.15
Prairie Naturalist	9	0.13
Canadian Journal of Zoology	8	0.12
Poultry Science	8	0.12
Oikos	8	0.12
Annual Review of Plant Physiology	7	0.10
Journal of Vegetation Science	5	0.07
Total	1411	20.64

published in the *Proceedings*). Of the *Proceedings* articles and abstracts that were cited, citation frequencies ranged from 1 to 12 citations each. Of those articles that were cited, 63% were cited just one time (Bremholm 2003).

The 485 articles published between 1983 and 2002 that were examined further were published in 223 unique source journals (Table 2).

Those journals cited 445 *Proceedings* articles 830 times. The journals most frequently citing the *Proceedings* did so 15 or fewer times between 1983 and 2002. Once again, the regional and topical focus is evident from the source journals, with a strong emphasis on natural history and ecology of the Southwest, and a stronger emphasis on fish and entomology than seen in the journals cited by the *Proceedings*. Nine journals appear on both lists of journals frequently cited by and frequently citing the *Proceedings* (*American Midland Naturalist, Canadian Journal of Zoology, Copeia, Ecology, Hydrobiologia, Journal of Range Management, Journal of Wildlife Management, Southwestern Naturalist*, and *Texas Journal of Science*) (Table 1 and Table 2). The *Proceedings* would also be at the top of the list of journals citing the *Proceedings* if it had been included in the ISI citation databases.

Does Indexing Have Any Relationship to Citations Received by the Proceedings?

UlrichsWeb.com, the online version of *Ulrich's Periodicals Directory,* lists 16 indexing and abstracting services that have included the *Proceedings* at any time, and the author identified another four (Table 3). Searches of each of the six indexes returned from 59 to 253 articles (Table 4). Although it is impossible to say whether any given citation resulted from indexing by a particular abstracting service, those evaluated did vary in the rate of citations received for the number of articles indexed. Indexing in GeoRef and PsycINFO has the least benefit as far as leading to citation. That corresponds to the paucity of journals in those fields that cite the *Proceedings* (Table 2). Articles indexed in CAB Abstracts have the highest citation rate at nearly 36%, followed by Wildlife & Ecology Studies Worldwide at about 28% and Zoological Record at about 23% (Table 4).

Because some articles were indexed in more than one database, the summary data are not the same as the sum of the results from the individual databases. Overall, 730 articles out of the total sample of 3,096 articles were indexed in the six databases examined. The results suggest that indexing does not have much of an effect on whether articles were cited or not. About 15% of those articles that were indexed were cited, while 14% that were not indexed were cited (Table 5). Indexed articles were cited an average 1.91 times and articles not indexed received an average of about 1.85 citations per article. A t-test produced a t-statistic of 0.26, indicating that at the 0.1 significance level no significant difference exists between the citations received per article for those indexed

TABLE 2. Journals Citing the *Proceedings of the Oklahoma Academy of Science* Three or More Times Between 1983 and 2002

Journal Title	Times Citing
American Midland Naturalist	15
Journal of Freshwater Ecology	15
Southwestern Naturalist	13
Copeia	12
Hydrobiologia	10
Journal of Herpetology	10
Canadian Journal of Zoology	9
Journal of the Kansas Entomological Society	7
Journal of Wildlife Management	7
Oecologia	6
Transactions of the American Fisheries Society	6
Canadian Journal of Fisheries and Aquatic Sciences	5
Behaviour	4
Environmental Biology of Fishes	4
Herpetologica	4
Journal of Raptor Research	4
Southwestern Entomologist	4
Texas Journal of Science	4
Wildlife Society Bulletin	4
Aquatic Botany	3
Archiv Fur Hydrobiologie	3
Conservation Biology	3
Crop Science	3
Ecology	3
Entomological News	3
Environmental Entomology	3
Environmental Pollution	3
Journal of Chemical Ecology	3
Journal of Fish Biology	3
Journal of Protozoology	3
Journal of Range Management	3
Nautilus	3
Proc. Helminthological Society of Washington	3
Total	185

TABLE 3. Abstracting and Indexing Services with Any Coverage of the *Proceedings of the Oklahoma Academy of Science*

Abstracting and Indexing Services
Bibliography and Index of Geology
Biological Abstracts
BIOSIS Previews
CAB Abstracts
Chemical Abstracts
Chemical Industry Notes
Chemical Titles
Field Crop Abstracts
Fisheries Review
GeoRef
Grasslands and Forage Abstracts
Oceanographic Literature Review
Plant Breeding Abstracts
PsycINFO
Review of Plant Pathology
Soils and Fertilizers
State Academies of Science Abstracts
Wildlife & Ecology Studies Worldwide
Wildlife Review Abstracts
Zoological Record

and those not indexed. It is possible that other abstracting services index parts of the *Proceedings* and that it has been cited by other journals that are also not indexed in the ISI citation databases.

These results suggest that authors learn about the research published in the *Proceedings* from a source other than the indexes examined here. One possible explanation is that interested researchers read the *Proceedings* rather than searching indexes. Another possibility is that authors who publish in the *Proceedings* and other journals cite their own work in more widely read journals, and those self-citations lead other researchers back to the *Proceedings*. An earlier study found that about 16% of the citations received by the *Proceedings* from other journals were self-citations, in which one or more authors cited his or her own work in the *Proceedings* (Bremholm 2003). What remains to be seen is whether posting the *Proceedings* online leads to more citations. The Google search engine has already indexed nearly all of the tables of con-

TABLE 4. Relationship Between Coverage of the *Proceedings of the Oklahoma Academy of Science* by Indexing and Abstracting Services and Citations Received in *Science Citation Index Expanded (SCI-EXPANDED)*–1966-2003 and *Social Sciences Citation Index (SSCI)*–1966-2003

Indexing and Abstracting Services (coverage through August 2003)	Articles Indexed	Indexed Articles Cited (through August 2003)	Times Cited (through August 2003)
BIOSIS Previews–[Web version]: Coverage begins 1993; Source; OVID	100	17 (17.0%)	24
CAB Abstracts: Coverage begins 1972; . Source: OVID	59	21 (35.6%)	32
GeoRef–[WebSpirs]: Coverage begins 1785; Source: SilverPlatter	245	8 (3.3%)	13
PsycINFO (PsycLit) [Web version]: Coverage begins 1872; Source: Cambridge Scientific Abstracts	105	5 (4.8%)	26
Wildlife & Ecology Studies Worldwide: Coverage begins 1935; Source: National Information Services Corporation (NISC) Biblioline	156	44 (28.2%)	88
Zoological Record–[WebSpirs]: Coverage begins 1970; Source: SilverPlatter	253	59 (23.3%)	110

TABLE 5. Relationship Between Indexing and Citations Received for Articles Published in the *Proceedings of the Oklahoma Academy of Science*

	Citations Received per Article	Articles Cited (percent)	Total Articles Sampled
Indexed	1.91	110 (15.1%)	730
Not Indexed	1.85	335 (14.2%)	2366
			3096

tents and full-text articles from the *Proceedings*, far surpassing the coverage by any abstracting and indexing service.

Are Articles Published in the Proceedings *That Are About Oklahoma Cited More or Less Often Than Those with a Broader Subject Focus?*

A higher percentage of articles with the word Oklahoma in the title were cited than articles without Oklahoma in the title, although articles without the word Oklahoma in the title were cited more frequently (Table 6). A t-test resulted in a t-statistic of -1.33, indicating that the difference between the mean citations received by articles with Oklahoma in the title and those without is not significant at the 0.1 level.

TABLE 6. Relationship Between Oklahoma Topics and Citations Received for Articles Published in the *Proceedings of the Oklahoma Academy of Science*

	Articles with Oklahoma in Title		Articles without Oklahoma in Title	
	Number of articles	Citations per article	Number of articles	Citations per article
Cited	183 (17.3%)	1.73	262 (12.9%)	1.96
Not Cited	876 (82.7%)		1775 (87.1%)	
Total Articles	1059		2037	

CHALLENGES AND OPPORTUNITIES FOR BIBLIOMETRICS IN THE ELECTRONIC ENVIRONMENT

The examples just discussed highlight the potential for using the tools of the digital age to conduct research on the growing body of scholarship available in electronic format. While the volume of print journals, journal back files, electronic-only journals, theses, and dissertations available online is growing, a number of factors in the electronic environment may actually limit the availability of that material for bibliometric research. As scholarly communication grows more digital, issues of access, copyright and fair use, file format and circumvention, and human factors such as variations in journal layout, citation styles, and human error create new challenges for bibliometrics research.

There is good news, however, for bibliometrics in the electronic environment. Publishers are making current issues of more print journals available online and adding more journal back files in the electronic format (Tenopir 2002). For example, the JSTOR project lists 353 journal titles in its collections including 87,769 journal issues and more than 2 million articles (JSTOR 2003a). Another 60 titles will be available by 2005 (JSTOR 2003b), with plans to add another 87 titles (JSTOR 2003c) in the future. ProQuest offers online full text of more than 100,000 dissertations through its Digital Dissertations product (ProQuest n.d.). The *Proquest Historical Newspapers* product offers digitized and searchable back files of 150 years of *The New York Times*, 97 years of *The Wall Street Journal*, 100 years of *The Washington Post*, and has projects underway to digitize the complete back files of the *Los Angeles Times* and the *Chicago Tribune* (ProQuest 2003; Tenopir 2002). Elsevier ScienceDirect® offers online access to over five million articles in 1,800 journals (Elsevier 2003a). The Elsevier backfiles project has as its goal the digitization of the entire back files for all of its journal titles, among them the entire run of the British medical journal *The Lancet* back to 1823 (Elsevier 2003b).

Digitizing those back files, producing PDF or TIFF image files, running the images through optical character recognition software to allow searching the text, and creating hypertext links cross-referencing articles takes time and resources. Despite claims about preserving knowledge for humankind, the publishers would not be doing it if they could not recover those costs by selling access. Libraries that had subscribed to the print version of any of those periodicals may find themselves paying again for access to the digitized version. Many libraries may find it too costly to maintain both print and electronic subscriptions, and, if pressed for space, may be tempted to forego their print back files and place their trust in the publishers for ongoing access to archived issues. However, the electronic version is not always the same as the print version. What this means to the bibliometrics researcher may depend on how wealthy his or her home institution is. In the past, the librarian or patron had access to the print version for bibliometric research. Now they may have access to both print and electronic. In the future, they may only have access to the electronic version, assuming the archived back issues remain accessible online.

Assuming that the librarian with bibliometric tendencies has access to the journals in electronic format through his or her home institution, is it legal and ethical to do the research? Copyright and licensing agreements limit what one may do with the electronic files for which libraries have paid to gain access, or even those posted freely on the Web, such as the *Proceedings of the Oklahoma Academy of Science*. Licensing agreements usually forbid the batch processes that would download the entire run of a journal, or a substantial part of it, to the researcher's computer. Publishers' Web servers can detect batch downloads and may cut off access to entire IP ranges until the problem is resolved. One would expect that academic research would be considered fair use; however, researchers are advised to read publishers' statements about conditions and terms of use, consult their electronic subscriptions manager, and seek permission of the publishers before undertaking a bibliometrics research project that involves capturing substantial content of electronic journals. Most publishers would probably welcome such studies if permission were sought in advance.

Not all of the digital scholarship on the Web is protected by copyright and licensing in the same way, however. Although still relatively small compared to established journals, alternative publishing models are emerging that make scholarly materials more readily available for research. For example, *PLoS Biology*, the open-access journal published by the Public Library of Science (Public Library of Science 2003), is licensed under a Creative Commons Attribution License. That license allows users to copy and distribute the work as long as they credit the original author (Creative Commons 2003).

Aside from issues of access and use, issues related to file format and anti-circumvention rules could make it difficult or impossible to extract information from electronic journals because of the file formats used. Most journals that are delivered electronically use HTML or PDF formats. HTML is essentially a text file, and the tools discussed here such as Perl scripts, databases, and spreadsheets will work for extracting and processing text from such files. PDF files, however, are images of the page. Users can copy and paste text from some PDF files, but that defeats the purpose of automating the bibliometric research process. Tools exist to convert PDF to plain text or rich text files, but doing so adds to the labor involved and raises questions about violating anticircumvention rules. Section 1201 of the Digital Millennium Copyright Act forbids circumventing any technological measure put in place to control access to copyrighted works (Library of Congress 2003). PDF files are desirable because they preserve the appearance of the printed page, which HTML does not, but one must also wonder if publishers prefer PDF format because it is more difficult for users to copy content.

The intention of the research method discussed here is to automate the extraction of data from large text files and long runs of journals. Without that automation, data extraction falls back into the manual methods that make bibliometric analysis of print journals difficult and time-consuming. For example, much of the research discussed here uses Perl scripts to match text strings, so when those strings vary, the matches fail. As one example, bibliographic citations in the *Proceedings* follow one style that does not match the format used by the ISI citation indexes. Matching references from the two sources requires parsing and rearranging bibliographic elements to create a citation format that allows automated comparisons. In addition, citation indexes may only name the first author of an article, which can be a problem if the researcher needs information about the entire research output of an author. Variant spellings in author names create yet another problem, as do variations in journal title abbreviations and erroneous citations.

All of these examples require manual intervention to check and correct errors, slowing the research substantially. Errors or variations within the HTML tags may also require manual intervention. When journals change their layout from one year to the next, the patterns in the HTML tags also change, requiring the researcher to modify the scripts. Typographical errors in HTML tags can also result in missing large sections of data.

The future of bibliometrics is far from clear. The potential exists for the next generation of bibliometrics research to couple readily available computational tools with a growing body of digitized scholarship. However, those same trends may ultimately complicate bibliometrics research, as issues of access, use, and format override the technical capabilities. As scholarly communication moves increasingly to the digital environment, librarians should support open access initiatives and work with publishers to ensure access for bibliometric research. Such research is in the best interest of all parties involved.

REFERENCES

ActiveState Tool Corporation. 1996-2001. ActivePerl version 5.6.1.631 Copyright (C) 1996-2001. Vancouver, BC: ActiveState Tool Corp.

Association of Research Libraries. 2000. *Directory of Scholarly Electronic Journals and Academic Discussion Lists*, first ed. Foreword. Washington, D.C.: Association of Research Libraries, 2000. http://db.arl.org/dsej/2000/foreword.html (accessed October 12, 2003).

Black, Steven. 2001. Using citation analysis to pursue a core collection of journals for communication disorders. *Library Resources and Technical Services* 45(1): 3-9.

Bremholm, Tony L. 2003. *Toward a Science of Place: Measures of Scientific Influence in the Proceedings of the Oklahoma Academy of Science*. Thesis (M.L.I.S.) University of Oklahoma, Norman, May 2003.

Chami.com. 1998. URL2File® Version 1.981208 Copyright (C) 1998, Chami.com Fort Walton Beach, FL. http://www.chami.com/free/url2file_wincon.html (accessed April 7, 2002).

Creative Commons. 2003. *Creative Commons Deed* http://creativecommons.org/licenses/by/1.0/ (accessed October 28, 2003).

Davis, Philip M. 2002. Where to spend our e-journal money? Defining a university library's core collection through citation analysis. *portal: Libraries and the Academy* 2(1): 155-166.

Dilevko, Juris and Esther Atkinson. 2002. Evaluating academic journals without impact factors for collection management decisions. *College & Research Libraries* 63 (November): 562-577.

Diodato, Virgil P. 1994. *Dictionary of Bibliometrics*. New York: The Haworth Press, Inc.

Edwards, Sherri. 1999. Citation analysis as a collection development tool: A bibliometric study of polymer science theses and dissertations. *Serials Review* 25: 11-20.

Elsevier. 2003a. ScienceDirect collection reaches five million full-text articles. Elsevier press release October 9, 2003. http://www.info.sciencedirect.com/sd_updates/press/archive2003/5million.shtml (Accessed July 15, 2004).

Elsevier 2003b. Elsevier launches *The Lancet* backfiles on ScienceDirect. News release October 8, 2003. http://www.elsevier.com/wps/find/authored_newsitem.cws_home/companynews05_00034 (Accessed July 15, 2004).

Harter, Stephen P. and Charlotte E. Ford. 2000. Web-based analysis of E-journal impact: Approaches, problems, and issues. *Journal of the American Society for Information Science* 51 (13): 1159-1176.

JSTOR. 2003a. JSTOR Facts & Figures. October 8, 2003. http://www.jstor.org/about/facts.html (accessed October 17, 2003).

JSTOR. 2003b. The Arts & Sciences III Collection–Title List. October 8, 2003. http://www.jstor.org/about/asIII.list.html (accessed October 17, 2003).

JSTOR. 2003c. Upcoming JSTOR Journals. October 14, 2003. http://www.jstor.org/about/upcoming.journals.html (accessed October 17, 2003).

King, Lisabeth A. and Diane Kovacs. 1994. *Directory of Electronic Journals, Newsletters and Academic Discussion Lists*. 4th ed. Washington, D.C.: Association of Research Libraries, Office of Scholarly Communication.

_____. 1995. *Directory of Electronic Journals, Newsletters and Academic Discussion Lists*. 5th ed. Washington, D.C.: Association of Research Libraries, Office of Scholarly Communication.

Library of Congress. 2003. *Circular 92. Copyright Law of the United States of America and Related Laws Contained in Title 17 of the United States Code.* June 2003. http://www.loc.gov/copyright/title17/circ92.pdf (accessed October 13, 2003).

National Science Foundation, Division of Science Resources Statistics. 2003. *The Implications of Information Technology for Scientific Journal Publishing: A Literature Review.* NSF 03-323, Project Director, Eileen L. Collins, NSF/SRS; Authors Amy Friedlander and Rändi S. Bessette. Arlington, VA: Directorate for Social, Behavioral, and Economic Sciences, National Science Foundation.

Oklahoma Academy of Science. *OAS Homepage* http://oas.ucok.edu/ (Accessed July 15, 2004).

Parker, Kimberly, Kathleen Bauer, and Paula Sullenger. 2003. E-journals and citation patterns: Is it all worth it? *The Serials Librarian* 44 (3/4): 209-213.

ProQuest. n.d. About ProQuest Digital Dissertations. http://wwwlib.umi.com/dissertations/about_pqdd (accessed October 17, 2003).

ProQuest Information and Learning. 2003. *Los Angeles Times* back file now available in *ProQuest Historical Newspapers*™. Press release, September 17, 2003. http://www.il.proquest.com/division/pr/03/20030917.shtml (accessed October 17, 2003).

Public Library of Science. 2003. *PLoS Biology: Open-Access Journal* http://www.plosbiology.org/ (accessed October 28, 2003).

Shannon, C. W. 1921. Oklahoma Academy of Science. *Proceedings of the Oklahoma Academy of Science* 1(1921): 11.

Stankus, Tony. 1999. The key trends emerging from the first decade of electronic journals in the sciences. *Science & Technology Libraries* 18 (2/3): 5-20.

Strangelove, Michael and Diane Kovacs. 1992. *Directory of Electronic Journals, Newsletters and Academic Discussion Lists*. 2nd ed. Washington, D.C.: Association of Research Libraries, Office of Scholarly Communication.

_____. 1993. *Directory of Electronic Journals, Newsletters and Academic Discussion Lists.* 3rd ed. Washington, D.C.: Association of Research Libraries, Office of Scholarly Communication.

Tenopir, Carol. 2002. Oldies but goodies: Publishers move to digitize older materials. *Library Journal* 127(November 1, 2002): 36, 38.

Tenopir, Carol and Donald W. King. 2000. *Towards Electronic Journals: Realities for Scientists, Librarians, and Publishers.* Washington, D.C.: Special Libraries Association.

UlrichsWeb.com. 2003. RR Bowker. http://www.ulrichsweb.com/ulrichsweb/ (accessed October 7, 2003).

Woodward, Hazel and Cliff McKnight. 1995. Electronic journals: Issues of access and bibliographic control. *Serials Review* 21 (Summer): 71-78.

Information Overload:
Keeping Current Without Being Overwhelmed

Patrick Sullivan

SUMMARY. With the rapid evolution of the Internet and the increased flow of information, it is difficult to keep current without the attendant problems of anxiety or overload. This article explores the issue of current awareness services (CAS) within the academic environment and the role librarians play in assisting university researchers to (1) keep current in their given subject area and (2) more effectively use other support tools to automate the handling of this increased flow of information. Selected CAS alerting services are mentioned as is the use of e-mail filtering technologies. *[Article copies available for a fee from The Haworth Document Delivery Service: 1-800-HAWORTH. E-mail address: <docdelivery@haworthpress.com> Website: <http://www.HaworthPress.com> © 2004 by The Haworth Press, Inc. All rights reserved.]*

KEYWORDS. Current awareness services, e-mail filtering, automated searches, faculty-librarian collaboration, Web page monitoring

---

Patrick Sullivan, MLIS, BS (Cross-Cultural Studies), is Reference Librarian, San Diego State University Library.

Address correspondence to: Patrick Sullivan, San Diego State University, University Library, 5500 Campanile Drive, San Diego, CA 92182-8050 (E-mail: sullivan@mail.sdsu.edu).

[Haworth co-indexing entry note]: "Information Overload: Keeping Current Without Being Overwhelmed." Sullivan, Patrick. Co-published simultaneously in *Science & Technology Libraries* (The Haworth Information Press, an imprint of The Haworth Press, Inc.) Vol. 25, No. 1/2, 2004, pp. 109-125; and: *Emerging Issues in the Electronic Environment: Challenges for Librarians and Researchers in the Sciences* (ed: Jeannie P. Miller) The Haworth Information Press, an imprint of The Haworth Press, Inc., 2004, pp. 109-125. Single or multiple copies of this article are available for a fee from The Haworth Document Delivery Service [1-800-HAWORTH, 9:00 a.m. - 5:00 p.m. (EST). E-mail address: docdelivery@haworthpress.com].

http://www.haworthpress.com/web/STL
© 2004 by The Haworth Press, Inc. All rights reserved.
Digital Object Identifier: 10.1300/J122v25n01_08

INTRODUCTION

With the explosion of information sources, does it seem a little more difficult these days to keep current with your subject areas? You're not alone. Regardless of discipline, today's abundance of electronic information has given rise to ever-louder cries of "information overload" combined with attendant anxiety on the part of librarians. As Paul Saffo, Director of the Institute for the Future, has stated, "Information overload is not a function of the volume of information . . . It's a gap between the volume of information and the tools we have to assimilate that information . . ." (Foley 1995). While it's obvious that the amount of information continues to expand exponentially, many times innovative tools that can help tame this increasing flow are simply overlooked.

This article explores a brief history of current awareness services (CAS) as well as recent enhancements to existing tools. More importantly, the role CAS can play in maintaining currency within the librarian's area of expertise and its simultaneous use in reaching out to faculty are discussed. Finally, management of the additional information influx through the use of focused filtering and bibliographic management software is examined. Although some of these services and tools have been in existence for years, from the author's personal experience, many librarians have only a token understanding of their capabilities, and countless faculties are completely unaware of their existence.

CURRENT AWARENESS SERVICES EVOLVE

Current awareness services have existed as long as libraries, but under an ever-changing nomenclature and with constantly evolving capabilities. They are basically those services which provide users with the latest research, publications, tables of contents (TOCs), Web sites or general developments in their area of interest, with very little effort on the researcher's part. In the early days of CAS, patrons relied almost completely on librarians to act as intermediaries, and the final product might have included a collection of photocopied TOCs, new book lists, indexing bulletins, extracts from abstracting services, or perhaps a printed clipping service provided by an outside vendor. From there, users would contact the information professional to discover how they could obtain the article, report, or book in its entirety.

Even when major online database vendors began to provide saved searches that could be rerun automatically, the process still generally involved a professional searcher. That individual was usually a librarian who had attended Dialog or DataStar training on their Selective Dissemination of Information (SDI) product. Librarians had to step through the process of developing a profile, selecting the correct databases and terms, and finally, after these searches had been run, they would need to review and revise these searches to ensure a targeted result set. Many of the CAS advances from manual to automated services have been well-documented in the literature, both on a global and individual campus scale (Fourie 2001; Housman 1973; Jax and Van Houlson 1988; Rowley 1985; Rowley 1994; Rowley 1998a; Rowley 1998b). Changes have occurred not only with respect to who runs the searches, but also with the scope of services offered and the number of vendors who have committed to CAS.

Current awareness services today can include the entire spectrum: TOC deliveries, saved searches, electronic clipping services, and alerting services which automatically run a user's search at regularly scheduled intervals. In addition to the services normally associated with libraries and their information resources, the growth of the Internet has engendered a number of other efforts, such as listservs, Web page monitoring, automated Web searches, newsletters, etc. While it is impossible to maintain an awareness of all these services, it is necessary for librarians and researchers to familiarize themselves with those in their areas of responsibility. Current awareness service efforts span the entire spectrum of disciplines but, luckily, a large percentage of these fall within the Science, Technology & Medicine (STM) environment. Because of the importance that timeliness plays in personalized information delivery, especially in STM, the rapid growth of CAS tools should continue into the foreseeable future and will present an ongoing challenge for information professionals.

WHAT CAS MEAN FOR RESEARCHERS AND LIBRARIANS

If many librarians have only a passing familiarity with CAS, it would be logical to assume that an even smaller percentage of faculty have discovered these offerings on their own. As information vendors began to target academic users directly through library databases and simpler search interfaces, librarians became the natural agents to provide instruction. As new features have been added to academic databases, such as CAS advances, librarians may be missing opportunities to reach out to their faculty. Rowley (1994) has noted that ". . . the more proactive provision of current awareness services may lead to the fuller involvement of the library in the activities of the academic community and lead to the further development of library services in a very appropriate direction." The role of CAS for both librarians and their discipline-specific faculty members can be immense and can allow for the forging of new partnerships based on an information agent model, allowing more active consultation with faculty.

Many times, the addition of new CAS features goes unnoticed or unpublicized within existing academic databases or search systems. The addition of CAS services to more traditional online databases that contain the valuable information professors regularly access presents one more opportunity for liaison librarians to demonstrate to faculty the added value that librarians bring to the academy. Introducing faculty to CAS can be as simple as explaining one online service to one professor or as complex as building an internal CAS structure with integrated, database-driven systems that map faculty interests and subject areas to newly received items (Schlembach 2001). This review focuses primarily on the collaborative aspects of CAS while also exploring some of the CAS capabilities available through existing electronic services in academic libraries.

In working with faculty, many of the historical goals and procedures associated with creating manual CAS efforts remain the same with newer electronic systems. As Cox and Hanson (1992) point out in their article on setting up a CAS, there are certain requirements that should be part of a librarian's service. First, the service needs to be promoted through workshops or group demonstrations. Once the existence of the service is established, profiles for users then have to be created using traditional reference interview techniques. After profiles are created, the searches will be run and results routed to the user, with hopefully some record of its successful completion, followed by any required modifications to the initial searches.

Introducing professors to the procedure for automatically running searches, with little or no effort on their part, can be truly rewarding, both personally and professionally. As Fourie (1999) observes in her article on using CAS as an empowerment tool, this is a "partnership between the information service and its users, and not merely an attempt to shift the workload of information specialists to their users." A medical researcher in the area of stroke rehabilitation had the following comments regarding the ongoing results of automated alerts that he has received. "The automated search results that I have received via e-mail have almost invariably contained citations that are very relevant to my research. Even when the results are not applicable to my specific projects they generally contain something of value to one of my colleagues" (Reker 2003). In this particular case, the delivery mechanism should also be explored. Many times the onus is placed on researchers to maintain their own CAS services, but services can vary based on the needs of the user and software capabilities. By combining the power of CAS services, in this case from Ingenta's Alerts, with the power of filtering capabilities built into most e-mail programs today, more sophisticated services can be offered. Here, the librarian created the alerting profile and automatically forwarded the incoming citations to the researcher's e-mail account using existing filters within the campus e-mail program. When working with professors who are hesitant to invest the time to learn how to navigate some of the CAS services, librarians may want to introduce them to the service by first capturing their alerts electronically in a special mail folder they can monitor to ensure that everything is working as planned. Next, the successful citations can be used as evidence that it may be worth the professors' time to take a more active role in this CAS process. If it makes sense to them, then it is a simple process of documenting the steps needed to personally implement the service. If they are still reticent, let the automated filters in your e-mail program take over and automatically route the results to the professor based on various header fields contained in the message which is received from the alerting database. While it may seem tedious at first, it is a simple process that requires minimal time to set up. E-mail filters will also be explored later in this article.

While librarians need to be constantly alert to the needs of faculty, they must also maintain their own professional readiness. Current awareness services are excellent resources for accomplishing this. Services are available today which allow us to not only monitor scholarly publishing efforts, but also to monitor granting agencies and see what other subject specialists are adding or removing from their resource Web pages, all automatically. The author uses a number of these services for exactly that purpose. For example, using one of the Web page monitoring services recently, the author was immediately apprised of a Call for Proposals that had gone out with a fairly short deadline. It probably would not have been discovered in time without the use of a CAS Web page monitoring tool. Sharing this awareness with fellow librarians and researchers makes the library a more actively engaged institution, both on campus and within the greater academic environment. Remember, librarians need to understand and employ CAS themselves before they can expect faculty to fully appreciate the role that these tools can play in research and professional development. The "passing familiarity" mentioned earlier needs to become a welcome acceptance for, and an in-depth knowledge of, the full spectrum of available CAS tools.

SPECTRUM OF SOURCES

It is difficult to properly classify the sources to be discussed and this, at best, will provide a sampling of the wealth of services that are available. Sources are listed with their Internet addresses under rather arbitrary headings. The difficulty in classifying these services arises from the way in which they can be accessed. Many librarians in the academic environment at larger institutions have the luxury of having access to a number of these products already. Many are very expensive, but contain advanced features that should be included in discussions with other information providers in relation to their future product development efforts. Faculty will also have ideas about how these services can be enhanced, and these, too, should be carried forward to vendors.

In the following services there are a number of different factors to take into consideration. First and foremost, does your campus subscribe to the service if it is a traditional online database vendor or publisher's site? If the answer is yes, has your campus subscribed to the specific product offering within the service mentioned? In many of the services, the current awareness features are built into the standard subscription, but in others an additional fee is charged. Some of the services require only a simple online registration to be able to proceed, while others provide limited free service, but a fuller-featured version at an additional cost. A limited trial period with the service is also another possible approach. Given all of the above, I still believe that librarians should familiarize themselves with the available services and their features. Remember that this is but a sampling of what is available. There may be very focused resources in a specific discipline that are beyond the scope of this article, but can nonetheless be uncovered through dialog with colleagues.

With respect to features, the sources below will range from the delivery of basic table of contents for journals to some very advanced features that allow the user to track specific citations within an article database. In the case of Elsevier's ScienceDirect, the user has the option of establishing an alert when an existing article in this database is later cited by another author. This is especially popular with professors who are trying to guarantee that they maintain a level of awareness regarding who is citing their work and in what context. The user in this scenario would receive an e-mail showing the basic information for the citing article, and from there the user could log on and review the entire citing article. Hopefully, other publishers will begin to provide these more advanced alerting options, so that users can take fuller advantage of these capabilities.

Recently, we have seen the emergence of what are sometimes referred to as broadcast searches, federated searches, or meta-searches being offered as part of systems like MetaLib from ExLibris (http://www.exlibrisgroup.com/metalib.htm). At user defined intervals, the system will search across multiple online article databases and the online catalog, subsequently sending a report to the user with a link that will reactivate the original query and display the results from the alert notification.

While these later efforts represent the cutting edge of alert services, there are other facets of the CAS market that bear a closer look. These include the more traditional table of contents and book alerting services, but have grown to embrace online database alerting services, Web page monitoring/automated Web searching, and finally, other miscellaneous services.

Journals–Electronic Table of Contents

Table of Contents (TOC) delivery has become a fairly common feature, with many publishers offering to e-mail researchers their most recent TOC. In addition to sending the citations they will often include a link to the actual article and options to download, or, if necessary, to purchase a copy online. The following list is merely a sampling of these services, and some of the vendors may also appear in one of the following categories since they offer both TOC services and Online Database Search Alerting Services.

CISTI–http://source.cisti.nrc.ca/cs/about_alerts_E.html
Provides a Journal Contents Alert with the TOC covering the 17,000 multidisciplinary titles in their database. Options to purchase online as well.

ELSEVIER ScienceDirect–http://www.sciencedirect.com
Journal Issue Alerts for over 1,700 journals that focus principally, but not exclusively, on the STM area.

Ingenta–http://www.ingenta.com and http://www.ingentaselect.com
Provides up to 5 free TOC alerts from the 5,400 titles in the Ingenta Select collection. Also available is a fee-based service (ingenta.com) that delivers a larger number of TOCs for a collection of over 27,000 journal titles, but requires a subscription.

Infotrieve–http://www.infotrieve.com
Offers a Table of Contents Alert service that covers more than 20,000 journals across a broad spectrum of disciplines.

Kluwer–http://www.kluweralert.com
For over 600 journals covering the areas of Biology, Chemistry, Computer Science, Engineering, Mathematics and a broad selection of other disciplines. The sign-up process is very simple.

SARA–http://www.tandf.co.uk/sara/
Scholarly Article Research Alerting (SARA) will send TOC for over 750 journals from Carfax, Psychology Press, Routledge, Spon Press and Taylor & Francis.

SpringerLink–http://www.springerlink.com/
Table of Contents Alert for over 500 peer-reviewed journals.

Wiley Interscience–http://www.interscience.wiley.com/
Table of Contents Alerts for over 450 scholarly journals.

Book Alerting Services

The following is only a sampling, but many publishers will allow users to establish keyword searches or subject area searches for new books that will run periodically. When a match is made, an e-mail alert will be sent announcing that a book matching the specified criteria has been released. Each vendor has a different approach to this, and it generally requires a visit to their page to review the type of service offered. Collection development librarians should be able to provide a more complete list of vendors with book alerting services.

- **Amazon Alerts–http://www.amazon.com/alerts/**
- **Blackwell Science–http://www.blackwellpublishing.com/ealerts/**
- **The Haworth Press, Inc.–**
  http://www.haworthpressinc.com/toc/

- **Kluwer–http://www.kluweralert.com**
- **Wiley–http://www.wileyeurope.com/legacy/utility/mailinglist/ wileyeurope/**

Online Database Search Alerting Services

Alerting services differ somewhat from more traditional Saved Searches. A Saved Search allows users to save their search and rerun it the next time they log on. While helpful, and sometimes part of the process for setting up a Search Alert, the alerting scheme takes the process one step further in that the user only has to perform the search the first time and then it runs automatically. The criteria for searching can be simple keyword or very advanced search criteria that allows pinpoint accuracy. Databases vary regarding how frequently a user's results are sent and in what form they are delivered. Some database providers will allow the researcher to determine how frequently a search is run and for how long the Search Alert remains active. On others, the frequency is fixed by the system, as is the case with Ingenta Reveal Alerts where the results are delivered once per week. The way the results are delivered varies among the database providers as well. Some will send a link via e-mail that takes users to their search system and allows them to see a list of results there, while others send a complete list of citations with links back to the full text of articles. This last approach is much more effective for librarians since they may be forwarding results to faculty members or other colleagues on campus, and having the link at the article level makes retrieval much easier.

Many of the systems offer alerts as a built-in part of their service, and others sell them as add-on services that a library can purchase separately. Even if the campus library subscribes to a database, often the user must register individually, establishing a unique username and password to take advantage of these personalization services. Since many database providers have very sophisticated systems requiring administrator involvement, librarians may have to ask their administrator to turn on the feature which provides access to a service mentioned below.

It should be noted that there are any number of other discipline-specific search alerting services such as the American Chemical Society's ASAP Alerts, BioMail, and the Cubby search alert service for PubMed. It is beyond the scope of this article to cover all of these, so only services provided by major vendors are included. To find out more about discipline-specific systems, use an Internet search system with phrases such as "current awareness" or "alerting services" and the name of the discipline of interest. Another strategy would be to add the word "library" and limit to "site=edu" so that the primary search results tend to be from the academic library world.

Cambridge Scientific Abstracts–http://www.csa.com
CSA Alerts run a search against all CSA indexes and returns whatever hits match the search criteria every week for up to six months, at which point the search alert can be renewed.

CISTI–http://source.cisti.nrc.ca/cs/about_alerts_E.html
Article Alert feature delivers, via e-mail, citations to new articles in a specified field of interest, with the option of purchasing the articles online.

ELSEVIER ScienceDirect–http://www.sciencedirect.com
My Alerts allows users to run their search from the main search screen, not the quick search, and then save that search as an alert with user-determined frequency. It also provides a cited article alert service.

Infotrieve–http://www.infotrieve.com
SDI (Selective Dissemination of Information) ALERTs allow users to save searches, group them, and then run them automatically to receive updates.

Ingenta–http://www.ingenta.com
(formerly UnCover and now including Catchword journals)
Reveal Alerts allow weekly delivery of search results for a large number of previously saved searches. An e-mail is generated for each saved search whether there are results or not.

ISI Web of Knowledge–
http://www.isiwebofknowledge.com/alertnotice/
Allows citation tracking as well as subject searches against the latest additions to the database.

Ovid–http://www.ovid.com/
The SDI feature must be turned on, but then users will be able to create their own SDIs that will be run as frequently as the administrator runs the scripts for the SDIs.

SpringerLink–http://www.springerlink.com/
Keyword Alerts will search the collection every time it is updated and send an e-mail with the results.

Wiley Interscience–http://interscience.wiley.com/
Profiled search alerts allow users to have their terms run against the Interscience database when it is updated.

Web Page Monitoring and Automated Web Searching

The services in this section are especially useful because of the ability not just to alert the user to the fact that something has changed, but also to, in many cases, highlight those changes. Imagine receiving a notice that a monitored Web page has changed and not having a clue about what has changed. With Infominder, for example, the free account holder can monitor up to 10 pages and will receive an e-mail with the option to see pages with all of the changes highlighted for easy review. TrackEngine, another service, will highlight the results, but also provides features like a drag and drop toolbar and online storage of bookmarks. Some of these services are free with a limited number of pages and others have trial periods. It is also possible to set up a sophisticated search at, for example, Google, and then monitor the search results for any changes that appear. Tyburski (2002), in her article on tracking trademarks, briefly discusses some of the default settings that may need to be changed to accomplish this reliably.

Infominder–http://www.infominder.com

TracerLock–http://www.tracerlock.com

TrackEngine–http://www.trackengine.com

WatchThatPage–http://www.watchthatpage.com

Miscellaneous Services

Biomail–http://biomail.sourceforge.net/biomail/
Automatically generates an e-mail with links to PubMed article abstracts based on a user's search terms. Very easy to use.

Blogtracker–http://www.dansanderson.com/blogtracker/about.php
Allows a user to track the latest updates on selected Weblogs.

INSPEC–
http://www.iee.org/oncomms/pn/management/inspec_alerts.cfm
INSPEC Alerts are standard profile searches, Subject Alerts are records grouped under subject headings and Custom Alerts are user-defined searches.

Office of Science–SC Alerts–http://scalerts.science.energy.gov/
SC Alerts was developed by the Office of Scientific and Technical Information (OSTI) and allows the user to set up a subject profile, sending a weekly alert on any new preprints that appear on the wide array of preprint Web sites.

Pubcrawler–http://www.pubcrawler.ie/
Allows a user to have searches run automatically against the PubMed and GenBank databases.

In the Appendix, the reader will find a sampling of Web pages that may prove useful in monitoring the future evolution of CAS. Using one of the Web page monitoring services mentioned earlier or the search alert services with "current awareness" as the search term will also assist users to keep current on new developments in this area.

MANAGING THE FLOW:
E-MAIL, BIBLIOGRAPHIC MANAGEMENT AND OTHER TIPS

While there are many benefits to the increased use of CAS, they are not without a downside. As Fourie (2001) notes, "There can also be negative aspects such as information overload, the time required to work through the information, the need to organize and manage the information provided by CAS, and cost implications." Users can also be overwhelmed if they use search terms that are too broad and/or the CAS interfaces are confusing. All of these are valid concerns and must be taken into consideration when approaching faculty. To assist in minimizing the "information overload" concern expressed by Fourie and the "gap" that Paul Saffo noted between the volume of information and the tools available, an examination of selected management tools and techniques may be of assistance.

E-Mail Filters

Since many of the services mentioned above direct the information flow through the individual user's e-mail box, that may be the appropriate place to start. Most e-mail services in use today allow some level of filtering. These filters allow the user to sort and automatically process incoming mail based on user-defined criteria. This processing can range from very simple to extremely complex, both in the *rules* that are applied to incoming mail and to the *actions* which are taken as a result of this filtering. A simple example might be if a certain word appears anywhere in the header or body of the message (e.g., rehabilitation in the subject line), then drop it in a predefined folder (e.g., rehabilitation research) so it can be reviewed later. A more complex example would select any incoming e-mail in which the sender equals the Ingenta service and which contains the search string "stroke and rehabilitation" and route these results to a faculty member across campus who is researching this subject area, print a copy for your personal file, and save a copy in a special folder on your computer. In addition to being able to properly distribute the tsunami of requested data that arrives daily, e-mail filters also allow the redirection of unwanted messages or "empty results straight to the trash folder" (Notess 1999) without any user intervention. For example, via the Ingenta service the author receives approximately 25 e-mail alerts on separate topics once a week. Since most journals are only published monthly, many of these weekly alerts contain the message "no articles were loaded in the last week that matched your search criteria." If the user pairs the wording of this message with the sender, which is always the same, or the subject line, a filter can be established to automatically route this to the trash folder or to another folder for subsequent review. By aptly employing the full power of the tools available, one can efficiently cull the critically needed information from the clutter. More in-depth information on how to use filters can be found at the following addresses, but a quick Web search on "filtering" and "e-mail" should deliver results that discuss methods for filtering in other e-mail programs.

Eudora–from Qualcomm
http://www.eudora.com/techsupport/tutorials/win_filters.html

MS Outlook–from Microsoft
http://www.microsoft.com/education/EmailTutorial.aspx

Other aspects of e-mail that should be discussed with faculty as part of outreach efforts are the organization of their mailboxes or folders, and their ability to effectively search mail that may be automatically placed in an unfamiliar location. The more effectively they can store and retrieve the incoming discipline-specific information, the more open they will be to hearing the message of current awareness.

Citation Management Software

While e-mail filtering has allowed us to deal with CAS data that arrives daily, it is still essential for librarians, and their faculty, to further manage the categorization of this information within personal information systems. While we would like to think that all librarians are familiar with and capable of training faculty in the area of bibliographic management software, sometimes referred to as reference management or citation management software, that is not currently the case. Faculty and librarians are often accustomed to doing things manually, even when writing lengthy monographs, but after other solutions are clearly explained, they usually respond positively. The ability to quickly change a reference list style for a different publication or use the cite-as-you-type feature of some packages is quite impressive if demonstrated effectively. The most popular software in this genre currently includes EndNote and ReferenceManager from ISI Researchsoft, and the newer Web-based RefWorks from Cambridge Scientific Abstracts (CSA). Each has its own benefits, but being aware of these and being able to assist faculty with them can help reduce the dreaded informational overload. The fact that most of the catalogs and online article databases used in libraries today have an option to export their results to one of these packages should substantiate the need for stronger efforts on the part of librarians. Through the use of bibliographic software packages, both librarians and faculty should be able to more efficiently file and retrieve incoming data for future use in professional publishing and research efforts. Faculty who have incorporated this software into their daily work routine have become much more skilled in building on previous work rather than starting from scratch each time a publication comes due.

Bookmarks

Continuing in the work smart theme, mention should be made of effective use of bookmarks. Logical hierarchical structures, customization of bookmark properties, so that they make sense to the user, and finally, a high level of comfort in using Web search systems are all important and should be emphasized. Other suggestions that fellow librarians have provided include: prioritize, visualize, group similar tasks and finally, be persistent, especially when making the connection with faculty. Some tips from Steven J. Bell for not being overwhelmed include the following: "Be a browser . . . concentrate on spotting the one or two items you need to know . . . Use your e-mail client to get organized . . . Print or capture and review later . . . Share the load and tackle it as a team" (Bell 2000). Using a mix of the tools mentioned above, along with a selection of productivity resources, should allow librarians to more effectively address the pressures brought to bear with the increased flow of information.

CONCLUSION

Technological changes are occurring at a dizzying pace in the world of information. We're beginning to see the incorporation of portable palm computing devices with interfaces to catalogs and databases. One of the predictions of de Stricker (2002) in her review of CAS challenges and opportunities is that "providers will probably find advantage in developing intelligent watch-me agents capable of adjusting a user profile based on the user's viewing and ordering choices." Additionally, she sees further refinement of filtering tools and the creation of "information visualization" tools. Already vendors have incorporated "more like this" and "see related articles" features, but with more active monitoring and incorporation of individual user preferences we could see massive changes in the personalization of CAS. Further research needs to be undertaken to document the role that alerting services will play in the future and also to determine the current level of awareness among faculty regarding these services. Working closely with the statistics received from the various database providers one should be able to gather existing baseline data from which to launch this type of research.

The plethora of services mentioned above is formidable, but not unmanageable. More effective use of the existing technologies will allow librarians to more easily move from the role of gatekeepers to the consultative role so often discussed, but less frequently employed, within the academic environment. Common-sense strategies, such as those outlined earlier by Bell, and appropriate technologies when operating in tandem will hopefully allow us to stay informed without being overwhelmed.

REFERENCES

Bell, Steven J. 2000. To keep up, go beyond. *College & Research Libraries News* 61 (7): 581-84.

Cox, John, and Terry Hanson. 1992. Setting up an electronic current awareness service. *Online* 16 (4): 36.

de Stricker, Ulla. 2002. 'Keep me posted . . . But not too much': Challenges and opportunities for STM current-awareness providers. *Searcher* 10 (1): 52-59.

Foley, John. 1995. Managing information: Infoglut. *Information Week* 551: 30.

Fourie, Ina. 1999. Empowering users–current awareness on the Internet. *The Electronic Library* 17 (6): 379-88.

_____. 2001. Current awareness services in an electronic age–the whole picture. In *Handbook of Information Management.* 8th ed., ed. Alison Scammell, 274-306. London: Aslib.

Housman, E. M. 1973. Selective dissemination of information. *Annual Review of Information Science and Technology* 8: 221-41.

Jax, J. J., and V. C. Van Houlson. 1988. A current awareness service for faculty and staff: The Stout experience. *College & Research Libraries* 49 (6): 514-22.

Notess, Greg R. 1999. On the net: Internet current awareness. *Online* 23 (2): 75.

Reker, Dean. 2003. "Alerts–stroke and rehab." E-mail to Patrick Sullivan, August 11, 2003.

Rowley, Jennifer. 1985. Bibliographic current awareness services. *Aslib Proceedings* 37 (9): 345-53.

_____. 1994. Revolution in current awareness services. *Journal of Librarianship and Information Science* 26 (1): 7-14.

_____. 1998a. Current awareness in an electronic age. *Online & CDROM Review* 22 (4): 277-79.

_____. 1998b. The changing face of current awareness services. *Journal of Librarianship and Information Science* 30 (3): 177-83.

Schlembach, Mary C. 2001. Trends in current awareness services. *Science & Technology Libraries* 20 (2/3): 121-32.

Tyburski, Genie. 2002. "Tracking trademarks on the web." Web page, http://www. virtualchase.com/articles/tracking_trademarks_print.html (accessed August 20, 2003).

APPENDIX. Selected Web Sites for Current Awareness Services

Note that many of these Web sites contain instructions specific to their organization for accessing the various alert services and may discuss databases that require licensed access.

Current Awareness Services and Saved Searches–
Library of Health Sciences
http://www.uic.edu/depts/lib/lhsu/resources/guides/current_awareness.shtml

Drexel University–Current Awareness/Alerting Services
http://www.library.drexel.edu/research/guides/pdfs/alertservices.html

Keeping Up With New Web Sites
http://lii.org/search/file/newsites

Keeping Your Research Up To Date
http://www.lboro.ac.uk/library/aware/

NIST Virtual Library–Alerting Services
http://nvl.nist.gov/nvl3.cfm?dynamic=alertservices&s_id=120

NSDL Scout Reports–Subscription Option
http://scout.wisc.edu/nsdl-reports/

Search Engine Showdown–Current Awareness Tools
http://www.searchengineshowdown.com/alerts/

Steven Bell's Keeping Up Web Site
http://staff.philau.edu/bells/keepup/

University of Toronto–Current Awareness Services
http://www.library.utoronto.ca/engineering-computer-science/resources/current_aware.html

The Impact
of Electronic Bibliographic Databases
and Electronic Journal Articles
on the Scholar's Information-Seeking Behavior
and Personal Collection of "Reprints"

Robert B. McGeachin

SUMMARY. This article examines the potential changes to the information-seeking behavior of scholars and how they manage their own collection of research article "reprints." With bibliographic databases and electronic journals provided by academic libraries now available at the science scholars' computer desktops, they can now locate and acquire a portion of needed research articles on their own at any time. They also, in some cases, have older paper copies scanned and delivered by libraries as image files at Web retrieval locations. Bibliographic citation management software is now in use by many scholars. Personal information management software is available and could also be used. This article reviews possible scenarios scholars can use to manage this new

---

Robert B. McGeachin, PhD, MS, MLIS, is Associate Professor and Coordinator for Agricultural Library Services, Medical Sciences Library, Texas A&M University, 4462 TAMU, College Station, TX 77843-4462 (E-mail: r-mcgeachin@tamu.edu).

Mention or use of commercial software products does not imply official institutional endorsement of them.

[Haworth co-indexing entry note]: "The Impact of Electronic Bibliographic Databases and Electronic Journal Articles on the Scholar's Information-Seeking Behavior and Personal Collection of 'Reprints.'" McGeachin, Robert B. Co-published simultaneously in *Science & Technology Libraries* (The Haworth Information Press, an imprint of The Haworth Press, Inc.) Vol. 25, No. 1/2, 2004, pp. 127-137; and: *Emerging Issues in the Electronic Environment: Challenges for Librarians and Researchers in the Sciences* (ed: Jeannie P. Miller) The Haworth Information Press, an imprint of The Haworth Press, Inc., 2004, pp. 127-137. Single or multiple copies of this article are available for a fee from The Haworth Document Delivery Service [1-800-HAWORTH, 9:00 a.m. - 5:00 p.m. (EST). E-mail address: docdelivery@haworthpress.com].

electronic collection of research articles and possible ways libraries can help them in this scholarly activity. *[Article copies available for a fee from The Haworth Document Delivery Service: 1-800-HAWORTH. E-mail address: <docdelivery@haworthpress.com> Website: <http://www.HaworthPress.com>*

KEYWORDS. Bibliographic citation managers, personal information managers, pim, ocr, reprint collection, scholar's workstation, remote access, library services

INTRODUCTION

Most academic scholars have usually amassed personal collections of works relevant to their scholarly research and communication. Books and journal articles have been available and collected for centuries. Published reprint copies and the advent of photocopiers greatly expanded the ability of scholars to collect large numbers of articles. Large collections have brought a need for organization of the collections and creation of access and retrieval mechanisms for them. Today, this is often accomplished by such traditional written and mechanical means as personal card catalogs to a collection of reproduced articles filed by author, title, or subject classified arrangements. Some scholars currently use bibliographic database software such as Pro-Cite, EndNote, or Reference Manager to replace card catalogs for organizing and gaining access to their personal print collections.

DREAM OF A SCHOLAR'S WORKSTATION COMING TO FRUITION

The advent of electronic databases and bibliographic software to replace physical card catalogs and the creation of large full-text databases of works have led to the verge of realizing Vannevar Bush's dream of the "memex" portion of a scholar's workstation (Bush 1945). Bush envisioned an increase in a scholar's work efficiency through the capability of full-text and image retrieval of a personal collection of scholarly information at the scholar's desk. Most scholars today deal with a narrowly focused subspecialty and need a large, organized personal collection of articles and information as well as access to acquiring new information in their field. They also need an efficient way to gather, store, and retrieve raw research data. The ability to do so electronically has been evolving over the last couple of decades. This is now technically possible, but the best means of acquiring and managing a personal full-text electronic collection needs to be determined by the scholar who now has more available options than ever for personal research information collection management. Ultimately individual scholars must decide what are the most convenient methods to use based on their level of comfort with physical print resources versus electronic resources.

MANAGING PRINT INFORMATION RESOURCES

Scholars have traditionally collected reprints by writing to the author of articles of interest and requesting a courtesy copy. They have also gone to their institution's library, browsed relevant journals and photocopied articles from these journals. Articles are then often indexed with some form of personal card catalog and stored according to an indexing scheme of choice. This is usually either alphabetically by author's name or some personal subject classification system devised by the scholar to fit specific research areas. If subject classified, they are often arranged alphabetically by author's name within the subjects. The average time to accomplish this traditional discovery, copying, cataloging, and storage is 7.4 minutes per article (note: this assumes multiple articles are retrieved in any session at the library, and this does not include travel time to and from the library which will vary for each scholar) (McGeachin 1998). This may still be a reasonable method for some scholars, especially if they have clerical or graduate assistant help available to help with the cataloging and storage tasks. Scholars also acquire a personal book collection, which may also be arranged alphabetically by author's name or alphabetically by title and cataloged as well. Most scholars are members of a relevant professional society which, in most cases, produces journal and/or trade publications that are either included in the cost of an annual membership dues package or available at a relatively low additional fee/s. This personal journal collection is not usually indexed or cataloged by the scholar, just arranged in chronological order by title on bookshelves, or perhaps, in pamphlet boxes on shelves. Most scholars have from one to five personal subscriptions to their most frequently used journals, as a convenience.

With the advent of growing amounts of information resources in electronic format provided by their institution's library and made remotely available at their desktops, scholars can find articles and print them on a local printer. This is preferable to trying to read the articles online for many scholars and produces a physical copy to add to their existing collection. Such electronic-to-print articles can be cataloged and filed into the existing reprint and photocopied article collection for later reference. These remotely accessible electronic articles are a great convenience for scholars, saving them large amounts of travel and photocopy time at the library. In many cases, if their local library provides remote electronic access to titles for which they have a personal subscription and pay extra above the base cost of their society membership, they are choosing to drop their personal print subscription and just use the equally convenient library supplied electronic version.

CONVERSION OF LEGACY PRINT COLLECTIONS TO ELECTRONIC FILES

For scholars with an existing collection of print resources that have taken up electronic storage and retrieval of new electronic resources, the question of whether to convert their existing print collection to electronic format is raised. They must decide if the time it would take to do so is worthwhile for them or not. To do so they would have two choices. The first is a conversion process of scanning their existing documents, followed by Optical Character Recognition (OCR) on the scans and cleanup editing on the OCR results before storing the new version of the document in some file format. But this can be a time-consuming process. A 1998 investigation found that using PageKeeper version 2.0 software (equivalent to about OmniPage version 6.0 OCR software) to scan and perform OCR took an average of 62 minutes per article to process, which is far too much of an effort to be worthwhile for most scholars (McGeachin 1998). Now, five years later, there have been increases in the OCR abilities of software. For example, OmniPage is currently in version 12.0, and a repeat of this time and effort study should be done to determine how long conversion of the average article would now take.

The second choice is to scan and convert the documents to Portable Document Format (PDF) files for storage. While this is relatively fast and the same file format in which many electronic resources are now being saved, the resulting files are relatively large and need a lot of storage space. Unless further processed with OCR, they are only image files that cannot be searched. One of the new native file output types of OmniPage version 12.0 is PDF with OCR done on the output files such that these combination image and OCR text PDF files are fully searchable. But the relatively large size of PDF image files may lead some scholars to save a smaller version. Products that can convert PDF files to much smaller file size Microsoft Word documents include OmniPage Pro version 12 (ScanSoft 2003a) and PDF Converter for Microsoft Windows (ScanSoft 2003c).

ELECTRONIC INFORMATION RESOURCES

Scholars read and most frequently cite in their publications those journals that are most convenient to them in terms of access. A bibliometric analysis of publications by molecular biologists at the University of Chicago showed that, on a campus with multiple libraries with scientific journals, they used and cited most frequently those titles that were in the library closest to them (Hurd, Blecic, and Vishwanatham 1999). So, the convenience of supplying electronic bibliographic databases for resource discovery and electronic journals and books for easy retrieval to the scholar's desktop is extremely important and will directly influence scholarly reading and citing habits and most likely the outcome of research efforts. Many scholars have not used print bibliographic indexes as their primary resource discovery tools. Rather they use easier methods, the most frequent of which are to consult with colleagues and/or just follow and use literature cited in articles they already have. Hallmark (1994) found that two/thirds of all citations in publications by scientists came from these two sources. Brown (1999) also found that scientists' most used means of finding current literature were browsing current journal issues, conversations with colleagues, and attending scientific conferences, with less than half using bibliographic indexes. So, with the provision of electronic bibliographic databases at their desktop, broader and more complete literature searches and reviews of the literature on an area of research can be performed by scholars, which should result in improved scholarly and scientific results. But more complete knowledge of the literature leads to increased acquisition of personal article copies and the need for more efficient retrieval of articles, personal indexing, and storage capabilities.

Scholars can now access electronic copies of articles at their desktop and have a number of choices on how to then deal with them. If they have confidence that they will have perpetual electronic access to articles, they may just want to maintain a personal index of bibliographic records with corresponding URLs included for easy future access to the articles. One group of software tools that can perform this function are bibliographic citation managers. There are now a growing number of these available for use by scholars. They usually include such features as the ability to:

- Create a database/s of records to a variety of resource types (articles, books, electronic resources, chapters, manuscripts, proceedings, AV materials, etc.)
- Import selected records from electronic bibliographic databases
- Search and retrieve records from bibliographic databases and online catalogs from within the citation management program
- Format the citations in any of hundreds of different journal or association citation styles and produce properly formatted, complete bibliographies of selected records in any of those styles
- Integrate with common word processing software such as Microsoft Word or WordPerfect in the creation of articles with inserted citations and final complete bibliographies (for example, this article was written using Microsoft Word 2000 integrated with EndNote 5.0 to create the citations and bibliography).

Available bibliographic citation-manager products now come as either purchased desktop software applications that operate from the local desktop computer and/or local area network server, or as subscription Web-based applications hosted on the vendor's Web server. The former do not require Internet access to operate, but the latter have the potential advantage of being accessible to users from anywhere they are located.

Desktop bibliographic citations managers include:

- EndNote version 7 (ISI ResearchSoft 2003a)
- ProCite version 5 (ISI ResearchSoft 2003b)
- Reference Manager version 10 (ISI ResearchSoft 2003c)
- Biblioscape version 5.3 (CG Information 2003)
- Reference Assistant (CrazySquirrel Complete Solutions 2003)
- Citation version 8.2 (askSam Systems 2003)
- Library Master (Balboa Software 2003)
- Scholar's Aid 4 AE (Scholar's Aid Inc. 2003).

Web-based bibliographic citation managers include:

- WriteNote (ISI ResearchSoft 2003d)
- RefWorks (RefWorks 2003)
- NoodleBib (NoodleTools 2003).

Most of these products have educational pricing available to make them more affordable in the academic scholarly environment.

One other option available to scholars that just want to capture an index of URLs to electronic resources is to use their Web browser's "bookmark" or "favorites" functionality to capture and store URLs. With the bookmark record editing features and hierarchical ability to create layers of folders, scholars can accumulate very extensive collections of links to both electronic articles and Web resources.

Another option now available to scholars, with the availability of accessing electronic versions of articles and books at the desktop, is to download a personal copy of the electronic file and store it locally. The increased availability of inexpensive desktop storage space or local area network storage space is one factor that makes this feasible for scholars. Again, the question of how to index, store, and retrieve these local file copies is raised. One simple possibility that might work for some scholars is to save the files with the resource title in the file name, and create a personal subject hierarchy of folders in file storage utilities such as Windows Explorer. A simple level of retrieval can be accomplished with the Windows search utility and word searching within titles or documents, or by browsing through the file names in the Windows Explorer file display.

A more elegant and robust solution is the use of Personal Information Management (PIM) software to store, index, and retrieve the electronic resource files. PIM is currently used to label and describe a wide range of software applications. These range from those focused on very specific types of information management such as Troopmaster which records and organizes information for Boy Scout Troops; to managing sales contact information; to managing personal calendars, address and phone books, e-mail and transfer of these to and from Personal Digital Assistant hardware; to the one this article focuses on, which is broad and comprehensive storage, indexing and retrieval of almost all files and file types in the personal computer. This class of software is designed to be a more holistic approach to managing many more types of personal files than the bibliographic citation managers that just focus on records about articles, books, and Web sources. Common types of files that PIMs are designed to store, index, and retrieve include: image files of many formats, PDF files, text files of many formats (sometimes including e-mail), and Web files. PIMs also usually allow existing files to be further annotated by the user. The user can also define the storage subjects/categories and create multiple cross-references among items.

Personal Information Manager programs include:

- PaperPort Pro 9 Office (ScanSoft 2003b)
- Enfish (Enfish Corp. 2003)
- TreePad (Freebyte.com 2003)
- CatClip version 2.5 (CatRunner LLC 2003).

Using PaperPort as an example, the scholar can use bibliographic indexes to identify relevant resources and link from them to the actual resources to examine online. If they choose to save an electronic copy they can "save as," copy and paste, or drag and drop the file to a PaperPort folder. Scholars can create and use a hierarchical file folder structure in PaperPort to store all of their downloaded and saved information resources. As this collection grows over time the extensive search capabilities of PaperPort allow scholars to locate and retrieve resources from their collection.

The scholar can use PaperPort to convert files from one type to another as it has a number of converters in its program functions, including the ability to do OCR processing on image files. For example, a scanned image can be moved with drag and drop from a PaperPort folder on to the Word icon in the "Send To" bar, and PaperPort will perform OCR and convert the results into a Word document. Resource item files can also be sent to other programs such as Internet e-mail, word processing, spreadsheet, fax, graphics, and online service programs. Other PaperPort functions include capturing Web pages as image files, the ability to add electronic annotations, as either text or yellow sticky notes, and the ability to add subjects, authors, and keywords to item properties to aid in search and retrieval.

THE ROLE OF LIBRARIANS IN ASSISTING SCHOLARS

A primary role for librarians is to continue to provide information resources to their client scholars in both print and electronic formats. But especially, providing remote access to electronic resources at the scholar's desktop computer should be facilitated for their client scholars to the degree that libraries are fiscally able. This includes providing electronic bibliographic indexes and databases, electronic journals and periodicals, electronic books, and access to the Internet. Since all literature that scholars need does not exist in electronic form yet (or, for what does exist, cannot be afforded as an electronic option yet), librarians can also create local electronic delivery systems to take requests electronically for their print journal items; retrieve these from their collections, scan and convert them to PDF documents, and place them in private Web-based storage for only the requesting user to retrieve. In this case, an e-mail is sent to the customer with a URL for the location of the PDF file to use for retrieval. The PDF file of the article would be removed after being accessible to the customer for one month. So scholars must either print it off or save the PDF file themselves if they need long-term access. (This service scheme ensures that scholarly "fair use" of the original material has been observed by only providing one copy on request to a single customer.) This makes essentially the entire print journal collection of the library accessible from the scholar's desktop.

Librarians can also play a role in assisting their customers manage electronic information once they have acquired it. They can assist in the usage of bibliographic citation managers either directly by providing access to them for library users, or indirectly by encouraging other computing-related entities at their institution to provide them. For example, the author of this paper is on a campus committee that has oversight of student open-access computing laboratories at the Texas A&M University campus, and he successfully made the case to the rest of the committee to include bibliographic citation management software as one of the applications made available in the student computing labs. Another librarian at Texas A&M University created a "connection file" for this software package that allows users to search the Texas A&M University Libraries' online catalog from within the bibliographic citation manager and directly import selected catalog records into their citation manager (Highsmith 2002). Librarians can be knowledgeable in the use of bibliographic citation management and personal information management applications and offer instruction to customers in one-on-one consultations, group classes, and by Web-based tutorials. Since the acquisition, classification, storage, and retrieval of information are at the heart of library science, librarians are a very appropriate group to advise scholars on how to manage their personal information collections.

CONCLUSION

Due to the efforts of their libraries, scholars now have many information resources available at their desktop in electronic format. Scholars now have a wider range of options in how to deal with personal information resources than ever before. These include a paper "reprint" article, journal and book collections with some form of cataloging and physical storage; using document scanning and OCR software to convert their existing print collections to electronic format; using bibliographic citation management software to catalog paper and/or electronic collections; using personal information management software to index and store electronic collections; or some combination of all of these methods. The degree to which scholars employ these various methods is a needed area of study by librarians.

REFERENCES

askSam Systems. 2003. *Citation Bibliographic and Research Note Software*, 15 February 2003, http://www.citationonline.net/ (accessed 20 September 2003).

Balboa Software. 2003. *Library Master for Windows* 2003, http://www.balboa-software.com/lmw.html (accessed 16 September 2003).

Brown, C. M. 1999. Information Seeking Behavior of Scientists in the Electronic Information Age: Astronomers, Chemists, Mathematicians, and Physicists. *Journal of the American Society for Information Science* 50(10): 929-943.

Bush, Vannevar. 1945. As We May Think. *Atlantic Monthly* 176:101-108.

CatRunner LLC. 2003. *CatClip 2.5–Your Personal Information Organization Solution*, 2003, http://www.catrunner.com/ (accessed 27 September 2003).

CG Information. 2003. *Biblioscape–Bibliographic Software for Citations and Bibliography Generation in APA, MLA, etc. The Best Reference Manager*, 13 August 2003, http://www.biblioscape.com/ (accessed 16 September 2003).

CrazySquirrel Complete Solutions. 2003. *Refas–The Reference Assistant*, 2002, http://www.crazysquirrel.com/refas/refas.php (accessed 16 September 2003).

Enfish Corp. 2003. *Enfish–Find Anything, Anywhere, Quickly*, 2003, http://www.enfish.com/ (accessed 10 September 2003).

Freebyte.com. 2003. *TreePad: Personal Information Manager, Notes Organizer, Word Processor, PIM, Database and More!*, 2003, http://www.treepad.com/ (accessed 27 September 2003).

Hallmark, Julie. 1994. Scientists' Access and Retrieval of References Cited in Their Recent Journal Articles. *College & Research Libraries* 55 (3):199-208.

Highsmith, Anne L. 2002. [Personal Communications] amdb.enz EndNote connection file for LibCat, Texas A&M University.

Hurd, Julie M., Deborah D. Blecic, and Rama Vishwanatham. 1999. Information Use by Molecular Biologists: Implications for Library Collections and Services. *College & Research Libraries* 60 (1):31-43.

ISI ResearchSoft. 2003a. *EndNote–Product Information*, 5 August 2003, http://www.endnote.com/eninfo.asp (accessed 20 September 2003).

_____. 2003b. *ProCite for Windows and Macintosh Product Information*, 19 August 2003, http://www.procite.com/pcinfo.asp (accessed 20 September 2003).

_____. 2003c. *Reference Manager for Windows Product Information*, 20 February 2003, http://www.refman.com/rminfo.asp (accessed 20 September 2003).

_____. 2003d. *WriteNote–Product Information*, 21 February 2003, http://www. writenote.com/wninfo.asp (accessed 20 September 2003).

McGeachin, Robert B. 1998. The Feasibility of Using Document Management Software in the Scholar's Workstation. *Journal of Academic Librarianship* 24 (6):449-553.

NoodleTools. 2003. *NoodleBib–The MLA and APA Bibliography Composer*, 2003, http://www.noodletools.com/noodlebib/index.php (accessed 16 September 2003).

RefWorks. 2003. *RefWorks Web Based Bibliographic Management Software*, 2003, http://www.refworks.com/productinfo.shtml (accessed 16 September 2003).

ScanSoft. 2003a. *ScanSoft–OmniPage Pro 12 Office*, 2003, http://www.scansoft.com/ omnipage/ (accessed 20 September 2003).

_____. 2003b. *ScanSoft–PaperPort Pro 9 Office*, 2003, http://www.scansoft.com/ paperport/pro/ (accessed 20 September 2003).

_____. 2003c. *ScanSoft–PDF Converter*, 2003, http://www.scansoft.com/pdfconverter/ (accessed 28 September 2003).

Scholar's Aid Inc. 2003. *Is Scholar's Aid Right For You?* 27 August 2003, http:// scholarsaid.com/right4you_research.html (accessed 20 September 2003).

Biology Databases
for the New Life Sciences

Katherine S. Chiang

SUMMARY. Hundreds of publicly-accessible biology data sites have appeared in the last twenty years. Sequence, microarray, and protein structure data are now stored in large complex databases. Bioinformatics, the computational manipulation of data to derive meaningful information, has emerged as a distinct field. Bioinformatics combines the subject expertise of the biologists with the data handling expertise of the computer scientists. There are information-science issues associated with these data: the databasing of information, the heterogeneity of the data, the complexity of the databases, the range of audiences being served, and the emergence of database standards. Librarians can make contributions in this developing area. *[Article copies available for a fee from The Haworth Document Delivery Service: 1-800-HAWORTH. E-mail address: <docdelivery@haworthpress.com> Website: <http://www.HaworthPress.com> © 2004 by The Haworth Press, Inc. All rights reserved.]*

KEYWORDS. Databases, genomics, bioinformatics, microarrays, data mining

Katherine S. Chiang, MA (Library Science), BA, is Head of Public Services, Albert R. Mann Library, Cornell University, Ithaca, NY 14853-4301 (E-mail: ksc3@cornell.edu).

[Haworth co-indexing entry note]: "Biology Databases for the New Life Sciences." Chiang, Katherine S. Co-published simultaneously in *Science & Technology Libraries* (The Haworth Information Press, an imprint of The Haworth Press, Inc.) Vol. 25, No. 1/2, 2004, pp. 139-170; and: *Emerging Issues in the Electronic Environment: Challenges for Librarians and Researchers in the Sciences* (ed: Jeannie P. Miller) The Haworth Information Press, an imprint of The Haworth Press, Inc., 2004, pp. 139-170. Single or multiple copies of this article are available for a fee from The Haworth Document Delivery Service [1-800-HAWORTH, 9:00 a.m. - 5:00 p.m. (EST). E-mail address: docdelivery@haworthpress.com].

http://www.haworthpress.com/web/STL
© 2004 by The Haworth Press, Inc. All rights reserved.
Digital Object Identifier: 10.1300/J122v25n01_10

INTRODUCTION

By 2003 a single microarray experiment could generate 400,000 to four million data points (Lin 2003). The *GenBank* database of DNA sequences, release 138.0, included 35 billion bases from 29 million reported sequences (Genbank 2003). The *PubMed* database of biological and medical literature was at over 12 million citations from 4,600 journals (National Center for Biotechnology Information 2003). The *Protein Data Bank* had over 20,000 protein and other biological macromolecular structures. It averaged over three million downloaded files each month (Research Collaboratory for Structural Bioinformatics 2002).

These databases are only the most well-known of the hundreds of publicly accessible biology data sites that have appeared in the last 20 years. Biology databases are numerous, huge, and significant. In 1996, the year the journal *Nucleic Acids Research* ran the first molecular biology databases inventory, there were 58 articles describing databases. By 2003, there were 67 databases in the A-D section of the alphabet alone. In addition to the number of databases, the other hallmarks of this development are that many of the databases run to millions of records; most are free and many have limited life spans.

The short life spans are a consequence of the trajectory of current molecular biology. The field is growing rapidly and the focus of effort is changing equally fast. The Human Genome Project to sequence the entire human genome was initiated in 1988. Ten years later the focus was on identifying genes from the sequences and functions for those genes. Now, the target is protein structures, functions, and even broader, complex biological systems elucidation. The holy grail of the enterprise is an understanding of how 'everything works in an organism' (Frazier et al. 2003). Databases feed into other databases; databases also merge or are integrated into other data. To an outsider, it seems like the leading edge of research is moving like the incoming tide on a nearly flat beach; one cannot run fast enough to keep up with it.

Why should non-researchers even care to keep up with the developments in biology databases? More specifically, why should librarians pay any attention; why should they care? Most of the data are free and scientists are finding and using the databases without assistance from librarians.

In spite of this, however, these databases should be of interest to librarians at several different levels. At least, they should have a passing interest in them as citizens. The impact of these databases on our lives could be profound and the potential usefulness of the data are infinite, powerful, and thought-provoking. A 2003 news article in *Science* describes "the first clinical trial to assign patients to standard or aggressive therapy based on a gene scan" (Branca 2003). In another real-world application, biosensors, using nucleic acid sequence-based amplification (NASBA), will soon be able to identify Dengue virus. Unlike other methods of testing for pathogens, biosensors are a hundredfold cheaper than laboratory tests, and they can identify pathogens in minutes or hours instead of days (Gabriel 2002).

It behooves science librarians to know what their patrons are using, as these databases are integral to research efforts today, and will inevitably make the transition into the teaching and learning processes tomorrow. Furthermore, these databases are growing at a pace where it seems likely that soon an individual researcher will not be able to stay knowledgeable about all of the databases of possible use. A comparable era was the 18th century when the librarian's role enlarged as scientists became overwhelmed with the volumes of print information in books and journals.

Finally, these large datasets and the computational techniques necessary to manage and understand the data are radically changing how some biology is done. In this era of large databases, the expertise of the librarian/information scientist will be even more central to research as the numbers and variety of biology databases proliferate. Bioinformatics innovations in large scale data manipulation have become a significant tool in biological research.

At the heart of the bioinformatics phenomenon is the decoupling of data collection from the experimental cycle. Classical life-sciences research is hypothesis-driven and biology has been characterized as a wet science, a laboratory, bench-based process. The researcher posits a hypothesis, creates an experiment, and gathers data that support or refute that hypothesis. Now a phase of pure data collection has altered the landscape by inserting yet another type of research into the cycle that leads to the production of knowledge. Simplistically reduced, data in these databases are analyzed, not to accept or reject a hypothesis, but to produce an inference that can then guide an experiment. The results of these data analyses are not the statistical confidences of the correlation, or experimental verification of a causal connection, but an identification of an area of interest within the datasets which may generate a hypothesis that can then drive the experimental research.

This rotation between massive data collection, then data analysis, which in turn guides the experiments that generate more specific data, is relatively new to biological science. Computationally controlled technologies make all of this possible, from the chip-controlled data collection to the completely computer-dominated data mining. Various terms have been used to describe this work including, *in silico* and the dry cycle (as contrasted with the 'wet' experimental phase), giving rise to the phrase 'wet/dry cycle' to describe the alternating process.

These large data collection efforts, and the subsequent analysis of patterns within the data, have loose parallels to some of the other sciences–atmospheric and space (with data collection from satellites and telescopes) and social sciences and marketing (with data collection from large-scale population surveys and consumer behavior). Researchers are 'mining' the *GenBank* database like the Census of Population or customer data is mined.[1]

The demographics in this research era are diverse. Multiple labs and large and small organizations are involved in data creation and manipulation. As such, there are various motives behind the generation and maintenance of the data and varied levels of economic stability to the servers and hosts of those data.

Compared to other data worlds (e.g., the social sciences, as illustrated by the history of the InterUniversity Consortium for Political and Social Research), these biological databases are early in their data-sharing life spans. However, they are maturing early, driven by accelerated research activity and the number of databases involved. Socio-economic elements have already appeared. Data producers, sponsors, and users are trying to create systems, standards, and agreements to reach the goal of database interoperability and consistency in the accessibility of the data. This is inevitable, given the numbers of researchers, labs, and organizations involved in data collection and sharing, and the speed with which the data are being collected and new databases are being created.

In the majority of data collection efforts, the advantages of having access to other data clearly outweigh those of data hoarding. The precedent and culture of data sharing set by the Human Genome Project and *PubMed*, as well as the public databases supported by granting agencies, is hard to compete with. Good intentions are more easily sustained as the Internet and network communication technologies reduce the overhead of actually shipping large amounts of data between researchers. Two high visibility attempts (Celera and Incyte) to sell data have not been profitable. However, data as intellectual property will continue. Genes can be patented.

Right now, the majority of this data discovery, retrieval, and acquisition is happening within the research community. Furthermore, the management of the databases and the efforts to increase data interoperability are also centered in the research community. But the need for information specialists is now emerging. The amount of data, their heterogeneity, and their scatter on computers across the world, will drive a need for specialists who will spend the majority of their energy managing and describing the data, rather than manipulating them. As the numbers, sizes, and variety of databases increase, the need for many of the solutions that libraries have developed is becoming obvious.

A quick example is illustrated by the following complaint: "The names used in the literature and those in the databases of molecular sequences differ widely due to a general lack of well-recognized standard nomenclature" (Blaschke and Valencia 2002). The idea of the authority record was probably created in response to a similar complaint.

Librarians have much to offer, especially as the interdisciplinary nature of these research problems puts researchers into unfamiliar territory. Bibliographers can identify pertinent datasets and help their organization license fee-based resources. Catalogers can create indexes, as the number of databases increases past what can be listed in a table or sorted into an hierarchical set of links. Reference librarians can help researchers find datasets outside their usual purview.

The approach of this paper is to swing the point-of-view on these databases, to look at them sideways, or perhaps more accurately, from overhead, as a way of comprehending their scope. There are many excellent papers and tutorials that talk about biology databases from a biologist's viewpoint, and others that talk about them from the stance of a computer scientist. Both of those viewpoints are application-centered. But there is value in taking a resource-based overview of these databases, in viewing them collectively.

Imagine the approach, creation, and use of each database as a country. Each lab group, grant-funded team, or research center is creating, populating, and manipulating a database or databases to meet their needs. Their connection to other databases (countries) is when they find one that has useful data for their project. Their approach to that data is out of self-interest, their transactions bilateral. Librarians are the international players, who regularly think in terms of multilateral agreements and see the trading at a collective level.

This information-internationalistic approach has two benefits when trying to comprehend the burgeoning world of biological databases. It is easier to hold the whole picture when working from commonalities between the databases, and it is easier to step into unfamiliar territory when stepping from the familiar. In this case, the concept of the database can help librarians understand the subjects of the databases.

In this paper, four major database types are used as examples: sequence data, protein data, microarray data, and the literature databases. Approaches to data manipulation are examined in the context of those data types, then the information and library issues are discussed.

THE DATABASES

Most biology databases are active collections, with the continual addition of new data. They were originally created for varying purposes. Animal breeders were early data collectors, and sought to improve domestic animal stocks by looking for genes in relation to traits of economic importance (e.g., litter size), and following traits through pedigrees (Law and Archibald 2000). The pharmacology industry is also a large producer of biological datasets.

The 'reference' efforts are perhaps the best-known biology databases. The most visible example is the Human Genome Project, but there are many other reference efforts. A coalition of institutions is sequencing the rice genome. The U.S. participants are: The Institute for Genomic Research (TIGR), Clemson University/Cold Spring Harbor Laboratory/Washington University consortium (CCW), Plant Genome Initiative at Rutgers (PGIR), and the University of Wisconsin (http:// www.usricegenome.org). The Mouse Genome has an even larger set of participants (http://www.ncbi.nlm.nih.gov/genome/seq/MmSeqCenters. html). Finally, there are the data warehousing efforts that assemble data from multiple sources under one format, such as the *Entrez Nucleotides* database (http://www.ncbi.nlm.nih.gov/entrez/query.fcgi?db=Nucleotide) and the *Protein Data Bank* (http://www.rcsb.org/pdb).

Historically, many of the databases (excluding the reference ones) were generated for local research programs and later opened to a wider group of potential users (Law and Archibald 2000). Similarly, the first library catalogs were created as automation tools to manage acquisitions and cataloging functions, and only later were they opened to public access. The databases have emerged out of a continuum running from data collection at the individual laboratory level, to data management for a collaborative lab project, to a depository for access by an even broader group of researchers interested in the data, to databases conceived and supported as a public warehouse (Schonbach 2000).

Most of the databases are Web accessible. Some databases are open to researchers who share their own data, others to researchers who have established accounts with the producer, and some are fee-based (Gardiner-Garden and Littlejohn 2001). In the late 1980s, *GenBank* tapes were available for local loading, and host institutions had to buy the software package to query the data. Now the *GenBank* database is available as an FTP download, and subsets from the database can be created via a search of the interface at the National Center for Biotechnology Information site (http://www.ncbi.nlm.nih.gov/entrez/query.fcgi?db=Nucleotide).

The result of all this data gathering and hosting is that there are many publicly available databases in biology. Most of them are easily accessible and thus attractive to a large body of researchers, from bench experimentalists, to bioinformaticists, to computer scientists.

Database Categories

The phrase *biology databases* is deliberately vague so as to cover a wide range of data types. There is no good estimate as to the number of databases that are publicly accessible and have some aspect of molecular biology/genomics in their contents, but it is easily double the number included in the *Nucleic Acids* database issue. The 2003 issue included approximately 400 titles, so there could easily be 800 to 1,000 databases. While numerous, the databases do cluster based on the type of data they include, or by some other scheme, such as organization, institution, or species.

Various articles about these resources have generated categorizations. Samples from the categories used by the *Nucleic Acids Research* in 2003 are:

major sequence repositories
comparative genomics
gene expression
gene identification and structure
genetic and physical maps
genomic databases
intermolecular interactions
metabolic pathways and cellular regulation
mutation databases
pathology
protein databases
protein sequence motifs
proteome resources
RNA sequences

retrieval systems and database structure
structure
transgenics
varied biomedical content.

Another resource sorted them into: biological literature, sequences, expression, protein interaction measurements, and metabolic expression (Marcotte and Date 2001). Another variation is: pathway, genome, protein, enzyme, chemical, and literature.

Some of the databases have print counterparts; most are purely electronic. There are hybrid databases, combining data from multiple sources. *KEGG*, the *Kyoto Encyclopedia of Genes and Genomes*, is an example of such a combination. "KEGG is a suite of databases and associated software, integrating our current knowledge on molecular interaction networks in biological processes, the information about the universe of genes and proteins, and the information about the universe of chemical compounds and reactions" (http://www.genome.ad.jp/kegg/kegg.html). Other databases are subsets from the larger databases with local value-added content.

This article focuses on four core database examples: sequence, microarray, protein, and literature databases. The last example needs no explanation for librarians. The sequence databases are the next easiest to explain–they contain DNA sequences and documentation on how that sequence was created, and often, links to articles and other information related to that sequence. The microarray data come from experiments looking at the 'interdependence of genes' (Hung and Kim 2000). The protein data come from both experiments and computational modeling of protein sequences and their structures.

It is impracticable to properly explain the science underlying the data being collected. Readers should consult a reputable textbook or the NCBI primer at http://www.ncbi.nlm.nih.gov/Education/index.html.

However, this metaphor might help. Let us say one seeks to understand how a library works. There is a set of job descriptions for each employee and functions for each piece of equipment in a library–but most users know only a few words of the language being used. Efforts to understand are further complicated, as the text of the descriptions has no "spacesbetweenthewords" and there are a lot of extraneous characters between some of the words and phrases. Somehow, one needs to decipher what constitutes a word among the string of characters, and what that word means. That is the metaphor for the efforts to discern genes within the sequence data and gene functions.

Once the description of a piece of equipment is known, it is possible to model what that equipment would look like, even if its use is unknown. For example the model might look like a container, leading to the speculation that it has some transport function within the library. Similarities between portions of two job descriptions could generate the inference that the two positions have some type of work in common. That is what gene function and protein modeling efforts are about.

Let us say that, in addition to the job descriptions, one is also able to collect snapshot data of who is working on something at any point in time. Through a series of experiments, those data can be collected. For example, a professor e-mails the library with a request that an item be put on reserve. At the time, one learns that machine A and person Z are 'active,' but one hour later equipment B and person Y and X are 'active,' then twelve hours later persons W, S, and T are active. Eventually, by doing enough of these experiments, one is able to identify which people and what equipment are involved in the reserve process at any particular point in time. It can be inferred that persons W, S, and T might have some interrelationship. That is what microarray data collection reveals about gene expression.

Sequence Databases

> The genome in a living organism consists of one or more long strings of deoxyribonucleic acids (DNAs), each of which is composed of millions of DNA 'letters' corresponding to the four nucleotide bases. A DNA string can be compared to a book containing tens of thousands of sentences. Each sentence (gene) is an instruction to construct, in most cases, a protein. Each sentence has a start code and an end code on the string, and, in between, every three DNA letters encrypt one of the 20 amino acids, which are the building blocks of proteins. (Hung and Kim 2000)

The genome has been described as a bounded dataset, the idea being that the dataset is the complete universe, rather than a sample (Birney et al. 2002). Automated gene sequencing technologies had developed in the early 1980s enough so that by 1989 the Human Genome Project could be considered a feasible undertaking. In 1995 the first full sequence for a living organism (the bacteria *Haemophilus influenzae*) was completed. In 1998 the first animal (*c. elegans*) was finished. The sequences for many of the model organisms (representative species) have been completed or are in process. The mouse, the fruit fly, the mustard *Arabidopsis thaliana* are all completed.

A press release on April 14, 2003 from the International Human Genome Sequencing Consortium (conveniently 50 years after the publication of Watson and Crick's paper) announced the completion of the human genome. It turns out to be much smaller than the initial estimates, only 21,000 base pairs, less than the puffer fish and only 1,000 base pairs more than the zebra fish. In 2000, at Cold Spring Harbor, the geneticists started a pool (Genesweep) on the number of genes in the human genome. The winner guessed 25,947 (the lowest estimate) and the bets clustered around 60,000. Much has been written about the competing projects, one commercial, one non-profit, and the eventual joint release of the data (Celera Groups 2000).

With many large sequence datasets completed, the research has moved to the next phase. As touched on in the introduction, this sequence of effort is unusual in the life sciences world of hypothesis-driven experiments. In the classical experiment-based process, a scientist generates a hypothesis, devises an experiment, collects data, and analyses those data in order to determine, with some level of statistical confidence, whether the null hypothesis can be rejected. Then one more bit of knowledge enters the discipline. But much of the current data collection runs independent of any experiment driven by any hypothesis. The analysis of these data is referred to as *in silico biology*, or hypothesis free. The former term is considerably less assumptive than the latter. The goal is, as it has always been, to extract significance from the data: an action, a function, a role in a pathway. But the approach must differ from classical methods simply because there is so much data. The only way to extract any sense from them is to apply highly computational approaches.

Life sciences researchers working with sequencing and other biology databases are using computation to identify the significances in each data collection. Their ultimate goal is an understanding of how everything works, at multiple levels of granularity, from the sequence coding a protein, to a protein functioning in a cell, to the cell's role in development, on up to the whole operation of the biological organism. In the case of sequence data, the goal is to identify genes within the sequence string. Once genes are identified the goal is to discover the function of the protein for which the genes code. The goal of microarray experiments is to identify which genes are active at particular times in the life of the organism.

Figure 1 is a string of sequence data from the Human Genome Project as submitted by the Welcome Trust, one of the participant sequencing organizations (Figures 1-5 are partial records from the *Entrez Nucleotide* (GenBank) database of the National Center for Biotechnology Information at http://www.ncbi.nlm.nih.gov/entrez/query.fcgi? db=Nucleotide). The complete sequence runs about 44 pages.

Figure 2 is a portion of a record indicating a computationally driven annotation. Note the layered conditionals in the description in the /product field: 'similar to hypothetical . . . '

Figure 3 is an example of a homology annotation—'similar to vomeronasal receptor V1RC3.' The gene V1RC3 has been identified in the mouse. The underlying theory for this annotation is that of 'conservation,' the annotation connection to the vomeronasal receptor gene identified in the mouse operates "on the principle that functionally linked genes will share common aspects of the contexts in which they occur" (Marcotte and Date 2001).

Figure 4 is the record for the V1RC3 gene in the mouse, which was identified experimentally.

Finally, Figure 5 is a sample of a curated record for a heavily studied gene. People with cystic fibrosis show mutations of this gene. The full record for this gene runs to 26 pages of sequence and literature citations.

As a reminder of the scale of this effort: the *Entrez Nucleotide* database is up to 20 billion of these sorts of entries.

Significant efforts are now being poured into distinguishing the genes from the non-coding sections of the sequence. Ideally an infinite number of laboratories with an infinite number of researchers would identify the genes experimentally. The *GenBank* database would then be a reference manual to each gene and that gene's function. Lacking that infinity of resource, researchers have turned to computational techniques to speed up the process.

Simplistically put, the computational techniques apply inference and induction techniques for the identification of possible genes in a sequence. The technique called *ab-initio* gene prediction uses "the statistical information contained within the genomic sequence to predict gene structures. The information used commonly includes compositional analysis of exons, introns, and splice sites which may vary according to the background composition of the full genomic sequence." Similarity-based comparison alignment involves "taking a protein or a cDNA and aligning it to the genomic sequence" (Birney et al. 2002). This technique could be thought of as a genetic cryptography to distinguish genes from non-genes in the sequence string.

FIGURE 1. Sequence Data from the Human Genome Project

```
LOCUS     AL391099        123083 bp   DNA    linear  PRI 02-APR-2003
DEFINITION  Human DNA sequence from clone RP11-178A10 on chromosome 10,
            complete sequence.
ACCESSION  AL391099
VERSION     AL391099.12  GI:29498303
KEYWORDS   HTG.
SOURCE     Homo sapiens (human)
  ORGANISM  Homo sapiens
            Eukaryota; Metazoa; Chordata; Craniata; Vertebrata; Euteleostomi;
            Mammalia; Eutheria; Primates; Catarrhini; Hominidae; Homo.
REFERENCE   1  (bases 1 to 123083)
  AUTHORS  Whitehead,S.
  TITLE     Direct Submission
  JOURNAL   Submitted (02-APR-2003) Wellcome Trust Sanger Institute, Hinxton,
            Cambridgeshire, CB10 1SA, UK. E-mail enquiries:
            humquery@sanger.ac.uk Clone requests: clonerequest@sanger.ac.uk
COMMENT     On Apr 2, 2003 this sequence version replaced gi:18642360.
            During sequence assembly data is compared from overlapping clones.
            Where differences are found these are annotated ...
FEATURES          Location/Qualifiers
    source        1..123083
                  /organism="Homo sapiens"
                  /mol_type="genomic DNA"
                  /db_xref="taxon:9606"
                  /chromosome="10"
                  /clone="RP11-178A10"
                  /clone_lib="RPCI-11.1"
BASE COUNT    38287 a  24949 c  25232 g  34615 t
ORIGIN
        1 atctaactga taattttgaa gccagttcta tttaccagga attttaaaac atgttttatt
       61 tacaacatat tgtcacatac acatagcaca aacacacaga cagaagcaga ...
```

Source: Nucleotide Database <www.ncbi.nlm.nih.gov/Entrez/index.htm>

FIGURE 2. Computational Annotation

```
    ...
    gene        complement(25938..93111)
                /gene="LOC338575"
                /db_xref="InterimID:338575"
    mRNA        complement(join(25938..27955,29461..29623,38525..38691,
                43080..43199,46878..46913,47920..47987,51016..51116,
                69371..69445,87844..88030,89956..90027,92996..93111))
                /gene="LOC338575"
                /product="similar to hypothetical protein FLJ40432"
                /note="Derived by automated computational analysis using
                gene prediction method: BLAST. Supporting evidence
                includes similarity to: 1 mRNA"
    ...
```

Source: Nucleotide Database <www.ncbi.nlm.nih.gov/Entrez/index.htm>

Alignments take the process one step further. Given a new sequence "rather than using a rule, law or equation to find the function of a protein, a biologist uses the knowledge that a similar sequence has a known function to make a judgment about the function of the new sequence" (Stevens et al. 2000).

FIGURE 3. Homology Annotation

```
...
gene       256377..279440
           /gene="LOC340752"
           /db_xref="InterimID:340752"
mRNA       join(256377..256478,272364..272452,279116..279440)
           /gene="LOC340752"
           /product="similar to vomeronasal receptor V1RC3"
           /note="Derived by automated computational analysis using
           gene prediction method: GenomeScan."
...
```

Source: Nucleotide Database <www.ncbi.nlm.nih.gov/Entrez/index.htm>

FIGURE 4. V1RC3 Gene in the Mouse

```
V1RC3 record
LOCUS      AF291499          900 bp   DNA   linear   ROD 22-DEC-2000
DEFINITION Mus musculus vomeronasal receptor V1RC3 (V1rc3) gene, complete cds.
ACCESSION  AF291499
VERSION    AF291499.1  GI:11967418
KEYWORDS   .
SOURCE     Mus musculus (house mouse)
 ORGANISM  Mus musculus
        Eukaryota; Metazoa; Chordata; Craniata; Vertebrata; Euteleostomi;
        Mammalia; Eutheria; Rodentia; Sciurognathi; Muridae; Murinae; Mus.
REFERENCE  1  (bases 1 to 900)
 AUTHORS   Del Punta, K., Rothman, A., Rodriguez, I. and Mombaerts, P.
 TITLE     Sequence diversity and genomic organization of vomeronasal receptor
        genes in the mouse
 JOURNAL   Genome Res. 10 (12), 1958-1967 (2000)
 MEDLINE   20568485
  PUBMED   11116090
REFERENCE  2  (bases 1 to 900)
 AUTHORS   Del Punta, K., Rothman, A., Rodriguez, I. and Mombaerts, P.
 TITLE     Direct Submission
 JOURNAL   Submitted (31-JUL-2000) The Rockefeller University, 1230 York
        Avenue, New York, NY 10021, USA
FEATURES            Location/Qualifiers
   source        1..900
              /organism="Mus musculus"
              /mol_type="genomic DNA"
              /strain="129/SvJ"
              /db_xref="taxon:10090"
   gene          <1..>900
              /gene="V1rc3"
   mRNA          <1..>900
              /gene="V1rc3"
              /product="vomeronasal receptor V1RC3"
...
PLVQISSDNRIINLLKNLQSKCH"
BASE COUNT     253 a   194 c   165 g   288 t
ORIGIN
     1 atgttctcat tggagaatgc tctttatatc caagctgggt taggagtcct agctaatatg
    61 tgtcttcttg ttttctatat ...
```

Source: Nucleotide Database <www.ncbi.nlm.nih.gov/Entrez/index.htm>

Again there are parallels to data analysis in the social sciences. For example, the work done by marketing firms trying to predict consumer behavior from databases of grocery purchases. They have a large dataset of all grocery purchases, by customer, store by store. Knowing the behavior of Consumer A, they try to extrapolate the behavior of con-

FIGURE 5. Curated Record

```
TITLE    Identification of the cystic fibrosis gene: cloning and
           characterization of complementary DNA
 JOURNAL   Science 245 (4922), 1066-1073 (1989)
 MEDLINE  89368940
 PUBMED   2475911
COMMENT    REVIEWED REFSEQ: This record has been curated by NCBI staff. The
           reference sequence was derived from M28668.1 and M55131.1.
           On Feb 17, 2000 this sequence version replaced gi:4502784.

           Summary: The protein encoded by this gene is a member of the
           superfamily of ATP-binding cassette (ABC) transporters. ABC
           proteins transport various molecules across extra- and
           intra-cellular membranes. ...
           CFTR gene.
           COMPLETENESS: full length.
...
```

Source: Nucleotide Database <www.ncbi.nlm.nih.gov/Entrez/index.htm>

sumer B based on B's similarity (in location and purchasing) to consumer A.

Protein Databases

Drastically simplified, the relation of sequences to proteins is: DNA is transcribed into RNA, then RNA is translated into amino acids that make up a protein. The amino acids are arranged into polypeptide chains that fold (like kinking a wire) into the repeatable structures of protein. To see samples of protein structures, do a Google image search on 'protein structure' or try the "Molecule of the Month" site at the *Protein Data Bank* (*PDB*): www.rcsb.org/pdb/molecules/molecule_list.html. Proteins 'do the bulk of the work' in a cell. Some are static, relatively long, and serve a structural function in the cell. Others are more compact and active, such as enzymes (NCBI 2003c). "Proteins are fundamental components of all living cells. They exhibit an enormous amount of chemical and structural diversity, enabling them to carry out an extraordinarily diverse range of biological functions . . . Identifying a protein's shape, or structure, is key to understanding its biological function and its role in health and disease" (NCBI 2003b).

Just as genomics is an encompassing term for sequence centered research, proteomics is used in a similar fashion for protein research.

Proteomics includes not only the identification and quantification of proteins, but also the determination of their localization, modifications, interactions, activities, and ultimately, their function. . . . Proteins are much more complicated than nucleic acids. Unlike the decoratively challenged DNA, proteins get phosphorylated, glycosylated, acetylated, ubiquitinated, farnesylated, sulphated, linked to glycophosphatidylinositol anchors, and embellished in numerous other ways. A single gene can encode multiple different proteins–these can be produced by alternative splicing of the mRNA transcript, by varying translation start of stop sites, or by frame shifting during which a different set of triplet codons in the mRNA is translated. All of these possibilities result in a proteome estimated to be an order of magnitude more complex than the genome. (Fields 2001)

The goal of proteomics is to know what a protein looks like (its structure) and what it does–its role in the operation of the organism.

As befitting their greater complexity, protein databases are varied, but with fewer records than are currently found in the sequence databases. Figure 6 is an extract from a record from the *Protein Data Bank* at http://www.rcsb.org/pdb/. The full record runs to 61+ pages.

There are databases for skin biology, hearts (human, rat, dog), yeast species and even maritime pine (Wojcik and Schachter 2000). The protein databases have a mix of information, just as the sequence databases. Some of the data are from experimental results; other portions are computer predictions.

The structure of a protein can be determined experimentally using x-ray crystallography or nuclear magnetic resonance spectroscopy. There are also *in silico* approaches. It is possible to predict a protein's structure using the knowledge of its sequence and 'rules' for how proteins fold. The theory underlying the *in silico* work is that "proteins that share a similar sequence generally share the same basic structure." By systematically working on clusters of proteins researchers are working to create a "set of sequences associated with each folding motif" (NCBI 2003b).

In turn, how a protein folds and what its range of motion could be are a clue to what its function might be. Protein A, with a known structure but unknown function, can be compared (computationally) to Proteins B-Z to find Protein N with a similar structure and a known function. Protein A could have a similar function to Protein N. An experiment could then be designed to confirm that prediction. See www.umass.edu/microbio/chime/explorer/morfdoc.htm for samples of animated visualizations of protein structure and movement.

Microarray Databases

As described previously, microarray data capture the expression activities of genes at different times. In the library metaphor on reserve

FIGURE 6. Extract from *Protein Data Bank* Record

```
HEADER        PLASMA PROTEIN
TITLE         HUMAN SERUM ALBUMIN COMPLEXED WITH OCTADECANOIC ACID
TITLE         2 (STEARIC ACID)
COMPND        MOL_ID: 1;
COMPND        2 MOLECULE: SERUM ALBUMIN;
COMPND        3 CHAIN: A;
COMPND        4 ENGINEERED: YES
SOURCE        MOL_ID: 1;
SOURCE        2 ORGANISM_SCIENTIFIC: HOMO SAPIENS;
SOURCE        3 ORGANISM_COMMON: HUMAN;
SOURCE        4 CELLULAR_LOCATION: SERUM;
SOURCE        5 GENE: ALB;
SOURCE        6 EXPRESSION_SYSTEM: SACCHAROMYCES CEREVISIAE
KEYWDS        PLASMA PROTEIN, METAL-BINDING, LIPID-BINDING
EXPDTA        X-DAY DIFFRACTION
AUTHOR        A.A. BHATTACHARYA, T. GRUENE, S. CURRY
REVDAT        1      06-NOV-00 1E71            0
JRNL                 AUTH       A.A. BHATTACHARYA, T. GRUNE, S. CURRY
JRNL                 TITLE      CRYSTALLOGRAPHIC ANALYSIS REVEALS COMMON
MODES OF
JRNL                 TITLE  2   BINDING OF MEDIUM AND LONG-CHAIN FATTY ACIDS TO
JRNL                 TITLE  3   HUMAN SERUM ALBUMIN
JRNL                 REF        J.MOL.BIOL.   V. 303  721  2000
JRNL                 REFN       ASTM JMOBAK  UK ISSN 0022-2836
REMARK        2
REMARK        2 RESOLUTION. 2.7 ANGSTROMS.
...
```

Source: *Protein Data Bank* <www.rcsb.org/pdb

reading processing, they are the snapshots of who was active when. The technology for production microarrays (the so-called 'gene on a chip') was developed about 1997. Microarrays are experimentally generated data, but at a much larger scale than datasets commonly generated in biology, as microarray experiments can produce millions of data points. Initially, the data were collected exclusively for local laboratories, but those efforts were quickly followed by the desire to compare or integrate datasets between labs and institutions. Libraries are familiar with that trajectory, as they may be one of the earliest examples of large scale data sharing. Instead of taking decades for that maturing and the development of standards and shared data, however, the self-organization of the microarray community began within four years of the automation of the technology.

To see examples of microarray slides do a Google image search on that term. The grid of small glowing green to orange to red dots is often used as an iconic image in genomics publicity. Each of those colored spots represents a gene.

"A microarray works by exploiting the ability of a given mRNA molecule to bind specifically to, or hybridize to, the DNA template from which it originated. By using an array containing many DNA samples, scientists can determine, in a single experiment, the expression levels of hundreds or thousands of genes within a cell by measuring the amount of mRNA bound to each site on the array. With the aid of a computer, the amount of mRNA bound to the spots on the microarray is precisely measured, generating a profile of gene expression in the cell" (NCBI 2003a).

The genes are 'spotted' in a systematic grid (thus 'array') on glass slides, silicon chips, or fabric membranes. The technique for some of the spotting machines is a spin-off from ink-jet printers, which gives a sense of how small the spots can be. In 2000 one of the high-end slides cost $1,000; in the spring of 2003 the cost was $350. The number of spots on each array can run into the tens of thousands. Fifty arrays can be run in an experiment, leading to huge datasets. Then, through hybridization probing "a technique that uses fluorescently labeled nucleic acid molecules as 'mobile probes' to identify complementary molecules, sequences that are able to base-pair with one another. . . . The labeled molecules bind to the sites on the array corresponding to the genes expressed in each cell" (NCBI 2003a). Some experiments capture the varying expression levels between spots in one array (Sherlock 2001). Others look at the differences in expression levels between two samples (Slonim 2002).

Expression based inference is the theory underlying microarray work; "the fact that 2 genes are co-expressed under many different conditions allows us to infer that the genes work together in some pathways and therefore have related function" (Marcotte and Date 2001).

A great amount of processing and data cleanup is required in order for the researcher to make the comparisons. The data must be normalized so as to minimize the non-biological variation, then transformed and analyzed to determine the set of genes that are statistically differentially expressed. Then they must be processed so as to create the clusters that indicate the co-expression. This is all designed to highlight potential significances–identifying similar expression patterns as a first step towards answering the question "Is there some real biological meaning behind the clustering?" (Tamames et al. 2002).

As mentioned, microarray datasets are a good illustration of the trend towards data sharing. The data are stored digitally, which makes them easy to transfer. They are all the products of somewhat similar methodologies. There is a base consistency in the technologies used. There is a definite value in seeing data from similar experiments. Researchers are aiming for a variation on meta-analysis, a combined analysis to "allow the parallel, quantitative comparison of the expression levels of almost all translated genes in two RNA samples" (Geschwind 2001). All of these elements lower the barriers to sharing the data. Data sharing will be discussed later.

Literature Databases

With the literature databases, librarians enter familiar territory. The primary literature database used by bioinformatics researchers is *Medline*, usually cited as *PubMed*. But instead of using the database to retrieve specific subsets of articles on a particular subject, or by a specific author, the bioinformatics researchers are using the database as something to be mined in and of itself. Researchers are deriving value from the citations and abstracts alone. One author calls it bibliomics (Uehling 2003a).

Any computationally amenable source of information about genes and gene functions is of interest to bioinformatics researchers. *Medline*, with its over 12 million citations and large abstract text mass, becomes an interesting resource. The entire file can be leased at no charge from the National Library of Medicine www.nlm.nih.gov/databases/leased. html. Researchers are manipulating *Medline* looking for relationships, anything that is shared. They are trying to find commonalities of attributes without knowing the attributes in advance. The existing attributes that organize the database, such as journal title, publication year, and pagination, are of secondary interest.

Three examples of text mining are: literature associations, shared references, and commonalities in entities.

Literature associations. In one example of this type of text mining, researchers looked at literature associations using the abstracts in *Medline* to identify co-mention of genes. Their method was "based on the assumption that if two genes are co-mentioned in a *Medline* record there is an underlying biological relationship" (Jenssen et al. 2001). This analysis required the creation of automated ways to identify 'biomedical nouns' and 'noun phrases' in order to determine if the use of a gene name could qualify as a 'co-mention.' Jenssen and colleagues mention the difficulties in processing natural language, as well as in quantifying changing biological terminology. They admit that it is unreasonable to expect scientists in different fields to adhere to naming standards, and demur that perfect precision and recall "is presently beyond our reach." Their research also acknowledged the need for 'ground truthing,' and they describe how they did a manual verification

of their core assumption (co-mention correlating to biological relationships) as part of the project.

Shared references. Another technique familiar to those who have
worked with some of the Institute of Scientific Information's bibliometric products is the identification of possible significances through
shared references. By looking at citations held in common across articles, the researchers hoped to avoid the problems in natural language in-
consistencies that text mining (such as in the previous research) must
overcome.

As they argue: "By relating documents talking about well understood
genes to documents discussing other genes, we can predict, detect and
explain the functional relationship among the many genes involved in
experiments." For each 'well understood gene' they identify a single
abstract, a 'kernel abstract for the gene.' They use a 'theme finding algorithm' to identify a body of related literature that clusters around that
kernel abstract. Then they perform an automated comparison within
that body of abstracts to 'derive functional relationships among the
genes.' Essentially, they are sorting genes into categories that may be
related to biological functions. "Our primary assumption is that common relevant literature strongly indicates common functionality among
genes. That is, genes that have similar lists of top-ranking documents
associated with them share some common biological function described
in the common literature" (Shatkay et al. 2002).

Common entities. This form of data mining consists of trying to discover commonalities in free text. It is another form of natural language
processing where researchers look speculatively "for common properties of entities belonging to different species" (Dicks 2000). They attempt to identify "groups of genes that are functionally coherent in
multiple organisms" (Raychaudhuri and Altman 2003). This form of
text mining relies on the functions of the genes being included in the
text, and in such a way that the machine algorithm can overcome variability in the way that function is described. It requires processing the
text to make sense of the terminology, then relating the terms to each
other, and then extracting ideas and concepts from the text (Yandell
and Majoros 2002). The goal of such an approach is to highlight areas
of interest out of the masses of data. They are "useful primarily as
tools of intellectual exploration and browsing, and not as comprehensive or definitive tools for global characterization of expression results" (Masys 2001).

Here again, the frustration with natural language processing is
voiced. Raychaudhuri and Altman (2003) write of the challenge of

"compensating for the great disparities in biological literature." Park (2002) referring to the *PubMed* database, goes so far as to complain: "This form's main problem is that the signal to noise ratio is poor owing to massively irrelevant and confusing text bodies."

In some cases, one wonders if the researchers doing text mining understand the *Medline* database, how it is created, and how it has changed over time. However, the way they are using the citations and abstracts as free text allows for significant levels of fuzziness without compromising the productivity of their approach.

DATA MINING AND MANIPULATION

Approaches

Current activities are in a chaotic phase. The ability of researchers to collect data outstrips the availability of techniques to analyze them. Bioinformatics researchers looking at the citation literature, at sequences, and at gene expression are trying to reduce the amount of data in an intelligent way so as to bubble up 'interesting data' that can then drive experiments. Researchers are trying to create high-level overviews of the data, "ideally in ways that impart additional information about its structure" (Slonim 2002). Several examples of this *dry* work of computational *in silico* data mining have been presented. The results of those efforts are intended to focus the subsequent work of the *wet* laboratory experiments.

Bioinformaticians are inventing techniques for data analysis. They are creating so many approaches to data analysis that the scene is reminiscent of the Wild West. There are multiple approaches to the same goals. The literature is full of articles describing new and better algorithms for data mining. Authors rarely cite anything outside of the field, and sometimes cite comparable approaches, even though much of the analysis (at least superficially) has parallels to data analysis in other domains. Most likely, a settling period will follow just as sequence comparisons have settled around some quasi-standard tools such as BLAST.

Meanwhile, authors jostle and engage in subtle salesmanship for their approach. In the proof-of-concept papers, phrases such as 'the advantage of,' 'a novel computational method,' and 'unlike other literature-based tools, the work we present here' appear (Shatkay et al. 2002; Raychaudhuri and Altman 2003; Raychaudhuri et al. 2000).

Occasionally, the frustration of the computational scientist at "the boundless chaos of a living speech" (Johnson 1773) will emerge as complaints about the imprecision of the terminology used by biologists, or in calls for standardization, usually to a format that would best suit the author's project. The most pragmatic papers recognize the inherent intractability of language and attempt to work around its variability. They tend to be papers that are jointly authored by researchers coming from the computational and biological domains.

Attempts to tame language aside, all the creativity and ingenuity pouring into this field has clearly transferable benefits to other information retrieval and database management arenas, making these developments even more interesting to librarians and information scientists in general.

Most of the approaches sort into some basic data reduction technique: classification, regression, clustering, association analysis, or alignment. Each technique requires identifying the information to be used in the analysis: the *Medline* database, or some subset; a portion of the sequence database; a set of microarrays. That identification is subject to the usual problem of precision/recall, or specificity/sensitivity– as some authors phrase it. Each technique addresses the minimization of that problem. Then that selected text must somehow be made amenable to computational manipulation. Yandell and Majoros (2002) described the challenge in terms of the *Medline* database at the time they worked with it: 11,450,302 abstracts, 1,130,223,622 words, 1,614,538 of them distinct. Only after that preparation can ideas and concepts be extracted from the text.

Some of the techniques are 'unsupervised,' meaning they rely on purely computational calculations to perform dimension reductions or clustering. Other techniques are primed, the so-called supervised methods that start from some known element or concept. An example would be the technique of identifying a 'kernel' abstract for a gene that then is used to identify a body of citations relating to the gene (Shatkay et al. 2002).

Some of the approaches are more complex. They combine separate manipulations into interlocking or mutually supporting combinations. Wu et al. (2002) describe a project involving the yeast database that is based on five different aspects of data relationships: physical association, genetic interaction, sequence relationships, sequence conservation, and patterns of gene expression.

All of the articles introducing techniques acknowledge the need for validation. In some cases, each approach is validated by comparing it against known results. For example, if it is an automated annotation technique, the researcher will strip the known annotations out of a dataset. They use their algorithm to create a set of annotations, then compare the results to the original annotations. In other cases, researchers are relying on the collective evaluative power of their colleagues. One article simply says: "Such links must be validated by the international research community" (Dicks 2000). Phrases like 'we rely on the fact,' 'the method is based on the assumption,' 'our primary assumptions' still abound in this world.

As bioinformatics approaches proliferate and the field matures, the question of validity will be answered in some form or another. Articles addressing these questions appear sporadically and will likely increase. Karp et al. (2001) describe the 'empirical study' of databases as "a new subfield of bioinformatics analysis that we call database verification." In the early days of statistical software packages, a statistician at Cornell presented the results of a series of benchmark tests on several programs. One program successfully divided zero into a number. Another program presented a calculation that was several degrees more precise than was justified by the data. Parallel assessments of the validity of the current crop of algorithmic approaches will need to be developed and applied in the -omics (genomics, proteomics, bibliomics) world.

Questions such as the following need to be asked. Compared to other approaches making the same claim, what is the quality of a particular data clustering or mining approach? Does the approach even do what it claims to do? Does the algorithm in the approach incorporate the theory adequately? Is the algorithm valid for the theory it assumes? Is the theory valid, given the data to which it is being applied? Do the data justify the inference being used on them?

Researchers will develop increasingly sophisticated computational methods that should compensate somewhat for heterogeneous data, and additional calculations for confidence measures are likely to develop as the bioinformatics field matures. But conclusions will still be only as reliable as the weakest data. Perhaps, eventually, certain clustering will 'win' and become the de facto standard manipulation for a particular function. Over time, that algorithm could be incorporated into the commonly used software and become invisible to users. At a simplistic level, the concept of a mean in linear statistics, and how it is calculated, and the embedding of that calculation into spreadsheet and statistical software packages is an example of this transition. It could be envisioned as an *in silica* recapitulation of evolutionary survival–the survival of the most efficient, most predictive/productive algorithmic approach.

Information Issues

It is time to step back and look at the databases collectively, almost decoupled from their content. This collective vantage point is a natural one for librarians, as they are the 'collectors,' and the social and economic issues that shape the growth of biology databases will, in turn, shape the scope of their involvement. Viewing the databases collectively allows librarians to see their parallels and differences when compared to the databases they are more familiar with. Some of the interesting (from a librarians' view) aspects of this arena are now discussed.

Databasing of information. A database could be considered the technological response to Johnson's 'boundless chaos' problem. "A database is a collection of electronic information or records organized, stored, and updated for the sole purpose of providing information. In this sense the computerized record of the human genome has become a database, and an online encyclopedia or dictionary is considered a database" (University of Chicago Press 2003). Within such a definition almost everything could be coded into a database. In the current world of computational biology, almost everything is.

The power of a database is in its consistency across a body of records. That consistency permits the retrieval of subsets, or sorting or clustering the data, based on specified criteria. A database enables the generation of new theories through the reorganization of its data, based on criteria other than how the database is stored. The *Medline* database stores data by author, title, abstract, source, and keywords. Researchers are extracting gene function by analyzing the text of the abstracts for particular patterns in the mention of genes and functions. That information is not coded into the database, it is in the *reorganization* of the text of the abstracts that the information about gene functions is elicited. No matter how large or small, or complex or simple the database may be, there still needs to be a consistency within the database so an operation on the data it contains will behave reliably.

Database heterogeneity. One approach to supporting consistency in a database has been the creation of the role of 'curator.' Examining the job descriptions of curators, one realizes that the term is an excellent one for the role. A database curator could be defined as the person responsible for the quality and integrity of the database. They ensure data are 'clean,' add records to the database, and maintain the database overall. Curators are also responsible for annotating the entries, and adding additional information about the entry entity (a protein or a gene) from the literature.

However, authorship varies wildly. The data records in a database can be from single experiments or from bulk sequencing or other highly automated technologies. Other records, or elements of a record, can be inferred, or summary annotations, or computationally generated annotations. Records can come from a few institutions or individuals in a research team, or anyone who fills in a data submission form.

There can be variability over time in how terms are used, even at the individual laboratory level (Jenssen et al. 2001). At the individual database level it would be possible to back correct the database. But there is still the problem of 'correcting' the information in other databases that derived information using the uncorrected terms. All sorts of things can go awry. Sequence errors, incomplete sequences, missing genes, or the wrong close match are examples of annotation limitations (Birney et al. 2002).

This variation has implications for the quality of any given database and thus any information produced from it. Wittig and Beuckelar (2001) call it the 'heterogeneity problem.' Errors can build and cumulate, or they can submerge under the countervailing weight of accurate data. Knowledgeable users working with adequate interfaces can select the types of data records they want to rely on. As the field of users expands, other users may not be as aware of these considerations of integrity. A quote from an article on taxonomic databases has equal relevance here. "Quality is an issue when releasing error-ridden data sets to point-and-click users who have little familiarity with the biases and errors in collection" (Winker 1999). Articles occasionally address the issues in data integrity (Brenner 1999; Pennisi 1999; Tsoka et al. 1999). At this time it is very much 'user beware.'

Database complexity. Yet another interesting aspect of these databases is their complexity. Many of the biology databases are at the *Chemical Abstracts*, and higher, level of specificity and sophistication. For example, the *Protein Data Bank* (*PDB*) is a combination of record types and entries. There are almost 50 record types including: CAVEAT "Severe error indicator. Entries with this record must be used with care." and CISPEP "Identification of peptide residues in cis conformation." As the *PDB* example demonstrates, the structure of each database and the individual records are customized to the discipline and the types of data. In the *PDB*, a researcher can retrieve a protein and then start up a 'viewer' to look at a color-animated model of that protein's structure.

Another aspect of database complexity is that most of the databases were born networked and born integrated. As mentioned before, databases cover the spectrum from those created and designed for use by one individual to those that were created by large consortiums and designed for use by thousands of students and researchers across the globe. With the easy availability of the network, and the option to make data accessible to a selected or unlimited group, most of the databases are advertised as available to all interested users. Some of these 'public' databases are quite idiosyncratic. Their interfaces approach the cryptic and assume users know exactly what they are looking for. Other interfaces acknowledge novice users.

With the availability of the open database comes the expectation that there will be interoperability between and amongst all of this networked information. The *Entrez* suite of resources from the National Center for Biotechnology Information (NCBI) is an example of interoperability. There are over 25 databases in the *Entrez* suite. Many of them were developed independently, but they all 'talk' to each other. This cross referencing capability is being developed for many of the large databases across publishers. The *GenBank* accession number is like the ISBN of the sequence world. Because most of the databases are freely accessible, database designers can be ambitious and generous about cross linking. The NCBI provides extensive instructions on how to link to the *Entrez* databases at: http://www.ncbi.nlm.nih.gov/entrez/query/static/linking.html.

Local vs. global databases. The final issue is the dichotomy of local to global, individual to community, or independence to standards. A defining characteristic of this arena is the speed of collection of huge amounts of data. In turn, the amount of data is driving the development of new technologies for data mining that work best when there are computational consistencies. Database creators are juggling their local needs against the community's needs. The development and adherence to consistencies requires additional work from each researcher working with a database. In addition to causing additional work for a researcher, consistency and standards can be barriers to individual creativity. The fields are growing and moving so rapidly that it is a real challenge to balance the two needs. A failure to exchange data would slow the field as a whole, while too many requirements for standardization could result in a premature 'normalization' which could hamper individual insights.

It is an interesting illustration of community to watch how these differing needs are playing out in the -omics world. The rapid growth of these databases within an entirely digital speed-of-electron-world has accelerated the process when compared to the development of standards in other research worlds. The -omicists have been able to skip the warehouse phase, best illustrated by looking at social science data in the 1970s. One of the reasons for the formation of the InterUniversity Consortium for Political and Social Research (ICPSR) was to enhance access to large social science datasets such as the Census of Population and Housing, and the various public opinion polls (Gallup, Roper, and NORC). The datasets were all housed at the University of Michigan, then duplicated and distributed on computer tapes to member institutions. The formation of the ICPSR structure took years. In contrast, the development of standards in the microarray community happened within four years of the publication of the core paper on the technology.

Database standards. The standards being discussed are familiar to most information specialists: data formats for interoperability, metadata, documentation, vocabulary, and sustainability. The interoperability discussions center around using more general format standards such as XML. The metadata development is still idiosyncratic. The microarray community is developing the MIAME (Minimum Information About a Microarray Experiment) standard: http://www.mged.org.

Documentation includes not only the broad documentation of how a database is defined, the fields, and the technical specifications of the database, but also documentation about individual records, how they have been changed, revised, annotated, or added to. Documentation is an emerging issue as researchers are starting to consider data quality. The desire for data quality is a first step towards the recognition that documentation matters. The Federal government has enacted data quality standards for Agency data. In October 2002 the Data Quality Act went into effect. From the reprint of February 22, 2002 in the *Federal Register*, subtitled *Guidelines for ensuring and maximizing the quality, objectivity, utility, and integrity of information disseminated by Federal agencies*:

> If an agency is responsible for disseminating influential scientific, financial, or statistical information, agency guidelines shall include a high degree of transparency about data and methods to facilitate the reproducibility of such information by qualified third

parties. . . . Each agency is authorized to define the type of robustness checks, and the level of detail for documentation thereof, in ways appropriate for it given the nature and multiplicity of issues for which the agency is responsible. (Office of Management and Budget 2002)

The pharmaceutical industry may be an early adopter, as their issues of data quality could have economic consequences. The FDA rejected a new drug application because of "deficiencies in 'data quality'" on the part of the submitting drug company (Uehling 2003b). Uehling goes on to posit "Section 515 [the Data Quality Act] may let Drug Company A challenge the data quality in any FDA publication based on information supplied by Drug Company B." Essentially, any drug company submitting data for FDA approval could find that data held to the same quality standards as for the Federal Agencies.

At a broader level, all researchers are concerned with the quality of the data they are using, as it affects the usefulness of the data. Referring to errors in gene annotations, Brenner (1999) notes "Subsequent searches against these databases then cause errors to propagate to future functional assignment. The procedure need cycle only a few times without corrections before the resources that made computational function determination possible–the annotation databases–are so polluted as to be almost useless." Tsoka et al. (1999) address the reproducibility issue: "Computational analysis of genome sequences is still largely an imprecise process and occasionally non-reproducible . . . The end result today is a vast collection of genome sequence annotations by various groups . . . that may be conflicting or inconsistent and usually impossible to compare." No doubt, as the field matures, documentation standards and tools will be developed and adopted.

The activity in vocabulary standardization further illustrates the tension between individual creativity and computational discovery. Computational approaches are possible only if the data are consistent, reliable and discrete elements. But humans converse in a language that is fuzzy and inconsistent. Furthermore, language, rhetoric, and syntax are idiosyncratic to the concepts and communication needs of a discipline. The jargon of the geologist is different from that of the horticulturist, even though they both use the term 'bedded.' The language of a discipline changes over time as the field matures, or is supplanted, or subdivides as specialties become distinct enough to be considered a separate discipline.

Even the organizing term used for this activity is an example of jargon. Researchers have adopted the term 'ontology.' It is a far stretch from the dictionary definition of ontology as: "The branch of metaphysics that studies the nature of existence or being as such" (Random House 1998).

An ontology in the -omics world is: "the concrete form of a conceptualization of a community's knowledge of a domain" (Stevens et al. 2000), "a classification methodology for formalizing a subject's knowledge in a structured way (typically for consumption by an electronic database)" . . . [For ontology-based terms] "their placement reflects the known or putative biological association" (Plant Ontology Consortium 2002), "the formalized specification of knowledge in a certain subject" (Xie et al. 2002), and "the specification of a conceptualization that can be computable . . . Ontologies are particularly beneficial because they compel the scientists to clarify the domains' semantics. . . . A formal ontology enforces the restriction of ambiguity in concept definitions" (Bernardi et al. 2002).

As a tenuous link to the original definition, ontology is being used in a way that clearly recognizes that theories drive classification and categorization schemes. Terms and relationships defined in an ontology are 'specifications' of the concepts and theories of a discipline. The quoted definitions also illustrate the individual versus community tension. Phrases such as 'compel the scientists' and 'enforces the restriction' evoke a martial approach to conformity.

In addition to concepts being constrained by formalization, there are additional challenges facing the efforts to 'formalize concepts.' Where does the ontology set the boundaries of the discipline to be 'specified'? If the goal is to expand an ontology, how can it change in response to additional disciplines? When plant scientists started working with the Gene Ontology (GO) they encountered a form of discipline provincialism. The concept of 'light sensitivity' sat in the hierarchy under the heading Vision. The Gene Ontology was developed by animal researchers.

The specification of concepts is the goal of an ontology. But if concepts are theory-based the specification will be very complex. While not a biological example, the potential diversity can be illustrated prosaically: hot oatmeal and cold pizza could fall within different people's concept of breakfast. Theories of what constitutes a first meal of the day vary considerably.

But perhaps the dangers of conformity are moot. The ontology effort will be an additional activity to that of the individual researchers. Individual researchers will still generate their articles or data as needed. The database curators and automated annotation efforts will construct and support the ontologies, much as catalogers use LCSH and *Medline* indexers assign MESH headings. Bioinformaticists will use the full text, or abstracts, or controlled vocabularies as appropriate.

Librarians' Roles

Visitors and travelers, librarians do well creating systems, structures, and services for the non expert–the student coming to a discipline or the researcher crossing boundaries to a new subject. Librarians take a comprehensive view of information, looking at the resources collectively. For most individuals, information is the single volume or database of direct use to them. Librarians see the forest and the trees, the library and the volumes. In the proliferation of biology databases there are unique roles for librarians, some that benefit the scientists that created them, and some that benefit other patrons.

The core role of a librarian is to know about the databases and the finding aids, and to help make them available. Presently, aside from the *Nucleic Acids Database* and lists at sites such as the NCBI, users are finding databases by word of mouth and happenstance. Archiving and preservation are still over the horizon. As the commercial issues of precedence and intellectual property ownership increase, methods of establishing history will have to be developed.

Librarians can be involved more deeply in this world. They have the skills to do so, and their primary interest is in the information as it permeates the scientific process. The researcher and student are primarily interested in the experimentation and processes of discovery and invention that generate new information. Librarians focus on the information first, rather than the problems it helps answer. They know about databases in their context: the social elements of how people use data systems and the political and economic elements of how databases are created and preserved.

It would be to everyone's advantage if librarians participated in building the information infrastructure of the -omics world. They could make contributions to the organization and interoperability of the resources that would ensure the information is integrated into existing structures. In turn, they would be able to help the increasingly widening audience for these databases.

In addition to helping the audiences for biology databases, librarians could be availing themselves of the informatics expertise of the people creating and manipulating these databases. The spin-off potential might rival the technologies generated from the 'space race.' The accomplishments of computer scientists are outright intriguing, both in the 'reach' of their attempts, and in the potential of their results. Hours of FTE are being expended in bioinformatics information manipulation. Some of these algorithms may turn out to be ineffectual for their original purpose, but wonderful for some other information application. The emerging strategies for mining the *Medline* database for genomics correlations (Uehling 2003a) might have transferability to other databases and other correlations. Perhaps what would be useful is an index of algorithms, a catalog of available routines with descriptions of types of data for which they are suited. Eventually these informatics routines might approach the structure and rigor of statistical procedures. If one has data of type X, the data mining algorithms X2 will reveal correlations of type Z.

Library systems for patrons in bioinformatics as well as other disciplines could benefit. Looking at the work in bioinformatics could bring a new source of creativity to our endeavors.

NOTE

1. See the PRIZM product from Claritas (www.claritas.com) for an example of consumer data mining.

REFERENCES

Bernardi, L., E. Ratsche, R. Kania, J. Saric and I. Rojas. 2002. Interdisciplinary work: The key to functional genomics. *IEEE Intelligent Systems* 17(3): 66-68.

Birney, E., M. Clamp and T. Hubbard. 2002. Databases and tools for browsing genomes. *Annual Review of Genomics and Human Genetics* 3: 293-310.

Blaschke, C. and A. Valencia. 2002. Molecular biology nomenclature thwarts information-extraction progress. *IEEE Intelligent Systems* 17(3): 73-76.

Branca, M. 2003. Putting gene arrays to the test. *Science* 300(11 April): 238.

Brenner, S. E. 1999. Errors in genome annotation. *TIG* 15(4): 132-133.

Celera Genomics. 2000. Celera Genomics: Groups Deny They are Racing. *Biotech Week* 5(July):18-19.

Dicks, J. 2000. Plant genome databases: From references to inference tools. *Briefings in Bioinformatics* 1(2): 138-150.

Fields, S. 2001. Proteomics in genomeland. *Science* 291(5507): 1221-1224.

Frazier, M. E., G. M. Johnson, D. G. Thomassen, C. E. Oliver and A. Patrinos. 2003. Realizing the potential of the genome revolution: The Genomes to Life Program. *Science* 300 (5617): 290-293.

Gabriel, J. 2002. Sensing trouble. *Cornell Engineering Magazine* 8 (1): 1.

Gardiner-Garden, M. and T. G. Littlejohn. 2001. A comparison of microarray databases. *Briefings in Bioinformatics* 2(2): 143-158.

Genbank. 2003. NCBI-GenBank Flat File Release 138.0. ftp://ftp.ncbi.nih.gov/genbank/gbrel.txt.

Geschwind, D. H. 2001. Sharing gene expression data: An array of options. *Nature Reviews Neuroscience* 2(6): 435-438.

Hung, L. W. and S. H. Kim. 2000. Genome, proteome, and the quest for a full structure-function description of an organism. *Nature Encyclopedia of Life Sciences*. London: Nature Publishing Group. http://www.els.net/ [doi:10.1038/npg.els.0003024].

Jenssen, T. K., A. Laegried, J. Kmorowski and E. Hovig. 2001. A literature network of human genes for high-throughput analysis of gene expression. *Nature Genetics* 28(1): 21-28.

Johnson, S. 1773. Preface to the English Dictionary. *Johnson Prose and Poetry*. Cambridge, MA: Harvard University Press: 302-323.

Karp, P. D., S. Paley and J. Zhu. 2001. Database verification studies of SWISS-PROT and GenBank. *Bioinformatics* 17(6): 526-532.

Law, A. S. and A. L. Archibald. 2000. Farm animal genome databases. *Briefings in Bioinformatics* 1(2): 151-160.

Lin, D. 2003. *Various Stuff About Microarrays*, Ithaca, NY: Cornell Computational Biology Service Unit.

Marcotte, E. M. and S. V. Date. 2001. Exploiting big biology: Integrating large-scale biological data for function inference. *Briefings in Bioinformatics* 2(4): 363-374.

Masys, D. R. 2001. Linking microarray data to the literature. *Nature Genetics* 28(1): 9-10.

National Center for Biotechnology Information. 2003. PubMed Overview. http://www.ncbi.nlm.nih.gov/entrez/query/static/overview.html.

NCBI 2003a. Microarrays: Chipping away at the mysteries of science and medicine. http://www.ncbi.nlm.nih.gov/About/primer/microarrays.html.

NCBI 2003b. Molecular modeling: A method for unraveling protein structure and function. www.ncbi.nlm.nih.gov/About/primer/molecularmod.html.

NCBI 2003c. What is a genome? http://www.ncbi.nlm.nih.gov/About/primer/genetics_genome.html.

Office of Management and Budget. 2002. Guidelines for ensuring and maximizing the quality, objectivity, utility, and integrity of information disseminated by Federal Agencies; Notice; Republication. *Federal Register* 67(36): 8451-8460.

Park, J. H. 2002. Network biology: Data mining biological networks. *IEEE Intelligent Systems* 17(3): 68-70.

Pennisi, E. 1999. Keeping genome database clean and up to date. *Science* 268(5439): 447-450.

Plant Ontology Consortium. 2002. Plant Ontology Consortium and plant ontology. *Comparative and Functional Genomics* 3(2): 137-142.

Random House. 1998. *Random House Webster's Unabridged Dictionary*. New York: Random House.

Raychaudhuri, S. and R. B. Altman. 2003. A literature-based method for assessing the functional coherence of a gene group. *Bioinformatics* 19(3): 1-6.

Raychaudhuri, S., P. D. Sutphin, J. M. Stuart and R. B. Altman. 2000. CLEAVER: Analyzing microarray data using known biological categories. http://www-smi.stanford. edu/pubs/SMI_Reports/SMI-2000-0839.pdf.

Research Collaboratory for Structural Bioinformatics. 2002. PDB Protein Data Bank Annual Report. http://www.rcsb.org/pdb/annual_report02.pdf.

Schonbach, C. 2000. Data warehousing in molecular biology. *Briefings in Bioinformatics* 1(2): 190-198.

Shatkay, H., S. Edwards and M. Boguski. 2002. Information retrieval meets gene analysis. *IEEE Intelligent Systems* 17(2): 45-53.

Sherlock, G. 2001. Analysis of large-scale gene expression data. *Briefings in Bioinformatics* 2(4): 350-362.

Slonim, D. K. 2002. From patterns to pathways: Gene expression data analysis comes of age. *Nature Genetics* 32(Supplement): 502-508.

Stevens, R., C. A. Goble and S. Bechhofer. 2000. Ontology-based knowledge representation for bioinformatics. *Briefings in Bioinformatics* 1(4): 398-414.

Tamames, J., D. Clark, J. Herrero, J. Dopazo, C. Blaschke, J. M. Fernandez, J. C. Oliveros and A. Valencia. 2002. Bioinformatics methods for the analysis of expression arrays: Data clustering and information extraction. *Journal of Biotechnology* 98(2-3): 269-283.

Tsoka, S., V. Promponas and C. A. Ouzounis. 1999. Reproducibility in genome sequence annotation: The *Plasmodium falciparum* chromosome 2 case. *FEBS Letters* 451(3): 354-355.

Uehling, M. D. 2003a. Digging into digital quarries. *Bio-IT World* (October 2003): 38-42.

Uehling, M. D. 2003b. Is data quality really job 1? *Bio-IT World* (February 2003): 11.

University of Chicago Press. 2003. *The Chicago Manual of Style*, 15th ed. Chicago: University of Chicago Press.

Winker, K. 1999. How to bring collections data into the net. *Nature* 401(7 October): 524.

Wittig, U. and A. Beuckelar. 2001. Analysis and comparison of metabolic pathway databases. *Briefings in Bioinformatics* 2(2): 126-142.

Wojcik, J. and V. Schachter. 2000. Proteomic databases and software on the Web. *Briefings in Bioinformatics* 1(3): 250-59.

Wu, L. F., T. R. Hughes, A. P. Davierwala, M. D. Robinson, R. Stoughton and S. J. Altschuler. 2002. Large-scale prediction of *Saccharomyces cerevisiae* gene function using overlapping transcriptional clusters. *Nature Genetics* 31(3): 255-265.

Xie, H., A. Wasserman, Z. Levine, A. Novik, V. Grebinskiy, A. Shoshan and L. Mintz. 2002. Large-scale protein annotation through Gene Ontology. *Genome Research* 12(5): 785-794.

Yandell, M. D. and W. H. Majoros. 2002. Genomics and natural language processing. *Nature Reviews Genetics* 3(8): 601-610.

Map and Spatial Data Acquisitions
in the Electronic Age

Joanne M. Perry

SUMMARY. Acquiring cartographic information has historically been complicated and time-consuming, but the Internet has provided librarians with a more efficient way to acquire these materials. Not only can cartographic materials be searched and ordered electronically, speeding the actual acquisitions process, but digital data as well as rare materials, that may or may not be for sale, can also be viewed, printed, or downloaded for research use. While many materials may be downloaded directly by users, circumventing the library altogether, identifying Web sites with cartographic materials remains a task that can be frustrating to those who do not have experience doing so. This paper discusses the changes in the cartographic acquisitions process and includes selected Web addresses and searching suggestions. *[Article copies available for a fee from The Haworth Document Delivery Service: 1-800-HAWORTH. E-mail address: <docdelivery@haworthpress.com> Website: <http://www.HaworthPress.com> © 2004 by The Haworth Press, Inc. All rights reserved.]*

KEYWORDS. Library acquisitions, maps, atlases, digital databases

Joanne M. Perry, MSLS, MA (Geography), is Maps Librarian and Head of Cartographic Information Services, University Libraries, The Pennsylvania State University, 001 Paterno Library, University Park, PA 16802-1807.

[Haworth co-indexing entry note]: "Map and Spatial Data Acquisitions in the Electronic Age." Perry, Joanne M. Co-published simultaneously in *Science & Technology Libraries* (The Haworth Information Press, an imprint of The Haworth Press, Inc.) Vol. 25, No. 1/2, 2004, pp. 171-184; and: *Emerging Issues in the Electronic Environment: Challenges for Librarians and Researchers in the Sciences* (ed: Jeannie P. Miller) The Haworth Information Press, an imprint of The Haworth Press, Inc., 2004, pp. 171-184. Single or multiple copies of this article are available for a fee from The Haworth Document Delivery Service [1-800-HAWORTH, 9:00 a.m. - 5:00 p.m. (EST). E-mail address: docdelivery@haworthpress.com].

Digital Object Identifier: 10.1300/J122v25n01_11

INTRODUCTION

Integral to many science disciplines, maps and other cartographic materials are frequently found in science and technology libraries. While these collections are often allied with the Government Documents Units or Social Sciences Departments, and many people automatically associate geography with history, nearly every discipline that does field work and has an interest in the locations of its variables will find maps and other cartographic materials of great value. In the past, however, acquiring maps was a time-consuming process, and acquisitions departments often felt at a disadvantage when trying to identify for purchase those items which had been requested by librarians and patrons.

Acquisitions departments may lack guidelines for locating cartographic materials or have few catalogs from map producers or other providers and, if there is not a geography or map specialist as part of the staff, may only have very generalized knowledge regarding how to locate cartographic materials. Even libraries with relatively large map collections might not have a formal work flow for map acquisitions if they depend upon government document depository agreements to provide maps for their collection.

The tools and strategies for identifying and acquiring maps and other cartographic materials are not fundamentally different than for acquiring books, but the process often seems overly complicated because those responsible for locating the requested items are often unfamiliar with the array of options available to them. Additionally, between the time an item is requested and received, there are a number of incremental steps that need to be accomplished in a systematic manner or the process will not be successfully completed.

While the electronic age of acquisitions, supported by the development of the Internet and Web services, has not made map acquisition easy, it has provided more tools and enabled librarians to identify cartographic materials more completely when requesting their purchase.

ACQUIRING MATERIALS, THEN AND NOW

Acquiring maps and cartographic materials in the pre-Internet age took time–most of it spent waiting for information to be received so that orders could be sent out. Publishers (commercial companies, government agencies, non-governmental organizations) had to be identified and their publication lists or catalogs acquired before purchase orders could be submitted by mail or by telephone. Often the items ordered were found to be out-of-print or, if received, not as expected or desired because the descriptions in the catalogs were erroneous or incomplete. Items might need to be returned and the process undertaken again before satisfying the librarian's original request. Additionally, identifying producers and dealers of specialty items, such as globes, aerial photographs, and raised relief maps, was often equally elusive and frustrating.

Certainly atlas orders worked more smoothly, as they were more likely to be reviewed in the literature or be listed in *Books In Print*, thus making them easier to identify. However, it must be noted that not everything referred to as an atlas fits the general understanding of a bound book of maps with some accompanying text. Still, without a robust bibliographic inventory method, similar to *Books In Print*, finding maps meant many inquiry letters sent to many publishers. Although Kenneth Winch published *International Maps & Atlases In Print* in 1974, with a 1976 revision, it could not be comprehensive for all commercial publishers, jurisdictions, and topics. Similarly, the more recent and expansive *World Mapping Today* by Parry and Perkins is currently the most comprehensive guide to topographic and geologic series and agency Web addresses, but is obviously unable to cite every map available at the time of publication, neither in 1987 nor 2000 (2nd ed.).

The Internet environment has changed the way maps and cartographic materials can be acquired, as many commercial publishers, dealers, government agencies, and non-governmental agencies (NGOs) now provide Web sites that include their publication lists or catalogs (see Appendix). Compared to paper catalogs, which are expensive to produce and mail, these Web catalogs are likely to be more up-to-date regarding out-of-print materials and may include thumbnail graphics of the items available for purchase. While full and proper bibliographic information is still highly variable, having a visual sample of the item is often enough to verify whether or not the piece is as wanted. Additionally, many publishers and dealers have sites that provide for direct ordering via purchase order or credit card, and shipping availability may be immediately known. Naturally, each library has its own acquisitions policy and work flow for online ordering but, at least, the time it takes to identify an item and locate a provider has been shortened.

CARTOGRAPHIC MATERIALS

Atlases

Atlas publications, the most well-known of cartographic materials, are the easiest to identify and purchase. While subject-oriented atlases might prove slightly more obscure, the ability to search online catalogs and online reference/catalog databases, such as *RLIN* and *WorldCat*, using the International Standard Book Number (ISBN) makes identifying materials quick and accurate. Certainly every librarian or acquisitions staff member who has struggled with generic, variant, or garbled titles (e.g., *World Atlas*, or *National Geographic Atlas of World History*) has been relieved to use an ISBN to speed the identification process.

Searching *GlobalBooksInPrint.com* (the newly expanded and electronic *Books In Print*) or *WorldCat*, both of which are library subscription databases, by ISBN, title, author, or subject, is an efficient way to identify the existence of particular atlases as well as noting atlas publishers. Subsequent searching of these publishers on the Web is often useful as their Web sites may provide extensive descriptions of their publications, as well as a direct ordering mechanism or information referring to other vendors.

Using commercial Internet resources is as easy for librarians as for the general public. For currently available atlases, certainly the more general ones, Amazon.com and BarnesandNoble.com are able to provide titles, often at a discount and in a relatively short time. Alibris.com is also an excellent site for atlases, contemporary or historical, since it has an out-of-print side to its business, as does Amazon and Barnes & Noble. Other useful as well as interesting sites are AddAll.com, Abebooks.com, and eBay.com. AddAll.com is an aggregate book search and price comparison site, Abebooks.com is an international site that sells used, rare, and out-of-print books, while eBay.com is the well-known auction site where atlases are for sale by commercial book dealers as well as laypersons. When dealing with out-of-print, Internet purchases, it is certainly a "buyer beware" situation, but the used book sites often enhance the traditional written condition description with color photographs of the item, a useful addition permitted by Web technology.

Standard approval plan profiles can be designed to allow for the automatic receipt of general and subject-specific atlases; however, some librarians prefer to receive slips rather than books due to the fact that each year a few of the largest publishing houses issue multiple versions of their general world and national road atlases. As a result, the approval plan profile might be overwhelmed by delivery of too many similar publications to the library, leading to an increase in returns which could be counter-productive to the approval agreement in the long run. Therefore, many atlases are purchased on a title-by-title basis, which necessitates knowing more about an item before it can be ordered. Although slips do not provide much content information, at least they provide the publisher's name, proper title, and ISBN for further searching at the publisher's Web site, or on *WorldCat* or *RLIN*.

Maps

Maps, in all their many variations, are available from hundreds, if not thousands, of dealers and publishers, presenting a veritable jungle of ordering pitfalls. Consequently, various strategies need to be used when searching for maps, as no single method will be successful every time.

While searching *WorldCat* or *RLIN* for bibliographic information on maps is certainly a useful route, using the ISBN may or may not be as helpful as in book searching. At an educational session at the 2003 International Map Trade Association annual conference and trade show in Santa Barbara, CA, several map-publishing representatives mentioned that reusing an ISBN for a subsequent map publication is not unheard of in the industry. This is not good news for either acquisitions or cataloging staff who rely upon such numeric codes to uniquely identify items. How often this re-issuance of ISBN numbers occurs is unknown, but it does cause one to consider that relying upon a single numerical search for requested items cannot be considered adequate in the case of maps. Titles, authors, subjects, scales, and publication dates will also need to be searched to insure a complete review of the reference source.

A well-known paper acquisitions tool, *GEO Katalog* (1900-), is a three volume, loose-leaf serial publication in German. Organized geographically, it lists maps, atlases, and selected books that are available for purchase from GeoCenter Internationales Landkartenhaus in Stuttgart, Germany. It is particularly useful for those trying to identify sheets that are part of large topographic or geologic series because series index maps are provided indicating sheet availability. Used in conjunction with *World Mapping Today* (Parry and Perkins, 2000), a 1,064-page reference source to maps and spatial data, these two traditional publications provide background information for maps and support online searching.

Typical searching strategies for maps require some knowledge about what exactly is being sought. Current, commercial publications can be searched at dealers' Web sites (such as MapLink, Omni Resources, Treaty Oak, or Wide World of Maps) or directly at the publisher's Web site (such as Rand-McNally, ITMB Publishing, or Benchmark Maps). These sites are less likely to list outdated maps, as they are in the business of making sure their products reflect the latest geographic information available, although they might market historical materials as well (e.g., National Geographic). Initially identifying publishers and map retailers can be difficult, but using the International Map Trade Association (IMTA) *Members Directory* or searching the Association's Web site (http://www.maptrade.org) will provide an international listing of over 800 members engaged in producing or selling maps. While the Web page permits searching for members by country and category of service provided, the paper directory has a number of access indices, including a geographic index by individual U.S. state (other countries sort by city).

If the items being sought are published by a government, searching the appropriate government agency's Web site is an excellent first step. While government agencies often keep their older maps in print somewhat longer than commercial companies, there is no law stating that all maps must remain in print forever. In addition, the U.S. government is trying to get out of the paper map business, although thousands of these maps are still produced annually and sold by the hundreds to dealers as well as singly to individual customers. This means that paper maps may still be ordered directly from the various government agencies or from dealers. In the past, when items went out-of-print, the only way to find stock was to contact dealers or ask for help from other librarians who might have duplicate copies they were willing to pass along. Today, computer technology is able to come to the rescue. As United States government publications are generally not copyrighted, there is no reason that a borrowed copy cannot be scanned, printed on an oversized printer, and then added to the collection. While this may not be the cheapest method of acquiring materials, for out-of-print items it might actually prove the fastest and most feasible method at this time.

DIGITAL DATA

The term digital data actually encompasses a wide-range of materials, from pre-packaged geographic information such as *StreetAtlas* by DeLorme or *Encarta Virtual Globe* by Microsoft to the downloading of maps or data directly from the Web. The major acquisitions problem continues to be identifying and locating the producers of appropriate digital data.

An excellent starting place is the book *GIS Data Sources* by Decker (2001). Aside from the clearly written text that discusses data and how to use them effectively, Decker has included a number of indices that have detailed annotations of data providers. His lists of providers cover U.S. federal, state, and local government sources, private and foreign sources, as well as associations and trade journal publishers.

If Decker's book is not available, then a search of GeoCommunity (http://search.geocomm.com), a GIS online site with 34,000 subscribers, owned and operated by ThinkBurst Media, should prove useful. Among its many offerings, GeoCommunity sponsors the GIS Data Depot (http://data.geocomm.com), a well established site where free data can be downloaded. An additional source for data is The Geography Network, supported by the Environmental Systems Research Institute (ESRI) (http://www.geographynetwork.com). Well-known among map librarians, Oddens Bookmarks (http://oddens.geog.uu.nl/index.html) is an international cartographic search engine with 21,500 links designed and supported by the Geography faculty at Utrecht University, The Netherlands.

Two basic search strategies present themselves initially. If it is probable that the data are from the United States government, searching the appropriate agency Web site will likely be the most productive search, as changes in technology have led to an increasing amount of government mapping being available to view or download over the Web. While government data are generally free, this new technology, which makes it very efficient to see maps, also makes the user responsible for the cost of the production of digital data into paper. This could require a substantial funding investment if an oversized printer needs to be purchased or if a commercial firm needs to be hired to print maps upon demand.

For state and local data, the state clearinghouse, a regional provider, or a city or borough planning commission might be the most useful. As each state has its own clearinghouse they will have to be accessed individually to identify what data they can provide. While 50 state clearinghouses and a number of regional associations are listed in Appendix B and C of the Decker book, the Geographic Information System Laboratory at MIT has posted a 12-page listing of GIS clearinghouses on their Web site (http://libraries.mit.edu/gis/data/statecenter.html) that should be more up-to-date and extensive.

Non-governmental agencies such as the United Nations (http://www.un.org), World Health Organization (http://www.who.int/en), and the World Bank (http://www.worldbank.org) either have map publications for sale or have maps that can be downloaded and printed from their Web sites. If identifying a likely NGO is difficult, there is a research guide to non-governmental organizations that has been posted by the Public Documents & Maps Department of Perkins Library, Duke University (http://docs.lib.duke.edu/igo/guides/ngo/) that includes an alphabetical list of hundreds of such organizations. While not every organization will have developed maps, it is worthwhile checking their Web sites when specialty maps are needed.

Public institutions such as libraries and museums frequently have historic or local maps available on their Web sites or for sale in paper form through their own Friends of the Library association or in-house store. Certainly the Perry-Castañeda Map Collection at the University of Texas, Austin (http://www.lib.utexas.edu/maps/index.html) is the most well-known in the United States, but other university and public libraries are also posting reproductions of items they own. Private collectors may also have Web sites showing their collections. David Rumsey's collection (http://www.davidrumsey.org) of over 8,800 historical maps is available online and has a GIS Browser that permits overlaying of maps and geospatial data as well as viewing or downloading the maps themselves. In addition, some 180 selected maps are also available for purchase as custom reproductions, mounted and framed.

In some cases, the alternative to official data is to locate a commercial provider who has repackaged government data or has developed its own. The 1:24,000-scale United States topographic map series is a case in point. Complete in approximately 55,000 sheets and produced by the U.S. Geological Survey as a paper product, the National Geographic has used this series to develop print-on-demand mapping kiosks where individuals are able to choose whichever topographic map they desire, and have it printed on waterproof paper for a charge. The actual size of the map is smaller than the official printed version and the cost is slightly more, but using a kiosk means no store has to hold large amounts of stock and the buyer doesn't have to be in the state where the map is held or contact USGS in Denver where the full paper stock is housed. Kiosks, located at camping and recreation retail stores such as G. I. Joe, REI, and EMS, are currently available in 25 states and the District of Columbia.

The National Geographic has also published the 1:24,000-scale U.S. topographic maps as state or regional coverage on CD-ROMs, both for the PC and the Mac operating systems, the latter available as of October 2003. As a result, libraries as well as the public can purchase any state coverage that they might desire. There is, however, a danger to purchasing digital data on CD-ROM. Certainly the lack of interoperability between PC and Mac operating systems has been well-known, but there is an additional problem with the relentless upgrading of Windows. As an example, in 1998, National Geographic produced *National Geographic Maps*, an eight-disc set of all folded maps included with the *National Geographic Magazine* from 1888 to 1997. A fascinating and potentially useful collection for map collectors and history buffs, it was designed to run on *Windows 95* and *Windows 98,* but upgrading to *Windows 2000* or *Windows NT* has led to access problems, with some people reporting difficult to no access at all. So, while it was once possible to reproduce these out-of-print maps using oversized color printers, if the software has been upgraded beyond *Windows 98*, it is probable that they are no longer accessible. It will be up to National Geographic to decide whether it is financially prudent to re-release these maps so that they can run in a different *Windows* environment.

The complexity of publication and identification of digital data is also illustrated by a global database on seven CD-ROMs. The U.S. Geological Survey began publishing these continental and regional atlases as part of their Digital Data Series in 2000. The first four atlases were *Global GIS Database, Digital Atlas of Central and South America* (2000), *Global GIS Database, Digital Atlas of Africa* (2001), *Global GIS Database, Digital Atlas of South Asia* (2001), and *Global GIS Database, Digital Atlas of the South Pacific* (2001). The remaining world coverage, *Global GIS Europe, Global GIS North Eurasia*, and *Global GIS North America*, was developed by the U.S. Geological Survey but published by the American Geological Institute (AGI) in 2003.

Naturally there are many commercial publishers that provide what might be called digital reference works, such as world atlases or travel routing programs, on CD-ROM. These materials are often available at bookstores and office supply stores as well as from the publisher, via Web sites. Rand McNally, Microsoft, and DeLorme are all well-known for these types of publications.

SPECIALTY ITEMS

Aerial Photographs

Aerial photographs, especially those of the decades from 1930-1980, are of interest to many disciplines that also use maps in their research. While maps are selective expressions of reality ruled by cartographic conventions and symbols, aerial photographs show everything their resolution will allow. As a result, researchers can identify those features most important to their projects, without the interpretation of an intervening party. Those interested in aerial photographs should contact the National Archives and Records Administration (NARA) (http://www.archives.gov/index.html) for photography before 1950 or the Department of Agriculture's Aerial Photography Field Office (APFO) (http://www.apfo.usda.gov/orderingimagery.html) for photography after 1950. Internet access for U.S. Geological Survey aerial photography may be found at Terraserver (http://terraserver-USA.com).

Globes

Globes are available in many sizes and styles. Once viewed only as educational items they can also serve as decorative items, made of acrylic or utilizing satellite imagery in place of traditional lines and colors. Currently available globes are produced by Cram Cartography & Globes (http://www.maps-eureka.com), National Geographic Maps (http://www.nationalgeographic.com), Raised Relief Map Company (http://www.rrmapco.com), Replogle Globes (http://www.replogleglobes.com) Spherical Concepts (http://www.sphericalconcepts.com) and Worldfx (http://www.realworldfx.com).

Raised Relief Maps

Raised relief maps, either in plaster or plastic, have been available for many decades. For the well-known U.S. topographic maps at 1:250,000-scale in raised relief or the National Park maps, contact map dealers such as: Global Map Store in Fresno, CA (505/224-9831), Hubbard Scientific (http://www.shnta.com), Omni Resources (http:// www.omnimap.com), or Zdansky Map Store in Corpus Christi, TX (361/855-9226). Trying to break into the raised relief market is the Raised Relief Map Company (http://www.rrmapco.com), a new firm currently producing mostly custom work.

Not surprisingly, computer technology and new modeling media have changed the way three dimensional products are now designed. Solid Terrain Modeling of Fillmore, CA (http://www.stm-usa.com) is producing physical models of terrain made from hi-density polyurethane foam overlaid with full-color aerial photography that is a vast improvement over the cardboard or plaster landscapes of the past. And Digital Wisdom (http://www.digiwis.com), a software company, specializes in ready-to-use graphics of maps and globes that look as if they are three dimensional instead of merely two dimensional.

Animated Maps

Urban Mapping (http://www.urbanmapping.com), a newly established company, has designed a new tourist map for Manhattan, *Dynamap for tourists: Manhattan*, using the older, lenticular image technology, formerly seen in children's toys. While still quite expensive and seen as a specialty item, this first map has attracted enough attention to be mentioned in the *The New York Times* and on CBS News, and a map for Chicago is under development.

CONCLUSIONS

It is clear that while the Internet provides a modern tool for cartographic acquisitions, finding and acquiring these items can still be extremely time-consuming, especially for digital data. However, the existence of Web sites enables laypersons, as well as subject specialists and acquisitions staff, to be more active in the pursuit of an item than ever before possible. Identifying cartographic materials will continue to be complicated simply because there are so many maps and so much data being produced and sold by government agencies, commercial publishers and dealers, but, once an item is identified, the process has become more manageable.

SELECTED RESOURCES

Decker, Drew. 2001. *GIS Data Sources*. New York: Wiley.
GEO Katalog. 1900- . Stuttgart: GeoCenter Internationales Landkartenhaus.
Global GIS. Europe. 2003. Alexandria, VA: American Geological Institute.
Global GIS. North America. 2003. Alexandria, VA: American Geological Institute.

Global GIS. North Eurasia. 2003. Alexandria, VA: American Geological Institute.

Global GIS Database, Digital Atlas of Africa. 2001. Flagstaff, AZ: U.S. Geological Survey. Digital data series DDS-62-B.

Global GIS Database, Digital Atlas of Central and South America. 2000. Reston, VA: U.S. Geological Survey. Digital data series DDS-62-A.

Global GIS Database, Digital Atlas of South Asia. 2001. Flagstaff, AZ: U.S. Geological Survey. Digital data series DDS-62-C.

Global GIS database, Digital Atlas of the South Pacific. 2001. Flagstaff, AZ: U.S. Geological Survey. Digital data Series DDS-62-D.

International Map Trade Association. 2001. *Members Directory.* Kankakee, IL: IMTA.

Parry, R.B. and C.R. Perkins. 2000. *World Mapping Today,* 2nd ed. London: Bowker-Saur.

Winch, Kenneth L. 1976. *International Maps and Atlases in Print,* 2nd ed. London: Bowker.

APPENDIX

Web Sites Mentioned

Associations:	URLS:
International Map Trade Association	http://www.maptrade.org

Atlas dealers:

AbeBooks	http://www.Abebooks.com
AddAll	http://www.AddAll.com
Alibris	http://www.Alibris.com
Amazon	http://www.Amazon.com
Barnes & Noble	http://www.Barnesandnoble.com
eBay	http://www.eBay.com

Cartographic data search engines:

GeoCommunity	http://search.geocomm.com
Oddens Bookmarks	http://oddens.geog.uu.nl/index.html

Data providers:

ESRI	http://www.esri.com
GIS Data Depot	http://data.geocomm.com
Terraserver	http://terraserver-USA.com
The Geography Network	http://www.geographynetwork.com
Tobin International	http://www.tobin.com
U.S. Dept. of Agriculture, Aerial Photography Field Office	http://www.apfo.usda.gov/orderingimagery.html
U.S. Census Bureau	http://www.census.gov/geo/www/maps
U.S. Geological Survey	http://ask.usgs.gov/products.html
U.S. National Archives and Records Administration	http://www.archives.gov/index.html

Globe dealers:

Cram Cartography & Globes	http://www.maps-eureka.com
National Geographic Maps	http://www.nationalgeographic.com
Replogle Globes	http://wwww.replogleglobes.com
Spherical Concepts	http://www.sphericalconcepts.com
Worldfx	http://www.realworldfx.com

Historic map site with GIS abilities:

David Rumsey Map Collection   http://www.davidrumsey.org

Map dealers:

Map Link   http://www.maplink.com
Omni Resources   http://www.omnimap.com
Treaty Oak   http://www.TreatyOak.com
Wide World of Maps   http://www.maps4u.com

Map publishers:

Benchmark Maps   http://www.benchmarkmaps.com
Michael Brein   http://www.MichaelBrein.com
DeLorme   http://www.delorme.com
Digital Wisdom   http://www.digiwis.com
IMTA (trade association)   http://www.maptrade.org
ITMB Publishing   http://www.itmb.com
Hedberg Maps   no URL; e-mail:
                               info@hedbergmaps.com
Microsoft   http://shop.microsoft.com
National Geographic   http://www.nationalgeographic.com
Rand McNally   http://www.randmcnally.com/rmc/home.jsp
Raven Maps & Images   http://www.ravenmaps.com
Urban Mapping   http://www.urbanmapping.com

Raised relief maps:

Hubbard Scientific   http://www.shnta.com
Omni Resources   http://www.omnimap.com
Raised Relief Map Company   http://www.rrmapco.com
Solid Terrain Modeling   http://www.stm-usa.com

University specialty sites:

Geographic Information System Laboratory at MIT
                http://libraries.mit.edu/gis/data/statecenter.html

Perry-Castañeda Map Collection, University of Texas at Austin
                http://www.lib.utexas.edu/maps/index.html

Public Documents & Maps Department, Perkins Library, Duke University
                http://docs.lib.duke.edu/igo/guides/ngo

The Virtual Patron

Lesley M. Moyo

SUMMARY. The modern academic library is characterized by technological innovation, optimum Internet connectivity, and boasts of numerous electronic resources and services that are accessible remotely.
Library patrons can now 'visit' the library and conduct research without
ever entering the library building. Furthermore, enabling technologies
have led to the exponential growth of distance education programs in
many higher education institutions. Students can now participate in college and university programs without leaving their geographical locations
because technology facilitates virtual delivery of academic programs.
This has in turn led to the emergence of virtual academic communities.
These virtual communities require the services and resources of various
academic support units much in the same way as traditional campus
communities. In order to remain relevant within this milieu, academic libraries are changing rapidly and being transformed to meet the changing
needs of the evolving academic communities they serve. To that end, libraries are increasingly providing services and support to virtual patrons, by facilitating access to and navigation of electronic resources and

Lesley M. Moyo is Head, Gateway Libraries (i.e., the *Gateway Commons*, an electronic
reference center and the *Pollock Laptop Library*), Penn State University, University Park,
PA 16802 (E-mail: lmm26@psu.edu). As a librarian in these facilities, Ms. Moyo assists
patrons in accessing and navigating the numerous electronic/Web-based resources, provides instruction and reference services both in person and virtually, and creates and packages information resources on the Web for use by patrons.

[Haworth co-indexing entry note]: "The Virtual Patron." Moyo, Lesley M. Co-published simultaneously
in *Science & Technology Libraries* (The Haworth Information Press, an imprint of The Haworth Press, Inc.)
Vol. 25, No. 1/2, 2004, pp. 185-209; and: *Emerging Issues in the Electronic Environment: Challenges for Librarians and Researchers in the Sciences* (ed: Jeannie P. Miller) The Haworth Information Press, an imprint
of The Haworth Press, Inc., 2004, pp. 185-209. Single or multiple copies of this article are available for a
fee from The Haworth Document Delivery Service [1-800-HAWORTH, 9:00 a.m. - 5:00 p.m. (EST). E-mail
address: docdelivery@haworthpress.com].

providing value-added support services that optimize effective use of these resources. The public service areas that have undergone the greatest technology-enabled transformation to meet the needs of virtual patrons are *access, reference,* and *instruction.* As technology changes, it will continue to define the capability of libraries to meet the changing needs of library patrons. This paper reviews some of the recent developments in electronic access, reference and instruction in light of services to virtual patrons, particularly college and university students. The paper focuses on virtual patrons in an academic setting and includes results of a survey on the perceptions and use of Web-based library resources and services by students of Penn State University's World Campus, a virtual campus with an enrollment of over 5,900 students. *[Article copies available for a fee from The Haworth Document Delivery Service: 1-800-HAWORTH. E-mail address: <docdelivery@haworthpress.com> Website: <http://www.HaworthPress.com> © 2004 by The Haworth Press, Inc. All rights reserved.]*

KEYWORDS. Virtual patrons, virtual libraries, online information services, virtual reference services, libraries–online instruction, libraries–electronic collections, academic libraries–technological developments

INTRODUCTION

Technology in libraries has not only transformed the way libraries do business, but has also changed the very nature of library work itself. The modern academic library environment, characterized by technological innovation, electronic communication, prevalence of Web-based resources and multimedia information, offers a host of electronic services and tools to patrons to facilitate their research. New service paradigms are emerging in response to the changing scholarship and scholarly communication patterns brought about by advanced technologies. Academic libraries are among the leading institutions in leveraging the power of technology to meet the needs of their patrons. Just over two decades ago, conducting library research involved visiting a library in person to search card catalogs and print indexes in order to locate books and journal articles. Now it is possible for library patrons to conduct research remotely, and have access to a myriad of quality electronic resources and collections. Library patrons can 'enter' the library both through the physical gateway and the electronic gateway. As a result, the building of electronic collections and development of virtual library services have become the focus of strategic development efforts in modern academic and research libraries. Furthermore, the growth of distance education programs in many higher education institutions has led to the emergence of virtual academic communities. These virtual communities require the services and resources of various academic support units much in the same way as traditional campus communities. In response to this trend, academic libraries are striving to provide equitable services to both in-person and virtual patrons. Over the past decade, many academic libraries have undergone significant technological transformation. The public service areas that have undergone the greatest technology-enabled transformation to meet the needs of virtual patrons are *access*, *reference*, and *instruction*. For instance, the increase in subscription databases, many of them full-text, e-books, and other electronic collections, as well as introduction of new and innovative ways of providing information literacy at a distance through creation of tutorials and other Web-based resources and services, are all typical characteristics of academic libraries of the 1990s and 2000s. Of particular note is the current proliferation of virtual reference services, providing libraries the capability for real-time communication with virtual patrons in order to assist them at their points of need.

Troll (2002) refers to the changes taking place in academic libraries as being of an evolutionary nature. She states that: "Academic libraries are changing in response to changes in the learning and research environment and changes in the behavior of library users. The changes are evolutionary. Libraries are adding new, digital resources and services while maintaining most of the old, traditional resources and services." Most of the changes taking place in today's academic libraries are technology-enabled. As a result of technological developments and changes taking place, the information-seeking behavior patterns of library patrons has also changed significantly. For instance, current research and professional literature indicates that the 'digital generation,' of which the majority of today's college and university students are a part, prefers to work in the online environment and increasingly prefers to conduct library research from their dorm rooms and at home, rather than inside the library building. This challenges the library to develop new content delivery modes to meet the needs of virtual patrons. However, although these college and university students largely consider themselves technologically savvy, most lack information literacy skills and competencies that enable them to be effective researchers. Troll (2002) says: "Even if undergraduate students turn to the scholarly electronic resources licensed by libraries, their search skills are poor. They seldom, if ever, use advanced search features, do not understand that result sets are not necessarily organized by relevance to their query, and look only at the first couple of Web pages of ten to twenty items retrieved." In order for these students to effectively access/navigate and retrieve quality information for their research, they need guidance and direction from librarians or other information professionals. Moreover, the exponential growth of electronic collections in many academic libraries has generated an even greater need for mediation and instructional support to virtual patrons.

THE VIRTUAL PATRON DEFINED

A virtual library patron is one whose accesses/use of library services and resources is unbounded by space or time. Hulshof (1999) refers to virtual library patrons as "people who use a library's resources and make requests for library assistance without actually setting foot in the library." Virtual patrons are generally the same people as any other library user and the services that they expect are similar to those that the library provides to in-person patrons. The only differences lie in the technology functionality that is required to provide access to library resources and services from a distance, and communicate with patrons synchronously or asynchronously. Virtual patrons may be located anywhere where there's Internet and electronic access to resources. In an academic library setting, patrons may be in their dorm room, classroom or office on campus, or they may be at home. They may be as near as the building next door or as far away as in a country across the globe. The primary factor is that they are accessing/using library services and resources remotely.

Who Is a Virtual Patron?

Graham and Grodzinski (2001) suggested that:

> In an academic setting, remote users may be separated into three primary groups: on-campus remote users, off-campus remote users, and distance education users. On-campus remote users include those accessing library resources from dorms, offices, classrooms, and computer laboratories. The off-campus remote user group consists primarily of traditional students, faculty, and

staff who access library resources from their homes or other locations away from the campus. In addition, this group may contain remote library users unaffiliated with the university. The final class of remote users consists of distance learners. These users are usually accessing the library's resources from greater distances than the members of the other two classes of remote users, and remote access is often their only means of attaining library materials.

This echoes Cooper and Dempsey (1998) who also suggested that there should be a differentiation between the remote user who is a few buildings away, and the remote user participating in a distance learning curriculum involving a distance of hundreds or thousands of miles, suggesting that knowledge and use of the library differs for each group. Graham and Grodzinski (2001) further argued that:

> Each of these remote user groups has distinct needs in terms of assistance and instruction, and vastly different methods are required to reach each group effectively. A student living in a dormitory, or a faculty member working in his or her office is more accessible than an off-site user working from home. In the case of the on-campus user, librarians may have opportunities to extend their services beyond the library's walls and to serve the user directly in his or her remote location. . . . In the case of distance learners, assistance may take the form of online tutorials and help screens, contact via telephone, and possibly video conferencing.

However, despite the different circumstances affecting each of these three remote-user subgroups, and the need to address the unique needs of each of them, there is, nevertheless, a lot of common ground in meeting their collective needs of access to collections, reference assistance, and instruction through effective online programs and services, and provision of appropriate electronic resources.

Needs/Desires of Virtual Patrons

Although virtual patrons can access a vast amount of electronic resources and information remotely, they still need assistance. They might have questions or need help in the use of these electronic resources. As Helfer (2003) pointed out, "Virtual patrons with access to electronic resources that the library offers will have questions, and the library has to have a means of responding to these questions and provide assistance within this virtual environment." In response, academic libraries are challenged to develop value-added services to support the use of electronic resources by virtual patrons. This demand on academic libraries will be increasingly heightened by the growth in numbers of virtual patrons. For instance, technological advancement has fueled the increase in numbers of distance education programs in many higher education institutions, contributing to the increase in numbers of distance learners and hence the surge in numbers of virtual patrons needing to use academic libraries. Furthermore, research has shown that even on-campus students prefer to use the library from their dorm rooms or from computer laboratories rather than visit the library in person. Consequently, every student enrolled in a college or university is a potential virtual patron of the academic library serving that community.

Virtual patrons in academic settings have certain expectations of the library. The 24/7 availability of the Web has enabled around-the-clock access to library electronic collections. This has, in turn, heightened user expectations for 24/7 access to not only the electronic collections, but also services and other library facilities that go with use of these electronic collections. The following are a sampling of articulated expectations of patrons accessing library resources and services remotely (compiled from various user surveys, of actual (verbatim) responses to questions on what patrons expect from the library):

- 24/7 service availability
- A Web site search engine that can find what I want
- A Web site that works
- Ability to conduct all library transactions online (library registration, request document delivery and interlibrary loan, renew library items, etc.)
- Easy access
- Easy-to-use Web resources permitting self-service
- Everything in full-text and downloadable or printable
- Everything should be in electronic format
- Faster service
- Offer study tips and guides
- Several options/alternatives to choose from
- Virtual reference service librarian available online 24/7.

As library users encounter innovative and convenient technology services in all sectors of their lives, their expectations of the library are elevated and they, in turn, place greater demand and pressure on the library to provide similar or corresponding services to those in other sectors. Their demands are often for a wider variety of information sources, services, and support. For instance, as library resources become increasingly available in electronic formats, librarians are under greater pressure to provide their patrons with access to full-text information online. Moreover, as noted from some of the expectations listed above, library users expect that they will not only be able to log on to electronic resources to access the information that they need at any time of day, and from any location, but they also expect to find real-time assistance (virtual reference librarian or other mediation service) at the time of access.

As libraries strive to meet these contemporary user demands/expectations with appropriate support, they find themselves grappling with a number of issues: not only is the nature of this support constantly in flux, but other issues such as funding, staff skills, and competencies in emerging service areas, etc., are prevalent. Libraries are challenged and motivated to continuously discover new ways of delivering services such as reference, instruction, and research support. The resultant developments, in turn, lead to growth of the electronic profile of the library and its capacity to serve virtual patrons.

Characteristics of Virtual Patrons

Serving virtual patrons within the electronic environment requires the library to provide personalized services because of the fact that the use of technology, for example, using a PC to access information on the Web, is a solitary activity in which the patron looking for information, conducting an online transaction, or accessing a service is often fulfilling an individual need or interest. Fritch and Mandernack (2001) stated that: "Technology has promoted a society characterized by independence and self-reliance, convenience and immediate gratification . . ." Librarians serving virtual patrons are now placing emphasis on training users to access and evaluate information sources for relevance and quality, independently, and also providing point-of-use assistance if and when users decide to seek help. Information literacy will continue to be a key aspect of the enduring reference paradigm within the virtual library environment. To facilitate development of services to virtual patrons, the library requires detailed information about their characteristics and instructional needs. Several studies have been conducted in recent years to establish profiles of students in the networked electronic environments of colleges and universities, including their use of online library resources and services. A study of the online habits of 2,060 full-time, American college and university students in October 1999 conducted by Yankelovich in partnership with netLibrary found that (as cited by Denise Troll, 2002):

- 82% of the students surveyed own a computer and "virtually all of them use the Internet."
- 93% claimed that finding information online makes more sense than going to the library.
- 83% said they were frequently unable to get the materials they need from the library because it was too late or too early to go to the library.
- 75% said they did not have enough time.
- 75% liked the convenience and 71% liked the time saved by finding information online any hour of the day.

According to the findings of another survey, *Pew Internet and American Life Project* (Jones et al. 2002): "Internet use is a staple of college students' educational experience. They use the Internet to communicate with professors and classmates, to do research, and to access library materials." However, the survey findings indicate that 73% of college students say the Internet, rather than the library, is the primary site of their information searches, while only 9% said they use the library more than the Internet for information searching, clearly showing the stronger preference that college students have for electronic access to information, especially via the Internet. However, although Jones and colleagues said students tend to use the Internet prior to going to the library to find information, they seemed to focus on use of the library as being synonymous with visiting the library in person. They did not acknowledge the fact that most of the library resources, including proprietary databases, are now accessible online via the Internet and students can complete a lot of their research from dorm rooms or at home using Internet-based library resources. It has been noted from observations and other anecdotal evidence that, when articulating their use of online information and resources, students often do not distinguish between the library online resources, such as databases, indexes, e-journals, etc., and the open Internet resources that are accessible via public Internet search engines. So, when they report using the Internet more than the library, there's a high possibility that they are including library databases accessible via the Internet in the 'Internet use' category, and only reporting in-person visits in the 'library use' category. This Pew Internet and American Life Project study emphasizes the Internet as a communication tool in the life of college students, and its impact on the students' overall academic experience. It reflects how electronic information and the Internet has become an integral part of college communication culture and has permeated every aspect of today's college life.

Another similar study of college students and their information-seeking behavior in an electronic environment articulates some of the concerns surrounding library services in a digital environment (OCLC, 2002). The OCLC (Online Computer Library Center, Inc.) white paper on the information habits of college students is based on a study conducted between December 11, 2001 and January 1, 2002 on U.S. college students representing all regions of the U.S. The study was conducted to determine Web-based information-seeking habits of college students and their use of campus library Web sites. The purpose of the study was to determine the profile of college and university students using Web-based library resources, and present their views of successful information delivery. The study provides recommendations for librarians on how to determine ways in which they can influence students' Web-based information choices. The study found that "college and university students look to campus libraries and library Web sites for their information needs." Seventy-eight percent of the respondents in this study preferred to access library Web sites remotely for their information. Sixty-two percent of the surveyed students responded that they would use online help available from librarians. The OCLC white paper also revealed that seven-in-ten students use the campus library Web site for at least some of their assignments. The most used Web-based library resources were full-text electronic journals (67%), library catalog (57%), databases (51%), and indexes to journal articles (51%). The survey profiles college students as "confident and savvy users of electronic information resources who value access to accurate, up-to-date information with easily identifiable authors." The overall results of the study showed that preferences of students included remote access because of the flexibility that it offers, and that this preference for remote access determined who they seek assistance from when using the Web. The results also showed that, in these settings, students tended to ask for help from friends and classmates (61%), their professors (36%), and from librarians (21%).

Impact on Quality of Work

These foregoing trends and characteristics of virtual patrons within the networked academic environment have led to some concerns about the quality of work by college/university students. The fact that a student can sit in his/her dorm room, access online library databases for articles, and write an assignment based on the articles retrieved without much consultation and guidance has led some professors to conclude that, in this new electronic environment, students do not need to be creative or exercise any critical thinking skills to complete their assignments. Instead, the students have a wealth of readily accessible information that they can obtain without much effort. Moreover, with this information being accessible electronically in full-text, students have the temptation to 'cut-and-paste' chunks of text from electronic articles and Web pages and literally 'compile' papers for their assignments, instead of composing original papers that express their individual thoughts and understanding. This trend calls for a greater effort, not only by academic libraries, but also by all other stakeholders in the academic community to highlight the value of intellectual integrity in scholarship and scholarly communication. Information literacy efforts in academic libraries should not only incorporate, but also emphasize, content on plagiarism and copyright issues as key components of their instruction. Another concern stems from students' use of general Internet content that is retrieved via Internet search engines such as Google. Whereas good quality articles are available on the open Internet, it takes good research and evaluative skills for a searcher to construct good search strategies that yield relevant results, and to 'sift' through items retrieved assessing the quality/relevance of each. Thompson (2003) recommends that students be taught how to evaluate Web resources and also basic search techniques such as boolean searching. He cites "a disturbing decline in both the quality of the writing and the originality of the thoughts expressed" which is attributed to use of the Web. Students must be helped to understand the difference between library databases and other online resources as opposed to the open Web. Librarians can and should influence students' search habits even in the virtual environment. Buchanan et al. (2002) emphasized the importance of library services, including user education, evolving to meet new user expectations in the virtual environment.

Some college/university faculty members believe that the quality of students' work is also being adversely impacted by students' strong preference for electronic information as opposed to print information. Tenopir (2003) cited a number of studies that have been conducted to determine student preferences when doing library research. The findings show overwhelmingly that students prefer electronic sources, with full-text being the most preferred. Some of the surveys cited by Tenopir show that faculty are also concerned about the impact that sources students choose may have on their quality of work. Full-text articles used for assignments may not necessarily contain the best information and research content for the topic being researched; however, a student conducting research from a dorm room or at home may prefer to use what is readily available in full-text online, rather than having to make a trip to the library to search for, perhaps more relevant, print sources. The time saved, the convenience of easy access, instant availability, and the flexibility of access location are all compelling factors that students have cited as the reason for preferring full-text online resources. When students access electronic resources remotely, they do not have as much opportunity for point-of-need assistance by librarians. Even when there are good-quality, electronic, full-text resources that are suitable for the assignment at hand, students may not have the information literacy skills and competency level to determine the best place to search, and be able to construct appropriate searches to find this information. For instance, students may not know which of the available databases is the best for their subject/topic. This may not be a critical issue in a situation where there are only a limited number of databases. However, in an institution like Penn State where the University Libraries subscribe to over 400 databases, students conducting research from their dorm room or at home would need some guidance or recommendation on what resources to use. Furthermore, even when students have identified the appropriate database, they may not be familiar with the search techniques applicable to that database, or they may need assistance in configuring a boolean search that would retrieve the best articles from the database. Many students are accustomed to searching the Internet using the *Google* search engine, which does not require the use of boolean operators to configure a search. All too often, students search library databases the same way that they search *Google* and end up with less relevant results. There is a clear need for mediation/guidance of researchers within the virtual library environment.

SERVING VIRTUAL PATRONS: EMERGING TRENDS

Virtual library service is a rapidly growing phenomenon that relates to library services and functions that are not limited by space or time. Libraries providing such services are sometimes referred to as virtual libraries, digital libraries, or electronic libraries. Burke (2001) defined the virtual library as one which "provides access to an integrated collection of print, electronic, and multimedia resources delivered seamlessly and transparently to users regardless either of their physical location or the location and ownership of the information." In a college/university, virtual libraries serve dispersed students, faculty and staff, as well as other affiliates and visitors. These categories of patrons constitute the key players in an academic community, and are all being impacted by the growth of electronic collections in libraries. Faculty as well as students have embraced electronic resources and are using them to varying degrees. Smith (2003) investigated faculty use of electronic journals and compared science and social science faculty at the University of Georgia. Results showed that there is a steady increase in electronic readership, and library subscription resources constituted the largest segment of literature read per week. Seventy-seven percent of science faculty reported using articles from electronic resources, while 69% of social science faculty reported the same. Other studies have been conducted to gauge the usage of electronic resources, and the findings reflect that library electronic resources usage by faculty as well as students is on the rise.

As academic libraries embrace the emerging virtual communities and the new scholarly communication patterns, new service modes are being developed to facilitate virtual access to resources and services. The traditional/core library services are increasingly being extended to the virtual space. The library public service areas that have undergone the greatest technology-enabled transformation to meet the needs of virtual patrons are *access*, *reference*, and *instruction*.

Electronic Access and Delivery

New scholarly communication patterns have emerged as a result of electronic publishing and the Web. Electronic collections, especially full-text databases, e-books, Web tools and resources, coupled with electronic document delivery systems, are expanding the scope of patrons that can be reached and served by libraries. Academic libraries are experiencing a surge in numbers of remote patrons that are being catered to via primarily electronic collections and services. The current trend in libraries is to move beyond just providing inventories of collections (catalogs) on the Web, but also providing full content through subscription to full-text electronic databases and e-books, and through digitization projects that are converting print material into digital formats that can be transmitted electronically. This trend improves access, as remote patrons can use the resources without having to come to the library building. Even in-person patrons are increasingly demanding full-text electronic resources in preference to surrogates, because accessing the information takes less effort and time. Moreover, once accessed, electronic information readily renders itself to manipulation, processing, and integration with other data/information, thus enhancing productivity. However, concerns remain in academic circles about students' 'cut and paste' tendencies when they have access to full-text resources. This has kept many faculty members vigilant in identifying plagiarism cases and taking disciplinary measures. Libraries' instructional efforts are also contributing to the education of students on issues of copyright and fair use, plagiarism, and intellectual integrity.

With the Web facilitating 24/7 access to library collections, virtual patrons are no longer restricted by library operational hours, distance, or location. They can access the Web at any time of the day or night and from any location where there is Internet access. This perpetual availability of the Web and the increase in electronic resources in many academic libraries has led to changes in collection development policies and practices. Libraries are shifting their focus from ownership of resources to access. Libraries no longer boast just on the size of their book and serial collections, but more on the size of both print collections that they own and electronic resources, including databases, e-books, and e-journals that they subscribe to. Libraries that have optimum connectivity and network bandwidth are able to provide access to vast amounts of information to their patrons. There is an overwhelming preference for full-text resources that enable patrons to complete their research online and retrieve articles without having to visit the library in person to search for print sources. However, there is concern among some librarians that this trend has led to patrons' devaluating print collections in libraries. This is a matter of concern in many academic libraries, because print sources still constitute the greater component of research collections. To extend the use of print sources to virtual patrons, libraries are employing new document delivery systems that provide electronic access to print information. The ILLiad electronic document delivery system in use at Penn State and many other libraries allows virtual patrons to register online and request articles from books and print journals to be sent to them electronically. Once user requests are received via ILLiad, the requested articles are scanned and converted into PDF files that are then sent to patrons electronically. Patrons can then view and print these documents.

Another development area that has greatly enhanced patron access to library collections is electronic reserves. Texts that were generally provided in print can now be scanned and made available in electronic format, permitting remote and multi-user access. In surveying students' perceptions of a new e-reserve system at Penn State Erie, Pilston and Hart (2002) found that students felt that e-reserves offer better access and flexibility. When students were asked which locations they accessed e-reserves from, home was the most used location for accessing e-reserves. Fifty-two percent of students accessed electronic reserves from more than one location, taking advantage of the flexibility of access. Regarding satisfaction rate, off-campus students showed a higher level of satisfaction with e-reserves than did on-campus students.

Facilitating access to electronic collections is based on individual libraries' technological capability to provide the necessary infrastructure for this access. In addition, the specific terms of access and use of individual databases and resources are determined by the terms of the license agreement. Depending on the stipulated terms, some resources may only be accessed within the library building, or may only permit a limited number of simultaneous users. Miller (2003) provided an anatomy of a library e-resource agreement and highlighted the considerations that a library makes before signing a contractual agreement with a vendor. These agreements ultimately govern the way respective electronic resources are accessed and used.

Virtual Reference Services

Library patrons working in a virtual environment still require assistance and guidance in order to fully utilize the library's resources. Point-of-need assistance to patrons working in the Web environment is increasingly being achieved through virtual reference services (VRS). Virtual reference services have exploded over the past five years. Based on a variety of models, such as collaborative reference efforts offered via a consortium, to outsourced services, libraries are grappling to address the need to communicate with virtual patrons in real-time and provide them with instruction and guidance. Although e-mail reference has been offered in many academic libraries for years, it has met with different levels of success. The main drawback to its application in the virtual library environment is the turnaround time between when the question is asked and the response is received. Patrons working in a virtual environment who encounter/experience difficulty finding information they require may need immediate assistance in order to be able to continue their research. Synchronous communication is the ideal for supporting virtual patrons, as they can get help at the time they need it. VRS offers the remote patron: a portable service accessible wherever they have access to the Web, just-in-time assistance, convenience (even local users need not come to the library physically), increased accessibility of librarians to assist and guide them, and another communication option in addition to other existing library communication facilities. VRS is an area that will continue evolving to meet the needs of patrons who are working primarily in a networked electronic environment. It offers the most personalized assistance in the virtual environment and provides virtual patrons the highest likelihood of getting their individual/unique needs met. Other options tend to be generalized; e.g., FAQs, tutorials, etc.

The development of VRS is related to the growth of electronic collections and resources. Electronic sources might have different user interfaces and require the use of different search techniques. When new sources are added to library collections, some patrons may require guidance on how to search them, and this generates the need for real-time support. As libraries continue to build their electronic collections and make them accessible over the Web, research will increasingly be conducted outside of the physical library building and there will be corresponding developments in VRS to increase and enhance support to dispersed patrons.

Information Literacy at a Distance

Research has shown that, very often, electronic resources provided by a library are used minimally because of a variety of factors, such as patrons not knowing that a particular source exists, or because they do not have the requisite skills for its use. These situations point to the need for marketing library services and resources to virtual communities, while at the same time providing appropriate mediation and instruction to equip patrons with the skills and competencies that enable them to make effective use of these resources. There are many approaches to providing information literacy at a distance; however, there is one factor in common. Information literacy at a distance is best achieved when tailored to the specific needs of a particular audience. Even in a virtual library environment, it is still necessary to get to know the library patrons' needs in detail. Hence, the need to evaluate services and survey the virtual patrons to obtain their input into the development of resources that best meet their needs. For instance, an understanding of the online learning characteristics of virtual patrons would provide a foundation for development of instructional content for them. Once patron needs have been established, the library has a number of ways to provide instruction virtually.

FAQs are one way that libraries provide instructional content virtually. Although FAQs usually provide answers and instructions on questions previously asked, they often include unasked questions that the library anticipates will arise in the use of their resources. Moreover, FAQs can facilitate the creation of knowledge bases that reflect common problems or areas where patrons have the greatest need for instruction or assistance. Information from these knowledge bases can be used to determine not only priority instruction areas, but also the best form of instruction to meet the patron needs. Online tutorials are another way in which many academic libraries serving virtual patrons have met the information literacy needs of their patrons. However, all tutorials should address specific instruction needs, and be geared to the information literacy skill level of the target audience. Dewald et al. (2000) emphasized the need for action, interaction, and application in the education process and suggested that one of the methods that librarians interact with patrons is through Web-based tutorials. "The interactivity of Web tutorials is the key to active learning and reinforcement."

Virtual reference services also play a role in information literacy. It has been noted from transaction logs that VRS sessions incorporate instructional content, and that instruction via VRS is particularly effective because it is provided at the point of need when the patron is most likely to be focused and attentive. Johnston (2003) discussed the University of New Brunswick's LIVE digital reference, which shows that 60% of transactions incorporate instruction. This convenient and personalized instruction is a good option for virtual patrons who may not have the opportunity to participate in a traditional library instruction session held inside the library building, or be able to visit a library in person for assistance.

In creating Web-based instructional resources, it is important to not only package the information appropriately, but also to understand the information-seeking behavior of the targeted audience. This should determine the way Web resources are packaged and presented for remote use. Virtual patrons may not have the opportunity to readily seek clarification and guidance when navigating the Web. Therefore, for Web-based instructional content to be effective, the Web sites on which they are presented should be intuitive and user-friendly. "With a growing number of patrons accessing library resources remotely, ease of access is an important issue. As the number of electronic resources has increased, the need for an intuitive and user-friendly interface for patrons to conduct productive research has emerged" (Crowley et al. 2002).

Libraries provide the necessary infrastructure inside the library building to access electronic collections. However, as many virtual patrons prefer to use library resources remotely, the library has no control on the technology resources at the remote access points. Often virtual patrons express their frustration with slow connections and the time it takes to download information. Some patrons connecting to library resources remotely via private ISPs may not be able to authenticate and may be denied access to resources. Libraries may offer a limited amount of technical support. Hulshof (1999) advised on the need for the library to establish the parameters of technical support to be provided to virtual patrons. He suggested putting together helpful resources such as help screens and FAQs that patrons can use to learn or troubleshoot their systems. Help desks may also be used to offer support to virtual patrons experiencing technical difficulty in accessing/navigating the library's electronic collections. In a high-tech library environment, it is often difficult to distinguish between technology literacy and information literacy needs among patrons. When patrons express difficulty in accessing and using an electronic source from a distance, the reason could be any one of many factors, or a combination, including lack of technical skills or lack of research skills or it could be due to limitations of the technology infrastructure at their remote location. The library can provide instructional support via Web tools to assist patrons experiencing difficulty. However, it may be difficult to ascertain whether problems arise from lack of information literacy skills or lack of technological skills.

To continue serving virtual patrons effectively and be able to tailor services to their needs, libraries must continuously assess and monitor changes in user needs and information-seeking behavior patterns that influence the way virtual patrons conduct online research. One way in which this assessment can be done is through surveys and focus groups. Information gathered through surveys of virtual patrons is useful in identifying priority areas and planning the future direction of services.

A SURVEY OF VIRTUAL PATRONS: PENN STATE WORLD CAMPUS

Penn State's World Campus, a virtual campus, was founded in 1998 and has grown significantly over the past five years. Now offering over

150 online courses in 30 certificate and degree programs, the Campus boasts an enrollment of over 5,900 students dispersed in all 50 states of the U.S. and in 44 other countries including, Malaysia, Costa Rica, Japan, Austria, and China. All of these students are potential virtual patrons of the Penn State University Libraries, who need access to research information and resources for their scholarly work and academic pursuits.

At Penn State, there is no separate unit within the University Libraries that serves distance education students and faculty or other virtual patrons. All electronic resources and virtual library services are fully integrated and centrally administered. Both in-person and virtual patrons can access and use these resources. However, to facilitate a 'one-stop-shopping' location, and for the convenience of World Campus students and other distance education students, an electronic gateway has been created on the Web to provide a single access point to the conglomeration of remotely accessible library resources and services (http://www.libraries.psu.edu/instruction/world/home.html). This gateway incorporates links to the CAT (Web catalog), the list of over 400 databases, as well as links to the online library registration forms, electronic document delivery service (ILLiad), Virtual Reference Service, and Web-based instructional tutorials. Although these resources are also available to in-person patrons, they constitute the core resources and support services used by virtual patrons.

To evaluate the use of these resources by virtual patrons, a survey of World Campus students was conducted in the Fall of 2001 and Spring of 2002. The objectives of the survey were to ascertain virtual patrons' perceptions, expectations, and use of Web-based library resources, as well as their information-seeking behavior patterns.

Methodology

A random sample of 200 students registered with World Campus was taken from a database of those who were registered with the University Libraries. Although the survey sample was small and the return rate low, the findings of the survey, nevertheless, provided insights into virtual patrons' levels of awareness of the availability of tools and resources that facilitate online research and transactions, and their use of them. The survey also revealed some information-seeking behavior patterns and preferences among the students that would significantly impact the way they access and use Web-based library information and services. This study was a Web-based survey in which the students sampled were e-mailed an invitation to participate in the survey. A link within the invitation e-mail led them to a Web-based questionnaire with 12 questions relating to their use of Penn State University Library Web-based services and resources, as well as their preferences, satisfaction in terms of adequacy of resources in meeting their needs, and how they rated the usefulness and ease of use of these sources based on their individual expectations (see Appendix 1). The survey questions focused on two broad categories of service: the first category related to the use of electronic resources such as the Web catalog, electronic databases, online reference tools, etc.; the second category related to the use of online support services, such as e-mail reference services, document delivery services, Web-based tutorials, etc.

Results

A total of 75 (37.5%) Web forms were returned. The data collected were analyzed using SPSS. The findings of the survey indicated that the most used resources were the Web catalog (76%) and full-text databases (64%). The comments shared by respondents also showed an overwhelming desire and preference for full-text articles and e-journals. Use of Web-based support services was limited, with interlibrary loan reflecting only a 26.7% usage rate, instructional resources/tutorials, 16%, and e-mail reference, 10.7% (the survey instrument was developed prior to the launching of the virtual reference service, which now reflects higher usage level among World Campus students).

In terms of satisfaction with Web-based library services, 65% of the respondents reported that their resources and service expectations were adequately met, 22% reported that the library resources and services were inadequate, while 13% did not respond to the questions on satisfaction with Web-based library resources and services. These and other findings led the researchers to make the following conclusions regarding virtual patrons:

- They use library Web-based resources heavily, yet they usually work with only a few resources and tend not to explore the full complement of resources available to them.
- They have a strong preference for full-text resources.
- They use Web-based support services moderately and largely do not ask for help.
- They have no significant difficulty in accessing and using Web-based resources, except when they experience connectivity problems relating to technology infrastructure at their remote location.

- Their satisfaction with Web resources and services offered is moderate to high.

It was also evident from the comments received that remote students do still need access to a library that they can visit in person. Many of the respondents indicated that, apart from using the Penn State University Libraries' electronic resources and virtual services, they also visited a local library in person and sought assistance with their research. Correlation analysis indicated that of those patrons who expressed satisfaction with current electronic resources and services, most of them also used a local library. On the other hand, of those who expressed dissatisfaction with the current resources and services, very few reported using a local library. This led to the conclusion that virtual patrons' research needs may not be fully met through exclusively virtual means, and that patrons may need to complement the use of virtual library services with in-person visits to a local library to get research assistance.

This survey of World Campus students was also seized as an opportunity to publicize the electronic resources and services of the University Libraries to remote patrons; therefore, the Web questionnaire included hyperlinks to all electronic resources and services that were mentioned in the survey. When respondents clicked the 'submit' button at the end of the Web survey, a new browser window popped up with a list of links, providing an opportunity for respondents to review all the sources referred to in the survey.

Discussion

Findings of the Penn State World Campus study, in comparison to findings of other similar studies covered by the literature, show similar trends in virtual patrons' perceptions of, and use of, the library. For instance, the OCLC (2002) white paper reports that the most used Web-based library resources were full-text electronic journals, the online catalog, and the electronic databases. Both of these studies also reveal a strong preference for full-text resources. The OCLC white paper, The University of Iowa study (Dew, 2001), and the Penn State World Campus study all indicate that students are fairly confident and savvy in navigating library Web resources and consider themselves adequately skilled to conduct online research. They did not perceive instruction in the use of electronic resources as a key need. Rather, they are more interested in full-text resources that provide instant access to online information. However, the findings of the present and other studies show that virtual patrons are not making optimum use of electronic resources and services available to them. Use of such resources as instructional tutorials and online research guides is very minimal. This may be due to the fact that virtual patrons consider themselves adequately equipped to perform research and do not need instruction or guidance. It is also possible that another reason for non-use of certain resources is that patrons are not aware that the resources are available in the first place. It could also be that patrons just determine, based on their own impression, that they do not need those resources. These possibilities underscore the importance of establishing a detailed understanding of the characteristics of virtual patrons in order to be able to provide services that match their profiles and needs.

CONCLUSION

Technological changes in academic libraries have enabled them to reach and serve patrons far beyond the library building. Virtual patrons can access library resources remotely and conduct their research from any location where there is Internet access, and with the perpetual availability of the Web, they can do so at any time of the day or night. However, evidence from surveys and observations has shown that these patrons still require assistance and guidance in conducting research. The vast amount of electronic resources and information accessible to them remotely has not eliminated the need for instructional support and guidance to enable them to retrieve quality, relevant information. In order for libraries to serve virtual patrons, they need to know them and understand their circumstances and research needs, much in the same way that they need to understand the needs of in-person patrons. The differences in serving virtual patrons compared to in-person patrons lie in the modes of delivery of the services. Access to collections is as important for in-person patrons as it is for virtual patrons. Similarly, the reference function remains basically the same, differing only in that virtual reference is defined by the technology that allows the service to transcend distance. This applies to instruction as well as many other functions within the virtual library environment. As technology continues to develop rapidly, the new capabilities that it offers will define the direction of services to virtual patrons in the academic library setting. However, the fundamental service principles and goals remain the same in both physical and virtual environments.

The characteristics/profile of today's virtual patron may not be the same as those of virtual patrons a few years down the road. The context of virtual library service is a dynamic one, and its parameters are largely defined by technological capabilities to provide electronic multimedia information over vast distances and in vast volumes, the ability to support virtual communities that emerge as a result of numerous online facilities, and the communication and interactions that take place between the library and patrons in the provision of access to this information. Within this environment, libraries create mechanisms that enhance access to collections, facilitate communication and dialog with patrons, and provide assistance and instruction. Trends show that service to virtual patrons is currently characterized by access to electronic collections, particularly full-text databases, e-journals, e-books, and e-reserves. Electronic delivery service systems are facilitating continued use of print collections by remote patrons. Virtual reference services and other electronic communication systems, both synchronous and asynchronous, provide a means of communication and dialog with patrons, and an avenue for libraries to develop detailed patron profiles and establish their needs. Web resources such as instructional modules, tutorials, and FAQs are good self-help resources for patrons to use independently to become efficient online researchers. However, effectiveness of such Web resources is dependent on the appropriateness of the design and content. To become efficient researchers, virtual patrons have to embrace these resources together with the support services that enhance their use. For instance, embracing electronic full-text resources in the absence of instruction or reference guidance may leave virtual patrons with inadequate skills to enable them make effective use of these resources. Moreover, virtual patrons must be cognizant of the issues surrounding the current electronic publishing and scholarly communication practices. Of particular note are intellectual integrity and adherence to copyright and fair use requirements as integral parts of the present day academic culture.

REFERENCES

Buchanan, Lori E., D. L. Luck and T. C. Jones. 2002. Integrating information literacy into the virtual university: A course model. *Library Trends* 51(2): 144-166.

Burke, L. 2001. The future role of librarians in the virtual library environment. *Australian Library Journal* 51(1). Journal available from World Wide Web: http://alia.org.au/publishing/alj/.

Cooper, R. and P. R. Dempsey. 1998. Remote library users-needs and expectations. *Library Trends* 47(1): 42-65.

Crowley, G. H., R. Leffel, D. Ramirez, J. L. Hart, and T. S. Armstrong, II. 2002. User perceptions of the library's Web pages: A focus group study at Texas A&M University. *The Journal of Academic Librarianship* 28(4): 205-210.

Dew, S. H. 2001. Knowing your users and what they want: Surveying off-campus students about library services. In *Off-Campus Library Services,* edited by Anne Marie Casey. New York: The Haworth Information Press, pp.177-193.

Dewald, N., A. Scholz-Crane, A. Booth, and C. Levine. 2000. Information literacy at a distance: Instructional design issues. *The Journal of Academic Librarianship* 26 (1): 33-44.

Fritch, J. W. and S. B. Mandernack. 2001. The emerging reference paradigm: A vision of reference services in a complex information environment. *Library Trends* 50(2): 286-305.

Graham, K. and A. Grodzinski. 2001. Defining the remote library user: An online survey. *portal: Libraries and the Academy* 1(3): 289-308.

Helfer, D. S. 2003. Virtual reference in libraries: Status and issues. *Searcher* 11(2): 63-65.

Hulshof, R. 1999. Providing services to virtual patrons. *Information Outlook* 3(1): 20-23.

Johnston, Patricia E. 2003. Digital reference as an instruction tool: Just in time and just enough. *Searcher* 11(3): 31-33.

Jones, S., M. Madden, L. N. Clarke, S. Cornish, M. Gonzales, C. Johnson, J. N. Lawson, S. Smith, S. H. Bickerton, M. Hansen, G. Lengauer, L. Oliveria, W. Prindle, J. Pyfer. 2002. The Internet goes to college: How students are living in the future with today's technology. Washington, D.C. Pew Internet and American Life Project, http://www.pewinternet.org (accessed July 6, 2003).

Miller, K. Metzinger. 2003. Behind every great virtual library stand many great licenses. *Library Journal* 128(1): 20-22.

OCLC (Online Computer Library Center, Inc.). 2002. How academic librarians can influence students' Web-based information choices. *White paper on the information habits of college students.*

Pilston, A. K. and R. L. Hart 2002. Student response to a new electronic reserves system. *The Journal of Academic Librarianship* 28(3): 147-151.

Smith, E. T. 2003. Changes in faculty reading behaviors: The impact of electronic journals on the University of Georgia. *The Journal of Academic Librarianship* 29(3): 162-168.

Tenopir, C. 2003. Electronic publishing: Research issues for academic librarians and users *Library Trends*, 51(4): 614-635.

Thompson, C. 2003. Information illiterate or lazy: How college students use the Web for research. *portal: Libraries and the Academy* 3(2): 259-268.

Troll, D. A. 2002. How and why libraries are changing: What we know and what we need to know. *portal: Libraries and the Academy* 2 (1): 99-123.

APPENDIX 1

(Web form used to survey virtual patrons: Penn State World Campus students)

Meeting the Needs of Remote Library Users

---

1) Which PSU library resource have you used? (Check as many as apply)

☐ The CAT (PSU online catalog)
☐ Fast Track (electronic database)
☐ Online Reference Shelf
☐ PSU Subject Libraries Home Pages
☐ None of the above

2) Have you ever visited the PSU Libraries' home page for World Campus students?

○ Yes
○ No

3) Have you ever used any of the PSU Libraries' **full-text** databases? (A full-text database provides access to entire articles online. An example of a full-text database is Proquest.)

○ Yes
○ No

4) Have you ever requested to have a book or journal article sent to you through the **Library Distance Learning Delivery** service (interlibrary loan)?

○ Yes
○ No

5) Have you ever e-mailed the **Electronic Reference Desk** for help with a research question?

○ Yes
○ No

6) Have you ever used any of PSU Libraries' online research tutorials, such as "Information Literacy and You?"

○ Yes
○ No

7) How easy is it for you to **find** the library resources that you need?

○ Very Easy
○ Easy
○ Difficult
○ Very Difficult

8) How easy is it for you to **get** the library resources that you need?

   ○ Very Easy
   ○ Easy
   ○ Difficult
   ○ Very Difficult

9) As a distance learner, does the library provide enough help for you to find and get the resources that you need?

   ○ Yes
   ○ No

10) If 'No' to above, what can we do to help you find and get the library resources that you need more easily? (check as many as apply)

   ☐ Provide more web-based tutorials on how to do library research
   ☐ Make available electronic, one-on-one research help
   ☐ Home delivery of books, journal articles and other materials

11) Do you visit a local library in person to do your research or get help?

   ○ Yes
   ○ No

12) If 'Yes' to above, which type of local library do you visit?

   ☐ PSU library (main library or branch campus)
   ☐ Public library in your area
   ☐ Other college or university library (non-PSU)
   ☐ Other type of library

13) Do you have any additional comments on the quality of library services to World Campus and other remote students? Please feel free to make suggestions!

Submit Form

Webinar Technology: Application in Libraries

Karen J. Docherty
Angi Herold Faiks

SUMMARY. This article reviews the current state of Webinar technology from a library perspective: what it is, how it works, and the many features Webinars commonly provide, including: polling, annotation tools, document sharing, recording, archiving, and reporting. The authors offer a brief look at types of organizations using Webinar technology, and which vendors are active in this rapidly developing market. Possible library applications are discussed and the authors' personal Webinar experiences are shared. A comparison to similar Web-based technologies such as Web tutorials, virtual reference, courseware management systems, videoconferencing, and Webcasting is also included. *[Article copies available for a fee from The Haworth Document Delivery Service: 1-800-HAWORTH. E-mail address: <docdelivery@haworthpress.com> Website: <http://www.HaworthPress.com> © 2004 by The Haworth Press, Inc. All rights reserved.]*

Karen J. Docherty, MA (Library and Information Studies), BA (Speech Communication), is an Electronic Resources Librarian, MINITEX Library Information Network, University of Minnesota, 15 Andersen Library, 222 21st Avenue South, Minneapolis, MN 55455-0439 (E-mail: kdochert@umn.edu). She works with all types of libraries in Minnesota, North Dakota, and South Dakota to assist in the review, selection, licensing, promotion, and evaluation of electronic information resources from various vendors. Angi Herold Faiks, MSLIS, BA (French, Philosophy), is Associate Library Director and Collection Management Team Leader, Dewitt Wallace Library, Macalester College, 1600 Grand Avenue, St. Paul, MN 55105 (E-mail: faiks@macalester.edu). At the time this article was written, she was an Electronic Resources Librarian, MINITEX Library Information Network.

[Haworth co-indexing entry note]: "Webinar Technology: Application in Libraries." Docherty, Karen J., and Angi Herold Faiks. Co-published simultaneously in *Science & Technology Libraries* (The Haworth Information Press, an imprint of The Haworth Press, Inc.) Vol. 25, No. 1/2, 2004, pp. 211-226; and: *Emerging Issues in the Electronic Environment: Challenges for Librarians and Researchers in the Sciences* (ed: Jeannie P. Miller) The Haworth Information Press, an imprint of The Haworth Press, Inc., 2004, pp. 211-226. Single or multiple copies of this article are available for a fee from The Haworth Document Delivery Service [1-800-HAWORTH, 9:00 a.m. - 5:00 p.m. (EST). E-mail address: docdelivery@haworthpress.com].

http://www.haworthpress.com/web/STL
© 2004 by The Haworth Press, Inc. All rights reserved.
Digital Object Identifier: 10.1300/J122v25n01_13

KEYWORDS. Web-conferencing, Web technologies, Web tutorials, distance education, virtual reference, library services, information technology

INTRODUCTION

Imagine the proverbial chemistry student, at one o'clock in the morning, preparing to search the chemistry database, *SciFinder Scholar*. She is seeking information about the structure and mechanisms of an enzyme for a class paper due the next day. Staring at the search screens, a mixture of confusion and panic sets in. The student remembers going to a library class on chemistry research techniques at the beginning of the semester, but now, months later, she cannot recall the process. If she really stretched her imagination, she might try looking at the *SciFinder* company Web page and use the tutorial for hints. Perhaps she could eventually figure out what to do by reading the help topics or by trial and error. Yet, she also remembers that the librarian instructor included other information in the class such as citation styles and suggestions for additional online resources useful in completing her paper. Wouldn't it be slick if the student could click on a button and replay that class? Sure!

Now, imagine three professors collaborating on a research project. They are each in different remote locations collecting data on crows. They are plotting their data using a geographical information system (GIS) and are working with the library expert to bring their data together for display on a map. The librarian needs to periodically meet with the professors, but has to do so remotely due to their off-site locations. Wouldn't it be great if they could all meet online to share documents, consult with the librarian, and have a group discussion? Certainly!

This article explores the application and usefulness of Web-based technology that can provide the services illustrated above and discusses the potential usefulness of such technology in libraries. Although various terms are employed to describe this technology–Web seminar, Web conferencing, Web sessions–this article uses the term 'Webinar,' as described in *The Webopedia online computer and Internet dictionary*:

> Short for Web-based seminar, a presentation, lecture, workshop or seminar that is transmitted over the Web.
>
> A key feature of a Webinar is its interactive elements–the ability to give, receive and discuss information. Contrast with Webcast, in

which the data transmission is one way and does not allow inter-action between the presenter and the audience. (http://www. Webopedia.com)

Webinar technology has the capability of bringing people together to share information using both visual and audio communication; this is the synchronous model. In addition, Webinar sessions can be recorded for later viewing; this is the asynchronous model. Perhaps the most at-tractive feature is that the learning curve and expertise required to use the software are minimal. The process takes about the same preparation time needed if the meeting, instruction, or collaboration was happening in person. Used in conjunction with traditional means of communica-tion, Webinars can extend the reach of those employing this technol-ogy much further than was previously possible. Webinars are an efficient and potentially cost-effective way to transmit and share in-formation with one or many individuals, no matter where they might be located.

WHY WEBINARS IN LIBRARIES?

Libraries have traditionally been early adopters of innovative tech-nologies. They implement, employ, and then instruct others in using complex systems and highly specialized software to store, retrieve, and manipulate information. Given libraries' commitment to outreach and teaching, and the increasing demands to bring services to users at the point of need, wherever that may be, it seems that interactive and real-time library user instruction via the Web makes perfect sense. Why, then, is there not great use of Webinar technology in libraries at the moment? In businesses today, Webinar systems are being used at an ever-increasing rate. Library consortia and networks are taking ad-vantage of the technology in order to train staff throughout large geo-graphic regions. With virtual reference software now being used in many libraries to answer questions from remote patrons, it makes sense that library staff would also teach patrons through interactive Webinar software.

Libraries have not avoided the idea of Web-based teaching. There are several articles and books on the topic. Yet, there is surprisingly little sophisticated development in this arena. Popular methods include static tutorials mounted on the Web and tutorials that have some interactive component such as animations or quizzes. Library instruction via the

Web remains largely text-based and static, while Webinar technology allows for interactive, real-time instruction in addition to asynchronous instruction using both video and audio components.

This article explains Webinar technology in detail in order to show its usefulness and practicality in a library setting.

HOW WEBINARS WORK

Webinars have both a visual component that is Web-based and an audio component that is most commonly delivered via telephone. Webinar attendees sit at a computer, usually their own, and participate in a live Web-based presentation. The presentation can be made up of *Microsoft PowerPoint* slides, a live Web searching or viewing session, a sharing of any desktop file (such as *Microsoft Word* or *Excel* documents), or any combination of these elements (Figure 1).

Some meetings allow for collaborative document sharing, which means that more than one person can edit the same file at the same time. A Webinar can be pre-scheduled or can be set up instantaneously at a time of need.

Most Webinars use a telephone for the audio connection, utilizing a conference call when there are more than two attendees. A telephone with a speaker-phone feature or the use of a headset is recommended– that way the presenter(s) and attendee(s) do not have to hold the handset during the presentation. The use of a speaker phone is also a great way for colleagues to participate in a session at one shared computer terminal.

Voice over Internet Protocol (IP) technology that facilitates delivery of voice or conversation over the Internet is also an option offered by many Webinar providers, but attendee hardware capability must be considered if this option is to be used. One of the most appealing aspects of Webinars is the ease of attending a session. Most service providers do not require that Webinar participants download any software, or if they do, it's typically a small, fast-loading plug-in. Then, users simply go to the URL provided to them by the Webinar presenter.

Webinar vendors usually host the service on their own servers, demanding little to no technical knowledge from users of the technology (presenters or attendees) and no hardware or software outlays beyond existing telephones and personal computers.

FIGURE 1. Example of an Instruction Slide Using Microsoft's *Live Meeting*

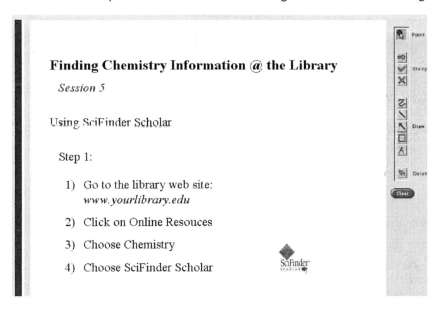

Screen shot reprinted by permission from Microsoft Corporation. SciFinder Scholar screen reproduced with permission of the American Chemical Society.

Session Size and Length

Webinar sessions vary greatly in both the capacity of attendees that can be accommodated and the length of sessions. Webinars can be used with as few as two people participating or with upwards of 2,000. Webinars are ideal for small group meetings and training sessions where participants require the opportunity to ask questions and provide feedback. Webinar technology is also suitable for large-group lecture-style presentations and demonstrations, where contributions by attendees are not critical, but large groups can still contribute and ask questions.

Session length also varies considerably and is at the discretion of the Webinar presenter and the demands of the content. Because attendees can be subject to a range of distractions at their computers, sessions shorter in length, for example, under an hour, will likely keep their attention. However, Webinars, depending on their purpose, can last for several hours. In such cases, it's advisable to make these sessions participatory in nature to keep attendees engaged throughout.

WEBINAR FEATURES

Polling–Most Webinar vendors provide the capability to poll attendees. The polling feature is useful on a few fronts: (1) polling engages session attendees; (2) it's a great mechanism for establishing the sophistication of session attendees on a particular topic; and (3) polling can serve as a way to quiz attendees, real-time, about the information presented during the Webinar.

Since participants attend a Webinar at their own workstation, office surroundings can be distracting. E-mail, the in-box, and colleagues all present challenges for keeping the undivided attention of the attendees. The use of polling slides requires that attendees interact with the Webinar presenter (Figure 2). Webinar technology often facilitates the capture of polling results. See the "Reports" section of this article for information on the feature.

Annotation and highlighting features–Most Webinar platforms offer the session presenter multiple tools for annotating and highlighting parts of the presentation in real time. These simple tools help direct the attention of the attendee to certain areas of the screen, and can be used to add additional information to an existing slide. For example, the presenter can circle or underline an important point, can check off topics covered, and can add additional text into the presentation as needed (Figure 3).

FIGURE 2. Example of a Polling Slide Using Microsoft's *Live Meeting*

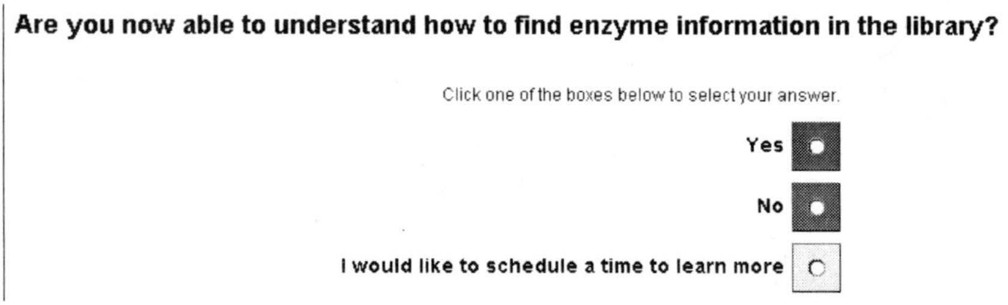

Are you now able to understand how to find enzyme information in the library?

Click one of the boxes below to select your answer.

Yes ▣

No ▣

I would like to schedule a time to learn more ▢

Screen shot reprinted by permission from Microsoft Corporation.

FIGURE 3. Example of a Microsoft *Live Meeting* Instruction Slide Marked on the Fly Up During a Webinar Session

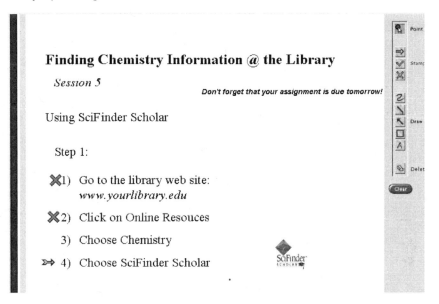

Screen shot reprinted by permission from Microsoft Corporation. SciFinder Scholar screen reproduced with permission of the American Chemical Society.

Document sharing–Some vendors provide the option for meeting participants to both share and co-edit documents with one another. This is particularly useful in a meeting-style setup rather than when Webinars are used for training or instruction. This option allows, for example, two people to view the exact same *Excel* document at the same time from their own computers and both can make changes and additions to the document together while also speaking to each other. It is a fantastic tool for collaborative work.

Recording and archiving–Most Webinar vendors provide a recording and archiving feature that allows for session playback at a time convenient for an attendee. This feature could be handy for the student who wants to review a session that he or she previously attended, or may be helpful to the person that could not attend the original session. Referring to the examples given at the beginning of this article, if one of the professors researching crow behavior was not able to attend the meeting to discuss plotting the GIS data with the librarian, he could review the recorded and archived Webinar to remain informed of the discussion and decisions. Perhaps the student looking for a refresher on how to search *SciFinder Scholar* could review the entire library instruction class during which she originally learned how to use the database.

It is important to note that the presenter of a recorded session may password-protect it, if he or she prefers for only a certain audience to review the content, or he or she may opt to share it with as broad an audience as possible. By not requiring a password, the presenter allows anyone in the world with Internet access, speakers, and recording format software, such as *Windows Media Player* or *RealPlayer Streamed Audio*, to review the session. For example, if all meetings of the crow data collecting team were recorded, they could share the URL(s) to these sessions with several other researchers who might have an interest in learning from their process. In the case of the *SciFinder Scholar* class, the librarian who recorded it could share the class with other colleagues to use as well. Or the librarian could post the archived session on the library's Web site, making it available for anybody to review it.

Reports–A variety of reports can be generated through most vendors' Webinar services. For example, presenters can gather data on who attended the session, how they responded to polling questions, how long they stayed for the meeting or presentation, and how many Webinar sessions were conducted by an organization. Most libraries capture a broad range of statistics to evaluate services and to share with funding bodies, boards, and other interested constituents. Webinars are another area where data can be gathered for a variety of uses.

SYSTEM REQUIREMENTS

Each service provider has a set of minimum system requirements for Webinar attendees. Most are able to accommodate hardware and software that is several years old. Webinar software is generally compatible with 166Mhz Pentium-based PCs with *Microsoft Windows* 95, 98, NT, ME, XP or 2000, Sun JVM 1.4 or Microsoft JVM, and Sun SPARCstation with Solaris 2.5.1, 2.6, 2.7 or 2.8. Either *Internet Explorer* 5.X or higher, or *Netscape* 4.5, 4.6, 4.7, 4.8 will work. *Macintosh* computers may or may not work, and usually require OS 9 or OS X. The technology required for presenting a Webinar is not often compatible with *Macintosh* computers. An Internet connection of 56.6K or faster is required. Since Webinar software is usually hosted by the provider–not the user–the requirements above are also applicable to Webinar presenters.

Security

According to the April 2003 "Web Conferencing Technologies" report by Lynne Jackson, "Security represents a major concern, as customers are wary that unauthorized people or even competitors can access a web conference" (Jackson 2003b). Many Webinar vendors are using secured socket layer (SSL) encryption for transmitting data between attendee and presenters and the vendor's server. Most vendors also have an option for requiring participants and presenters to authenticate themselves when entering a session. Meeting identification numbers, passwords, and other login information may be required for participation. Other security measures may be used, varying from vendor to vendor. Alternatively, if security is not an issue, and the goal of the presenter is to reach as broad an audience as possible, meetings can be left open to let anybody participate.

WHO IS USING THE TECHNOLOGY?

Increasingly, organizations are realizing the cost- and time-savings benefits of Webinar technology and appreciating the ability to share information with colleagues, students, and others in an efficient and timely manner. Many large corporations such as Hewlett Packard, CISCO, Prudential, American Express, Dow Jones, Capital One, Kodak, PeopleSoft, Agilent, and thousands of others, are using Webinars to communicate with and instruct staff and customers. "Oracle's [Judy] Sim says it costs her company 58 cents per person to set up a Webinar presentation, a dramatically lower cost than the $350 per head that the company was accustomed to paying for a real-world seminar" (Swoyer 2000). A sample of library and educational organizations that are currently using Webinar technology include OCLC Online Computer Library Center, The MINITEX Library and Information Network, AMIGOS Library Services, the University of Wisconsin–Extension Broadcasting and Media Innovations Unit, the University of Michigan, and many others. Several library product vendors like OCLC, Lexis-Nexis, OVID, Cambridge Scientific, to name a few, are also taking advantage of the power of Webinar technology, using it to demonstrate products for sales and training purposes.

MARKET TRENDS AND CURRENT VENDORS

There are a variety of Webinar products on the market today, and the number of vendors is expected to grow as more organizations grasp the benefits of this technology. Jackson (2003a) states that "[web conferencing] represents one of the few technologies able to exploit economic problems because it does what a lot of Internet-related companies promised to do but failed: Cuts costs and raises quality." She goes on to note that the market is growing at around 50% a year. A sampling of products in today's marketplace includes: *Microsoft Office Live Meeting: A PlaceWare Service, WebEx, Raindance* and others.

SUBSCRIPTION MODELS AND COSTS

No doubt a variety of subscription models exist. The most common model is based on the number of seats that an organization purchases, providing an unlimited number of meetings in a year for up to a set number of attendees. For example, a university might purchase ten seats to accommodate small classes and meetings or 100 seats to accommodate large gatherings. Another common model is the per-minute model, allowing organizations to schedule meetings on an as-needed basis, charging the organization for each participant per each minute of attendance.

While Webinar technology might sound very attractive, it is certain that many will be concerned with the costs, especially in times of tight budgets. Vendors often offer discounts to educational organizations. Real costs may actually be eliminated if this technology is adopted. For example, a class delivered via a Webinar could save travel costs and time for attendees and presenters, presentation room and equipment rental fees, and supplemental material printing fees. In addition, a significant amount of staff time and money could be required if a library creates its own method of offering Web-based instruction. These costs should be evaluated to see if, in the long run, Webinar technology would be less expensive to purchase than offering traditional meeting and training options or developing one's own Web-conferencing/training system.

COMPARISON TO OTHER WEB-BASED TECHNOLOGIES

A variety of Web-based learning technologies are available on the market today. Many librarians are familiar with virtual reference services, classroom management systems like *WebCT* and *BlackBoard*, and video conferencing. How do these packages compare to Web-conferencing technology? Although they do share some common features and purposes, the focus or strength of each is quite different. Currently, the various technologies do not replace one another, and in fact, complement each other when used together to provide instruction or meeting support. The dynamic nature of the Web-based solutions market may result in a convergence of many of the features and functionalities of the following tools.

Web Tutorials vs. Webinars

Web tutorials are canned presentations designed for use at the convenience and pace of the library user. "Relatively simple-to-use software packages allow text, document files, images, sound, animation, and video to be integrated into web-based training materials" (Allan 2002). They can be interactive, inviting the user to make choices and select responses, or they can be passive, allowing the user to watch or "forward through" the presentation. They can offer both an audio and video component, as do Webinars. While there are software packages that can be purchased to facilitate the creation of a tutorial, most examples found in the library are "home grown" and largely text-based. Differing from Webinars, they do not allow for live interaction with others. Web tutorials can reach many users at once, with each user having an individual experience with the tutorial, similar to an archived Webinar session.

Virtual Reference vs. Webinars

Both virtual reference software and Webinars allow librarians to communicate with library users, but there are substantial differences. The most obvious difference is that virtual reference software offers primarily a text-based and visual interaction, whereas Webinars provide both audio and visual components. Although many virtual reference service providers do offer voice over IP to customers, few libraries are using this technology at the present. Another main difference is that a user activates the virtual reference process by submitting an e-mail message or Web form or by clicking on a chat button, whereas the presenter actually initiates the Webinar session. Where virtual reference is most often a one-to-one interaction and is either asynchronous (e-mail or Web form) or synchronous (live chat), Webinars are designed primarily to communicate one-to-many or many-to-many in a meeting-style set up in either real-time (synchronous) or in an archived session (asynchronous).

Many virtual reference systems now allow for page pushing, application sharing, and co-browsing. The same features exist for Webinars. Features available with Webinar technology that are not available in virtual reference packages are polling and the ability to record and archive a session, although chat software does have a record in the form of a transcript.

Courseware Management Systems vs. Webinars

According to Shank and Dewald (2003), "Most courseware (software) shares a certain set of basic features, including powerful resource sharing, communication and assessment tools." Courseware provides access points for readings and other related material, including links to library resources, and can facilitate student and instructor communication via distribution lists and chat forums. "Built in assessment tools allow instructors to create simple, auto-marked web quizzes and tests, create auto-marked web surveys, and monitor their students' progress and interaction with the courseware-enhanced quizzes, materials, and communication features" (Shank and Dewald 2003).

Webinars and courseware systems both offer the ability to share files among participants, but to date, Webinars alone allow for the real-time co-editing of any file on the presenter(s) workstation with other Webinar participants and co-presenters. Webinars also allow for live Web demonstrations. Webinars and some courseware systems offer recording and subsequent archived playback of sessions at the convenience of attendees, and certain courseware packages do offer this feature as well.

Webinar participants can chat with other attendees, ask questions by typing and sending them to the presenter, or verbally ask questions. This feature is also built into some courseware packages. There is no built in post-session communication mechanism for Webinar participants. This is a main difference with courseware systems, where distribution lists and chat forums are core strengths.

Webinar technology offers a polling feature that can be used as a quizzing or testing function. Although responses are captured and can be shared with other participants instantaneously, they do not automatically indicate whether a response is correct or incorrect. The presenter can either give the correct answer during the session or can retrieve responses at the end of a session and follow up with the students afterwards. This illustrates a difference from courseware management systems that allow for built-in automatic and immediate feedback to instructor-created quizzes.

Courseware systems allow instructors to grade and track student performance throughout the duration of a course and share records with systems such as *Peoplesoft*. Webinar technologies do not accommodate this type of ongoing record keeping.

California State University, Chico, uses *HorizonLive*, a form of Webinar technology, to complement their university's *WebCT* courseware package. Authors Blakeslee and Johnson (2002) describe a project where CSU library staff used *HorizonLive* to create archived library tutorials with enhanced screenshots to demonstrate library skills to selected classes. They state, "*HorizonLive*, especially when used in a class that is already using the (*WebCT*) technology, is an excellent way to deliver library instruction."

In sum, because the intent of courseware software is generally to deliver or supplement an entire course online over a period of time such as a semester, in many cases it will offer a more sophisticated suite of tools and features. The choice of which method to use depends upon the content, format, and intent of the instruction being delivered. Kraemer (2003) adds, "Due to the complexity and power of . . . course management software, [instructors] must go through training in order to begin constructing a class." While training is also needed to use Webinar technology, it is minimal, perhaps requiring only a few hours.

Videoconferencing and Webcasting vs. Webinars

Videoconferencing and Webcasting are probably the closest relatives to Web-conferencing. All are designed to allow users in different locations to participate in meetings or training with both audio and visual components. The focus of videoconferencing and Webcasting is on showing recordings of participants and instructors, whereas the Webinar focus is on the presentation content or material being shared. In other words, users of videoconferencing or Webcasting consider the ability to see the presenter and attendees during a session important. "Webcasts depend heavily on the video transmission and often focus on the *talking head* instead of the information being transmitted" (Hendersen 2003). Many Webinar packages allow presenters to include images of themselves in the display area. Alternatively, some Webinar packages may allow for streaming video of the presenter, but the capacity to shift between presenter and document does not exist at this time. Webinar technology also provides special annotation tools, co-editing of documents, and the polling and reporting features that are not available in video-conferencing.

Another major difference between Webinars and videoconferencing or Webcasting is the equipment, hardware and software required for each of these means of instruction. Webinars do not require any equipment other than a computer, standard Web browser, Internet connection with a speed of 56K or faster, and a telephone. In addition to the computer, Web browser, and fast Internet connection, desktop video-conferencing, for example, requires at the very least a video camera, a microphone, speakers, viewing software, and video streaming software.

CURRENT WEBINAR APPLICATIONS

Most current users of Webinar technology are using the application in at least one of three ways: training, sales demonstrations, and meetings. The introduction to this article mentioned two possible applications: the student wishing to replay an archived session on how to use library resources, and the librarian and professors in disparate locations needing to meet to collaborate on their research. Many other applications are conceivable. Libraries could not only record live bibliographic instruction sessions, they could also record "canned" sessions on any number of topics for students to use on an as-needed basis. To facilitate staff training within a single library, on a campus with multiple libraries or even on separate campuses, Webinars provide an opportunity for everyone to gain the same information without the time and expense of moving people around or between campuses or the hassles of scheduling. Perhaps a library has updated several human resources policies or has implemented a new integrated library system. Both of these topics could be addressed either via the meeting or instruction capabilities of a Webinar. Similar to the example of the library and professors working on plotting spatial data, Webinars are an excellent meeting tool for telecommuting staff or for individuals spread across the country or world. Meetings can take place as usual, regardless of location. Webinar technology also offers an easy way to demonstrate to either library patrons or staff how to perform a task such as resolving a technical problem, illustrating a new procedure, or learning a new skill. For example, if a library was switching to new e-mail software for their employees, an instructional session could be recorded once for each employee to review on their own time.

RESPONSE TO WEBINARS:
THE AUTHORS' EXPERIENCE

Many benefits of Webinar instruction and meetings in a library setting are illustrated. Whether it is used in place of, or as a supplement to, face-to-face meetings or classes, it can serve as a powerful and practical tool for reaching a variety of audiences.

There are some less obvious benefits to the technology as well. Those who find it stressful to talk in front of people might be more comfortable presenting or participating in this format. It should also be mentioned, however, that for those who need a lot of feedback, especially visual, this mode of communication might prove more difficult. Neither attendees nor presenters have to worry about how they look during a session. Attendees, for example, could be wearing their pajamas, have their feet up on their desk, and be sipping a cup of coffee and no one would ever know. The authors of this paper often poll Webinar attendees and have repeatedly found that most attendees are thrilled with the technology. One librarian commented, "My first experience with a Webinar was very positive. I think that the Webinar format will allow MINITEX participants to gain knowledge in a variety of areas that they might not otherwise study. Taking an hour out of a workday does not require the commitment that traveling to a half-day seminar takes. I was surprised; I hadn't anticipated enjoying the Webinar format so much." Another librarian stated, "I really like the WEBINAR sessions. The pace is fine and the group is small enough so that I don't feel a question slows the session down too much." The authors' organization has also been able to reach several individuals who would have otherwise not been able to attend in-person instruction or meetings if either would have required any travel. One librarian in a remote location commented, "The Web seminar gave me what I needed to know about a particular vendor's services. I would not have attended this informational session in person." In sum, the experience of Webinar usage in the authors' organization has been highly positive.

CONCLUSION

Optimally, Webinars will be used to complement traditional instruction or meeting formats. A Webinar can never replace the interaction and communication that takes place when people are physically together. Yet, when meeting face-to-face is not possible or practical, or as an alternative format to meet certain instructional, collaborative or meeting needs, Webinars can be a tremendously effective tool. Libraries, in particular, can employ this technology to serve and instruct patrons and staff when and where they need it.

REFERENCES

Allan, Barbara. 2002. *E-learning and teaching in library and information services.* London: Facet Publishing.

Blakeslee, Sarah, and Kristin Johnson. 2002. Using HorizonLive to deliver library instruction to distance and online students. *Reference Services Review* 30(4): 324-329.

Henderson, Allan J. 2003. *The e-learning question and answer book: A survival guide for trainers and business managers.* New York: AMACOM.

Jackson, Lynn. 2003a. Web conferencing market trends. *Faulkner's Advisory on Computer and Communications Technologies.* http://www.faulkner.com (accessed September 2003).

Jackson, Lynn. 2003b. Web conferencing technologies. *Faulkner's Advisory on Computer and Communications Technologies.* http://www.faulkner.com (accessed September 2003).

Kraemer, Elizabeth W. 2003. Developing the online learning environment: the pros and cons of using WebCT for library instruction. *Information Technology and Libraries* 22(2): 87-92.

Shank, John D., and Nancy H. Dewald. 2003. Establishing our presence in courseware: Adding library services to the virtual classroom. *Information Technology and Libraries* 22(1): 38-43.

Swoyer, Stephen. 2000. Web seminars catch on. *MC Technology Marketing Intelligence* 20(6): 26.

Webopedia. http://www.Webopedia.com (accessed September 2003).

Preserving Digital Libraries: Determining "What?" Before Deciding "How?"

Jean Marie Deken

SUMMARY. Preservation of digital libraries is a complicated process that must begin with an appraisal of what is to be preserved before it moves on to the question of how to best preserve it. In order to fully understand the nature and attributes of digital documents and digital libraries, it is necessary to place them in the context of some of the other types of cultural artifacts that have been preserved over time, and to look at how the issues of fixity (stability) and durability (longevity) of these other artifacts have been addressed. Cultural artifacts are products of the "processing" of "parts" into "products" of varying fixity and durability. Efforts to define digital documents and digital libraries are at the root of current research into the best ways of preserving both, and have been deeply affected by the blurred boundaries between parts, processes, and products; by the continually changing nature of digital entities; and by the entities' low fixity and low durability. Current research projects into the preservation of digital entities have concluded that a necessary first

Jean Marie Deken, MA, MLIS, CA, is Archivist and Head, Archives and History Office, Stanford Linear Accelerator Center, Stanford, CA 94025 (E-mail: jmdeken@slac.stanford.edu).

The author would like to thank Professor Ziming Liu, San Jose State University School of Library and Information Science, for his assistance in preparing this manuscript.

[Haworth co-indexing entry note]: "Preserving Digital Libraries: Determining 'What?' Before Deciding 'How?' " Deken, Jean Marie. Co-published simultaneously in *Science & Technology Libraries* (The Haworth Information Press, an imprint of The Haworth Press, Inc.) Vol. 25, No. 1/2, 2004, pp. 227-241; and: *Emerging Issues in the Electronic Environment: Challenges for Librarians and Researchers in the Sciences* (ed: Jeannie P. Miller) The Haworth Information Press, an imprint of The Haworth Press, Inc., 2004, pp. 227-241. Single or multiple copies of this article are available for a fee from The Haworth Document Delivery Service [1-800-HAWORTH, 9:00 a.m. - 5:00 p.m. (EST). E-mail address: docdelivery@haworthpress.com].

Digital Object Identifier: 10.1300/J122v25n01_14

step is the appraisal of the "significant properties" of digital objects. Now is the time for the creation of a range of digital-derivative products of high fixity and high durability that each effectively captures some significant property of the original "digital performance" or "digital organism." *[Article copies available for a fee from The Haworth Document Delivery Service: 1-800-HAWORTH. E-mail address: <docdelivery@haworthpress.com> Website: <http://www.HaworthPress.com> © 2004 by The Haworth Press, Inc. All rights reserved.]*

KEYWORDS. Digital libraries–preservation, digital media–preservation

INTRODUCTION

Preservation of digital libraries is a complicated process involving issues of storage media, hardware and software fixity and longevity. Because of the complex nature of digital library preservation, it is best to begin with an appraisal of what is to be preserved before moving on to the question of how to best preserve it. Ongoing and completed digital preservation research projects are making valuable contributions to our understanding of the issues involved with preserving digital materials in an authentic manner, but before real-world libraries and archives attempt to adopt the strategies and tools developed by these projects, librarians and archivists must answer the question: Is it always necessary, worthwhile, and the best practice to preserve digital materials digitally? Underlying this question are two other questions that preservation researchers, as well as librarians and archivists, need to answer: What sort of cultural and actual artifact is a "digital document" or a "digital library"? And, what is it we are preserving when we preserve the "digital document" or the "digital library"?

CREATION AND PRESERVATION
OF ANALOG CULTURAL ARTIFACTS

In order to fully understand the nature and attributes of digital documents and digital libraries, it is necessary to place them in the context of some of the other types of cultural artifacts that have been preserved over time, and to look at how the issues of fixity and durability of these other artifacts have been addressed. In general terms, cultural artifacts are products resulting from the processing of parts (see Figure 1). Parts are elements that are manipulated; process is the act of manipulating parts; and product is the result of the processing of parts. Products can be thought of as having two primary qualities: fixity and durability. The quality of fixity relates to the stability of the artifact over time, while durability relates to its temporal longevity (Arms 2000, p. 254; Brown and Duguid 2000). For example, a one-hundred-year-old oak tree is durable but not fixed: it has survived a long time, but it has changed continuously over that period of survival. A Babylonian clay tablet, by contrast, is both fixed and durable: it has survived for millennia in an unchanged form (Boorstin 1987).

Musical performances are short-lived vocal and instrumental activities that can be captured through musical notation (symbols used to make a written record of musical sounds). The first known western musical notation system was developed in the first century C.E. (Musical Notation 2001). Much later, devices were developed to make a material chronicle of musical passages and to allow later mechanical reproduction (music boxes, player piano rolls). Still later, more sophisticated and accurate devices were invented to capture more fully and precisely the sounds of performed music and to fix them in a medium (sound recording) that would remain relatively stable in storage and could faithfully reproduce the performance when mounted on the appropriate playback device at a later time. Recognized musical genres include folk, classical, opera, jazz, etc. Actual individual performances in the recognized gen-

FIGURE 1. Basic Elements of Cultural Artifacts, in Sequence

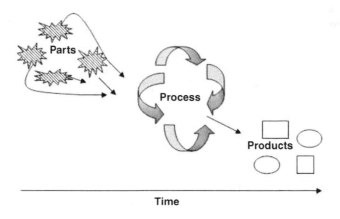

Time

res are preserved through sound recordings, which may last up to 100 years depending upon the storage medium (St-Laurent 1996). Musical performances are also recreated to a close approximation based upon both study with traditionally trained practitioners, and interpretation of surviving written documentation and artifacts (sheet music, librettos, surviving musical instruments, historic opera houses). Placing musical performance into the construct of parts, process, and product delineated in Figure 1, it is clear that the voice or instrument are "parts"; the played or sung performance is "process"; and the sheet music, libretto, or recording is "product." The relative fixity and durability of musical performance products (the recordings of the performances) varies according to the durability of the recording medium. Parts of musical performance–the voices and instruments–move on to other processes once a product is completed, and eventually lose their processing utility (singers lose their voices and eventually die; instruments wear out or break). The individual products of music–sheet music, librettos and/or recordings–persist and can be retained for future use as products or re-utilized as parts in later musical performance processes. Their fixity and durability depend upon the medium on which they are recorded: Sheet music and librettos on paper media tend to be more fixed and durable than recordings.

Theater and oratory are also transient vocal and physical performances. These sometimes involve devices for voice amplification, costumes, props, and staging. Recognized theatrical genres include comedy, tragedy, and satire; recognized genres of oratory include funeral orations, sermons, and political speeches (Oratory 2001). Theatrical and oratorical works were originally captured by the author or the listener by means of rote memorization. Later means of capture included inscription on various media (including paper) of the spoken text and of instructions and notations concerning movements to be performed in conjunction with the verbal presentation (Drama, Western 2001). Later, more sophisticated and accurate devices were invented to capture the sounds and the images of theatrical and oratorical performances and to fix them in a medium (audio recordings, moving picture film, videotape, DVD) that would remain relatively stable in storage and would faithfully reproduce the performance when mounted on the appropriate playback device. The vocal portions of actual individual theatrical and oratorical performances can be preserved through audio recordings, which, as noted above, may last up to 100 years. The combined vocal and visual aspects of performances are preserved through moving picture film, videotape, and the more recently developed DVD technology.

The oldest of these media, moving picture film, has been successfully preserved for 70 to 90 years under optimal storage conditions (Association of Moving Image Archivists 2000).

Theatrical and oratorical performances are also recreated to a close approximation based upon study with traditionally trained practitioners and study and interpretation of surviving written documentation and artifacts (scripts; stage, set, and costume designs documented in writing or printing on paper; historic costumes, stage sets and theater buildings; etc.). In theatrical and oratorical performance, the "parts" are the voices, bodies, and gestures of the actors or speakers, and the play performed or recited. The acted or spoken performance is the "process"; and the text, script, and movie, video, or DVD recording are the "products." The relative fixity and durability of theatrical and oratorical performance products vary according to the recording medium. The component parts of theatrical and oratorical performance–the voices, bodies, and gestures of the speakers and actors–move on to other processes at the completion of a performance, and their durability, like that of musicians, is bounded by the limitations of human biology. The products of theater and oratory–texts, scripts, audio recordings, and movies–are retained as cultural artifacts. Their durability varies depending upon the durability of the medium upon which they are recorded.

Literary works were originally created orally and preserved through rote memorization, in much the same manner as musical, theatrical, and oratorical works. They were later created using a brush or pen dipped into ink and applied to papyrus, wood, vellum, or paper (Brookfield 1993). Still later, mechanical methods of printing with ink on paper were developed. In printing, an individual or machine mounts moveable type in chases that are locked into presses, inked and then manipulated against paper to deposit recognizable marks. Printed pages are cut, folded, and sometimes sewn and cased in bindings. After the printed product is created, the moveable type is broken out of the chases, returned to sorted stock to be reused, or, in later processes, melted down and reformed into new letters (Katz 1995). In the mid-nineteenth century, literary works also began to be created by means of the typewriter (Brookfield 1993), which is a device operated by one person and utilizing alphabetic keys which, when pressed, cause type bars to strike an inking mechanism and deposit ink on paper in the shape of letters or symbols.

Literary works are conventionally shaped into one of many recognizable genres: letter, diary, broadside, poster, history, novel, memorandum, receipt, contract, newspaper, magazine, map, etc. (Levy 2001).

Singly-produced literary works have been preserved by individuals who have either copied them by hand or have utilized one of the mechanical copy processes (photocopying) (Katz 1995). Printed texts have usually been preserved through the production of many multiples, some of which have been collected by libraries and research centers. In the creation of literary works, pen and ink, moveable type, printing presses, and typewriters are some of the "parts" which can go on to be used in other processes until they are worn out, or used up and eventually discarded. The processed, marked paper–whether collated into books, magazines, and newspapers or fashioned into single sheets as letters, receipts, etc.–is the "product." The fixity and durability of literary "products"–letters, diaries, novels, memos, etc.–are dependent, as with all other cultural artifacts discussed thus far, upon the characteristics of the recording medium. Until the present, the most common medium for literary "products" has been paper, a medium of high fixity and varying durability. Alkaline papers stored under optimal conditions can last several hundred years without significant deterioration; acid papers or papers stored under adverse conditions will only last for several decades, if that long (American Library Association 1993).

This very brief and condensed history of a few of the myriad types of cultural artifacts is provided in order to demonstrate some characteristics common to their creation and preservation. As has been shown, the cultural artifacts discussed result from the "processing" of "parts" into "products" of varying fixity and durability. Preservation efforts for most cultural artifacts have centered on the products, while inanimate parts used in the processes of creating the artifacts have generally been retained only for re-use in subsequent processes. It is useful to note here that museums have traditionally collected and preserved noteworthy or unique individual specimens of parts used in the creation of cultural artifacts. However, even when inanimate parts have high levels of stability and fixity (lead type, for example) the vast majority are not preserved: they are re-formed or repeatedly re-used and ultimately used up in the creation of additional artifacts.

CREATION OF DIGITAL CULTURAL ARTIFACTS

Digital entities are collections of "bits stored on a floppy disk, on the hard drive embedded in [a] . . . workstation, or on a fileserver" (Levy 2001). They are also the "perceptible display[s]" of such collections on a screen or on paper. Because a digital entity is imperceptible to humans, a tangible display must render it perceptible and useable. In the early days of computing (1940s to 1960s), perceptible displays of bit collections were generated in paper form as punched cards, punched paper tape, and continuous-feed paper printouts. Later innovations allowed displays to occur on CRT (cathode-ray-tube) and more recently, flat-screen monitors. Computer programmers write code (called programs, software programs, or simply software) which directs computer hardware to manipulate collections of bits in specific ways in order to complete calculations or sort and manipulate data, and to subsequently generate visible displays of the processed data in formats structured according to software instructions. Emerging genres of digital output include e-mail, traditional mail, bulletin boards, listservs, news groups, textual reports, database reports, spreadsheets, and Web pages, as well as digital forms of previously analog cultural artifacts, such as musical performances, theatrical performances, and all of the previously mentioned literary genres.

Perceptible displays of digital information can range from the relatively fixed (PDF files) to the continuously updated (Webcasts, online chat rooms). Presently (mid-2003) identifiable parts of the digital environment are: collections of bits, interpretive and processing software, hardware, and perceptible displays. Processes are the electronic interactions of software and hardware directed by individuals or set in motion automatically at the direction of software. Products include perceptible displays of processed bits on CRT monitors, new bit collections in storage, new software programs, and outputs to magnetic, paper, film, and digital media. One difficulty in analyzing and managing digital parts, processes and products is their continuously changing nature: "Already the addition of new capabilities to existing software make[s] it difficult in some cases to identify where one format or genre ends and another begins. Many of these formats and genres will become obsolete with developing technology, while some will continue to evolve and become more complex" (Gilliland-Swetland 1995).

Besides the continuously changing nature of the elements of the digital environment, two other crucial difficulties exist. One is the fact that the clear boundaries and distinctions between parts, process, and products that exist in the analog worlds of previous cultural artifacts are blurred in the digital environment (see Figure 2). The second is that no part of the digital construct–the parts, processes, or products–possesses either a high degree of fixity or a high level of durability.

FIGURE 2. Basic Elements of Digital Cultural Artifacts, in Sequence

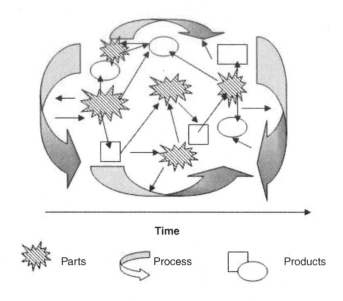

Time

Parts   Process   Products

WHAT NEEDS PRESERVATION: WHAT IS A "DIGITAL LIBRARY" OR A "DIGITAL DOCUMENT"?

Efforts to define digital documents and digital libraries are at the root of current research into the best ways of preserving both. These efforts have been deeply affected by the blurred boundaries between parts, processes, and products; by the continually changing nature of digital entities; and by the entities' low fixity and low durability. The National Information Infrastructure (NII) definition of a digital library holds that "the essence of the digital library concept is that: heterogeneous and distributed files and databases are available, linked together, and frequently annotatable; library contents comprise multiple digital media (text, images, graphics, audio, video); library contents are universally accessible from work, school, and home through telecommunications networks; the library is designed for multiple and diverse user communities; the library is dynamic, in that the nature of both the digital library and its user communities should change as a direct result of their interaction with one another . . ." (Gilliland-Swetland 1995). This "digital library" entity is so different from the traditional library in its qualities of fixity and durability that using the same name for both contributes added confusion to an area where what is required is enhanced clarity.

In the realm of analog cultural artifacts, "libraries" can be defined as organized collections of relatively long-lived, fixed products. When fixity and durability are plotted as in Figure 3, analog library materials are located somewhere in the upper right-hand quadrant of the matrix. The NII definition of a "digital library" establishes it as a relatively fluid entity, which, because of its digital components, is also relatively short-lived (unless some sort of preservation intervention is undertaken). The low fixity and low durability of digital libraries places them in the lower left-hand quadrant of the fixity-durability matrix (see Figure 4). To call a digital library a "library" is to run the risk of ignoring the fact that one of the most important attributes of a library is its durability—that is—its persistence over time. A further problem with calling a "digital library" a "library" is that the traditional library conventionally collects cultural *products*, not cultural *parts* or *processes* (see Figure 1). Cultural products are "products" precisely because of their relative fixity and durability, and they are also products because they have been consciously developed to be carriers of cultural content to future generations. Documents, for example, "do not merely convey information, they help make it, structure it, validate it" (Arms 2000).

While the parts that are processed into analog cultural products are sometimes durable and fixed, they have not normally been preserved, nor has their preservation even been attempted, for chiefly economic reasons.[1] Voices, bodies, costumes and sets, for example, have fairly short natural life spans, and are used to better advantage if they participate serially in a number of processes over their lifetimes. Typewriters and printing presses have much longer physical life spans, but their useful life spans are significantly shorter than their physical life spans, because economics usually dictates that they be replaced with newer technologies that are both cheaper and more productive. But parts and processes are distinguished from products chiefly by the expectation that they will be ephemeral, that no extraordinary effort will be needed or expended to preserve them, and that it is not their function to carry cultural content into the future.

The digital realm is both too compressed (in time and in space) and too new to have yet sorted out its parts, processes, and products. In fact, it is an important feature of the digital realm of the present time that its processes are ongoing and its products are transient (Levy 2001). The situation might be clarified if what are now being called "digital librar-

FIGURE 3. Relative Longevity of Original *Analog* Cultural Artifacts Under Optimum Conditions

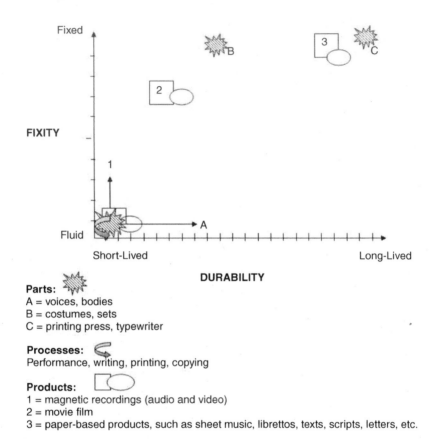

Parts:
A = voices, bodies
B = costumes, sets
C = printing press, typewriter

Processes:
Performance, writing, printing, copying

Products:
1 = magnetic recordings (audio and video)
2 = movie film
3 = paper-based products, such as sheet music, librettos, texts, scripts, letters, etc.

ies" were named something like "digital conservatories," "digital exchanges," or "digital studios"; and if "digital documents" were called, for example, "digital performances" or "digital moments." These vocabulary corrections would significantly sharpen the now-blurred distinctions between parts, process, and products in the digital realm. Digital products created to date are almost uniformly not sufficiently fixed and durable to qualify them to carry cultural content into the future. Two exceptions are paper-based and film-based outputs (Figure 4). While both can be sufficiently durable and fixed for long-term retention, paper- and film-based outputs do not satisfy the requirements of

FIGURE 4. Relative Longevity of Original *Digital* Cultural Artifacts Under Optimum Conditions

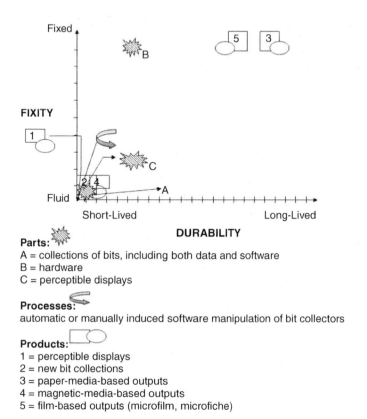

Parts:
A = collections of bits, including both data and software
B = hardware
C = perceptible displays

Processes:
automatic or manually induced software manipulation of bit collectors

Products:
1 = perceptible displays
2 = new bit collections
3 = paper-media-based outputs
4 = magnetic-media-based outputs
5 = film-based outputs (microfilm, microfiche)

those who wish to capture and convey all of the dimensions of digital originals (Commission on Preservation and Access 1996). Balancing fixity and durability with ongoing full functionality and dimensionality turns out to be the central quandary facing those who would undertake to preserve digital artifacts. If one examines the historical record, however, one realizes that never before has any civilization successfully preserved the processes and parts of its cultural activities *on an ongoing basis*. Yet, that is what we now seem to be attempting in the digital realm. We may, in fact, be able to successfully preserve digital parts and processes, but we must undertake to do so very carefully, and with a full understanding of the enormity of the undertaking at hand.

DECIDING "HOW":
PRESERVING THE RIGHT THINGS IN THE RIGHT WAYS

Current research projects into the preservation of digital entities have concluded that a necessary first step is the appraisal of the "significant properties" of digital objects (Holdsworth and Seargeant 2000). One working definition of the distinctive qualities of digital entities lists them as ease of replication, ease of transmission and multiple use, plasticity/fluidity, equivalence of works, compactness, and non-linearity (Samuelson 1991). According to a recent research project, the first task of those undertaking to preserve digital entities is to determine which of the distinctive qualities of the digital entity is significant enough to warrant its long-term maintenance in viable form (Cedars Project 2001). Digital preservation research projects are also investigating and developing procedures for maintaining the viability of the distinctive qualities of digital entities over time (Moore et al. 1999; Cedars 2001). While the results of these projects are encouraging, the solutions toward which they currently point are neither easy nor inexpensive. For these reasons, such solutions should be undertaken only when the digital material is truly valuable, when the long-term resources of the creating or custodial organization are sufficient, and when there is no other acceptable preservation alternative. Even when future long-term digital preservation solutions become less labor and resource intensive, it may still be worthwhile for organizations to take a much more traditional approach to preservation of digital materials.

The "traditional" form of digital preservation that should be seriously explored is "multi-tracking." Using multi-tracking, an organization will exploit digital entities' most distinctive characteristics (ease of replication, ease of transmission and multiple use, and plasticity/fluidity) to periodically, and at regular intervals, intentionally create fixed and durable products that capture those attributes of the digital material that can be successfully fixed and extended. This process would be similar to the process of creating periodic system "backups," but unlike backups, the products of multi-tracking would be self-contained, complete, and system-independent entities. One need only look to the analog realm to locate many precedents for this type of preservation. Musical works are performed by living musicians, they are recorded (and played back) in a variety of media, and they are documented with ink on paper using musical notation systems. In the realm of science, students of natural history have traditionally maintained small, living collections (aquaria, zoos, greenhouses), as well as collections of non-living specimens (skeletal remains, dried plants, preserved tissue collections, etc.) and detailed illustrations. No one of these preservation "tracks" preserves every attribute of the original entity, but used together they provide good enough information at a reasonable cost and in a sustainable way. Multi-tracking for preservation tacitly acknowledges that different media have different strengths and weaknesses, and it allows preservation of various attributes of cultural artifacts to be accomplished across a range of media. Preservation studies have repeatedly pointed out that digital preservation efforts must realistically account for institutional priorities, available resources, and the limits of technical feasibility (CLIR 2001; Commission on Preservation 1996; Chen 2001; Hedstrom 1991, 1997; MacLean and Davis 1998). Now is the time for the creation of a range of digital-derivative products of high fixity and high durability that each effectively captures some significant property of the original "digital performance" or "digital organism." Some of these fixed and durable products may be digital, and some may be analog. Some may be high-maintenance, but most should probably be relatively low-maintenance.

CONCLUSION

The most threatened records in the current age are the newest (Brown and Duguid 2000), and it is incumbent on us to not wait for some future "perfect" preservation solution to save our present-day digital entities. Daniel Boorstin, historian and former Librarian of Congress, has written: "The limits of historical discovery come from the physical qualities of objects as much as from the human activities which they suggest" (1987). He proposes that what survives to inform and delight future generations is "collected and protected" information. It is the task of those who would preserve today's digital entities for tomorrow's generations to accurately and realistically determine how best to collect and protect the works of the digital realm that have been entrusted to their care.

NOTE

1. Exceptions are the individual specimens that are collected by museums and used in historical displays and studies.

REFERENCES

American Library Association (ALA). 1993. "Recycled and Permanent: An ALA Washington Office Fact Sheet." *Alkaline Paper Advocate* 6:3 (September), http://palimpsest.stanford.edu/byorg/abbey/ap/ap06/ap06-3/ap06-308.html.

Arms, William Y. 2000. *Digital Libraries.* Cambridge: MIT Press.

Association of Moving Image Archivists (AMIA). 2000. *Storage Standards and Guidelines, Motion Picture Film,* http://www.amianet.org/publication/resources/guidelines/storage/mopic.html (accessed July 16, 2004).

Boorstin, Daniel J. 1987. A Wrestler with the Angel. In *Hidden History.* New York: Harper & Row.

Brookfield, Karen. 1993. *Book.* London: Dorling Kindersley.

Brown, John Seely and Paul Duguid. 2000. *The Social Life of Information.* Boston: Harvard Business School Press.

The Cedars Project. 2001. CURL Exemplars in Digital Archives. *Digital Preservation and Further Information.* Consortium of University Research Libraries: United Kingdom, http://www.leeds.ac.uk/cedars/DigPres.htm (accessed September 15, 2003).

Chen, Su-Shing. 2001. The Paradox of Digital Preservation. *IEEE Computer* 34(3): 24-28.

Commission on Preservation and Access and The Research Libraries Group. 1996, May. *Preserving Digital Information: Report of the Task Force on Archiving of Digital Information,* http://www.rlg.org/ArchTF/.

Council on Library and Information Resources. 2001. *The Evidence in Hand: The Report of the Task Force on the Artifact in Library Collections,* http://www.clir.org/pubs/reports/pub103/contents.html.

Drama, Western. 2001. In *The Columbia Encyclopedia,* 6th ed., http://www.bartleby.com/65/dr/drama-We.html (accessed September 15, 2003).

Gilliland-Swetland, Ann. 1995. Digital Communications: Documentary Opportunities Not to Be Missed. *Archival Issues* 20(1): 39-50.

Hedstrom, Margaret. 1991. Understanding Electronic Incunabula: A Framework for Research on Electronic Records. *The American Archivist,* 54(3): 334-354.

Hedstrom, Margaret. 1997. Digital Preservation: A time bomb for digital libraries, http://www.uky.edu/~kiernan/DL/hedstrom.html.

Holdsworth, David and Derek M. Seargeant. 2000. *A Blueprint for Representation Information in the OAIS Model,* http://www.personal.leeds.ac.uk/~ecldh/cedars/ieee00.html.

Katz, Bill. 1995. Printing and the Renaissance. In *Dahl's History of the Book, Third English Edition: The History of the Book No. 2.* Metuchen, NJ: Scarecrow Press.

Levy, David M. 2001. *Scrolling Forward: Making Sense of Documents in the Digital Age.* New York: Arcade.

MacLean, Margaret and Ben H. Davis, eds. 1998. *Time and Bits: Managing Digital Continuity.* Los Angeles: Getty Conservation Institute.

Moore, Reagan, Chaitan Baru, Amarnath Gupta, Bertram Ludaescher, Richard Marciano, and Arcot Rajasekar. 1999. *Collection-Based Long-Term Preservation.* San Diego Supercomputer Center. San Diego, California. Submitted to National Archives and Records Administration, http://www.sdsc.edu/NARA/Publications/nara.pdf.

Musical Notation. 2001. In *The Columbia Encyclopedia*, 6th ed., http://www.bartleby.com/65/mu/musicaln.html (accessed September 15, 2003).

Oratory. 2001. In *The Columbia Encyclopedia*, 6th ed., http://www.bartleby.com/65/or/oratory.html (accessed September 15, 2003).

Samuelson, Pamela. 1991. Digital Media and the Law. *Communications of the ACM* 34(10): 23-28.

St-Laurent, Gilles. 1996. *The Care and Handling of Recorded Sound Materials*. Music Division: National Library Of Canada, http://palimpsest.stanford.edu/byauth/st-laurent/care.html (accessed September 16, 2003).

Index

Page numbers followed by f indicate figures; those followed by t indicate tables.

BOOK ORDER FORM!

Order a copy of this book with this form or online at:
http://www.haworthpress.com/store/product.asp?sku=5340

Emerging Issues in the Electronic Environment
Challenges for Librarians and Researchers in the Sciences

____ in softbound at $29.95 (ISBN: 0-7890-2578-7)

____ in hardbound at $49.95 (ISBN: 0-7890-2577-9)

COST OF BOOKS _____

POSTAGE & HANDLING _____
US: $4.00 for first book & $1.50
for each additional book.
Outside US: $5.00 for first book
& $2.00 for each additional book.

SUBTOTAL _____

In Canada: add 7% GST. _____

STATE TAX _____
CA, IL, IN, MN, NJ, NY, OH & SD residents
please add appropriate local sales tax.

FINAL TOTAL _____
If paying in Canadian funds, convert
using the current exchange rate,
UNESCO coupons welcome.

❑ BILL ME LATER:
Bill-me option is good on US/Canada/
Mexico orders only; not good to jobbers,
wholesalers, or subscription agencies.

❑ Signature _____

❑ Payment Enclosed: $ _____

❑ PLEASE CHARGE TO MY CREDIT CARD:
❑ Visa ❑ MasterCard ❑ AmEx ❑ Discover
❑ Diner's Club ❑ Eurocard ❑ JCB

Account # _____

Exp Date _____

Signature _____
(Prices in US dollars and subject to change without notice.)

PLEASE PRINT ALL INFORMATION OR ATTACH YOUR BUSINESS CARD

Name

Address

City State/Province Zip/Postal Code

Country

Tel Fax

E-Mail

May we use your e-mail address for confirmations and other types of information? ❑ Yes ❑ No We appreciate receiving
your e-mail address. Haworth would like to e-mail special discount offers to you, as a preferred customer.
We will never share, rent, or exchange your e-mail address. We regard such actions as an invasion of your privacy.

Order From Your **Local Bookstore** or Directly From
The Haworth Press, Inc. 10 Alice Street, Binghamton, New York 13904-1580 • USA
Call Our toll-free number (1-800-429-6784) / Outside US/Canada: (607) 722-5857
Fax: 1-800-895-0582 / Outside US/Canada: (607) 771-0012
E-mail your order to us: orders@haworthpress.com

For orders outside US and Canada, you may wish to order through your local
sales representative, distributor, or bookseller.
For information, see http://haworthpress.com/distributors

(Discounts are available for individual orders in US and Canada only, not booksellers/distributors.)

Please photocopy this form for your personal use.
www.HaworthPress.com

BOF04

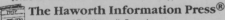